CHANGING CAREERS IN SCIENCE AND ENGINEERING

The M I T Press

Cambridge, Massachusetts, and London, England

CHANGING CAREERS IN SCIENCE AND ENGINEERING

Edited by Sanborn C. Brown

Library of Congress Cataloging in Publication Data

Career Seminar for M.I.T. Alumni, Massachusetts
   Institute of Technology, 1971.
   Changing careers in science and engineering.

   The seminar was conducted by the M.I.T. Alumni
Association.
   Includes bibliographical references.
   1. Engineering as a profession--Congresses.
2. Science as a profession--Congresses. I. Brown,
Sanborn Conner, 1913-   ed. II. Massachusetts
Institute of Technology. Alumni Association.
III. Title.

TA157.C48   1971   502'.3   72-8840

ISBN 0-262-02090-4

CONTENTS

With shifting national priorities, opportunities are appearing for engineers and scientists in such new fields as
environmental protection, urban affairs, housing, education,
health care, and ocean engineering, while other fields,
such as aerospace and electronics, suffer retrenchment.
Unfortunately, too few of those who are equipped to move
into new positions realize their opportunity, and many are
cautious about entering areas whose future potential they
do not fully understand.

On April 17 and 18, 1971, the Massachusetts Institute of
Technology Alumni Association conducted a "Career Seminar"
for scientists and engineers who were considering a change
in career orientation. The emphasis was placed on long-
range personal career planning and training rather than on
immediate job placement. Almost all those who attended
were employed, and the audience fell into two main groups,
about equally divided. There were those who felt that
their engineering careers were threatened by changes in
national priorities, and others were mostly younger individuals who were advancing in their careers but had decided that they did not intend to stay in the same place
the rest of their lives and were looking for information
to help them make their decisions.

The speakers provided forecasts of overall needs for
engineering, scientific, and managerial talent in the
coming decade as well as forecasts in specific professional
areas. They examined the impact of changing federal funding policy on future employment opportunities. There was
also discussion of personal adjustment problems of shifting

careers, when and how to use placement services, and where
to look for career information to make better-informed
career decisions.

It seemed to those who attended this seminar that much
of what was being said was of permanent value. Therefore
it was decided to transcribe the tapes that were made and,
after suitable editing, to produce this volume of the proceedings. The seminar was held under the auspices of the
M.I.T. Alumni Association, and the proceedings were supported by the M.I.T. Graduate School.

The invited speakers were the following:

John D. Alden
Executive Secretary, Engineering Manpower
Commission of Engineers Joint Council,
New York

Robert O. Bigelow
Assistant Chief Engineer
New England Electric System

John Blair
Director of Research
Raytheon Manufacturing Company

Phillips R. Brooks, Jr.
Manager, Digital Instruments Research
American Optical Corporation

Secor D. Browne
Chairman, Civil Aeronautics Board

M. Louise Curley
Vice President
Scudder, Stevens and Clark

Daniel F. Fairbanks
Manager, Research Division
Dennison Manufacturing Company

Robert G. Foster
Technical Director, Technical Products Group
Corning Glass Works

Lee Grodzins
Professor of Physics, M.I.T.

Ward J. Haas
Vice President
Warner-Lambert, Inc.

Arthur W. Heineck, Jr.
Vice President
Inforex, Inc.

Antony Herrey
Director, Real Estate Office, M.I.T.

Alfred A. H. Keil
Head, Department of Naval Architecture and Marine
Engineering, M.I.T.

Donald W. Kenny
Vice President for Engineering and Licensing
Robin and Haas Company

Franco Modigliani
Institute Professor, Professor of Economics and
Professor of Finance, M.I.T.

Charles A. Myers
Sloan Fellows Professor of Management
Director of Industrial Relations Section, M.I.T.

Paul Penfield, Jr.
Professor of Electrical Engineering, M.I.T.

Robert W. Puffer
Manager, Peripherals Engineering
Digital Equipment Corporation

Paul A. Samuelson
Institute Professor, Professor of Economics, M.I.T.

Harvey M. Sapolsky
Associate Professor of Political Science, M.I.T.

Edgar H. Schein
Professor of Organizational Psychology and Management,
M.I.T.

Irvin W. Sizer
Dean of the Graduate School, M.I.T.

Glenn P. Strehle
Vice President
Colonial Management Associates, Inc.

Lester C. Thurow
Professor of Management and Professor of Economics, M.I.T.

Robert S. Timmins
Executive Vice President, Abcor

Wallace E. Vander Velde
Professor of Aeronautics and Astronautics, M.I.T.

Robert K. Weatherall
Assistant Dean of the Graduate School and
Director of Placement, M.I.T.

Jerome B. Wiesner
President-elect, M.I.T.

Sanborn C. Brown
Cambridge, Massachusetts
June 1972

Chapter 1

OPENING REMARKS

Dean Robert K. Weatherall, assistant dean of the Graduate School and director of Placement at M.I.T., after a few general remarks, introduced Dr. Jerome B. Wiesner, president-elect of M.I.T. Dr. Wiesner, recalling his responsibilities as the Science Advisor to President Kennedy, reviewed some of the decisions that had been made in Washington to commit the country to the space program. He also touched briefly on the questions of science and technology in our society.

Robert K. Weatherall: We are at what seems to be, and perhaps is, a turning point in the history of science and engineering in this country. In 1969 we reached the moon, after a tremendous decade of effort, and the nation is wondering where to go next, if anywhere. We have cut back on our defense spending after a longer period, perhaps a quarter of a century, of intense activity, and the nation is unsure what kind of investment in defense is called for, whether indeed there should not be more cutbacks. There is questioning by the scientists themselves. I was struck by Dr. Bentley Glass, president of the American Association for the Advancement of Science, talking in Chicago in December about the status of genetics, quoting colleagues in his field, asking whether the subject of Molecular Genetics has reached some kind of an end point. Scientists are not sure where their disciplines are headed.

In the nation at large there is a strong feeling that
perhaps technology has gone as far as it should go, that
society is spoiled by technology, that the environment is
hurt by technology. In recent months we voted down the
SST, a particularly striking illustration of that national feeling at work.

Compounding the situation is the state of the economy.
We are caught in an inflationary recession, and the universities, which are a major employer of scientists and
engineers, are having to cut back on their hiring of new
people. The financial outlook in the universities is
bleak. Industry too has been hurt by the economy, and
commercial firms as well as defense companies have been
letting people go.

Many scientists and engineers who have lost their jobs
or who are in danger of losing their jobs are wondering
whether they can continue in the career for which they
were trained. Should they make a change, and if they
change to some other part of science or engineering, what
change should they make? What other sector of the science economy is in better shape than the one they are in?
This is really the focus of this seminar. In planning
the seminar we have addressed ourselves not to the immediate predicament of the man who has lost his job, who
wants to know how to find another one, but more to the
longer-range implications for scientists and engineers of
the cutbacks in so many areas. What does the present situation really amount to, where is the economy headed in
the next 5 years or so, what are the prospects in the

different branches of science and engineering? These are
the questions with which we are concerned.

It may be that the present distress in the science economy will turn out to be only a perturbation. I have had
occasion to read recently an account of measures taken in
the thirties to help science through the depression. The
scientific agencies of the federal government suffered
serious cutbacks, and our own President Compton was ap-
pointed chairman of a committee to see what could be done
to rally support for science in Washington and to seek out
new ways of supporting science. The ring of the situation
is strikingly familiar to us today. In retrospect, the
situation that President Compton and his committee were
worried about looks like a little wobble on the curve, not
such a serious thing as they felt it to be. It would be
nice if we could feel that our present situation is a similar wobble on the upward curve of the science. We can
hope to learn something about this during these next 2
days.

Jerome B. Wiesner: I have the courage to stand up here
and talk on this subject because my favorite philosopher
is Thurber and my favorite line from him is that "It is
better to know some of the questions than all of the answers." There is no problem that I have spent time with
in my professional career that has more uncertainty to it
than projections and predictions about manpower needs in
the field of science and technology. I remember a Satur-
day afternoon in April 1961, a decade ago, I sat for an

afternoon with President Kennedy while we studied all the
memos and charts provided us by people from the Labor Department, National Science Foundation, Bureau of Labor
Statistics, National Academy of Sciences, and other agencies that kept statistics on scientific manpower problems
and tried to decide whether if we were to launch into the
lunar program there would be manpower enough to do the
job. We came to a very interesting conclusion that we
never told anyone about. We observed from our analysis
that because of the stabilization of the cold war, which
had begun under President Eisenhower, and the consequent
leveling off of the defense budget, which we expected to
continue during the decade in which we hoped we would have
some influence on the world affairs, in 3 or 4 years there
would be indeed a manpower surplus, given the rate at
which schools were turning people out and the rate industry was then absorbing them. This was rather a startling
conclusion to us, but it was clearly indicated in the
material that the people had supplied to us. As a matter
of fact, those conclusions motivated some other things
that we did in the years immediately ahead which relate
directly to the questions you are talking about here today. We concluded that, as a matter of fact, a technical
program of a magnitude we were contemplating was almost
necessary to take up the manpower surplus, or we would be
facing a very different kind of problem. On the other
hand, I think some of the problems we face today stem
from the decision we made later that spring to go ahead
with an accelerated space program.

Some of the problems we are facing stem from the fact that there has been a more rapid increase in salaries for workers in these science-oriented categories than there had been in the society at large.

I am basically optimistic about this problem on the longer pull, but that does not help the people who are caught in the present bind very much nor does it help institutions like ours that have to live through these difficult periods. But there have been other difficult times in the postwar period. I remember the 1958-1959 recession in science and engineering which was due entirely to a cutback in federal spending. That occasion was dictated largely by fiscal constraints because President Eisenhower was not anxious to increase the debt ceiling, and therefore he imposed budgetary controls largely to stay below the debt ceiling.

My view is that the proportion of highly skilled people who will be needed to continue the growth and development of our economy will go on increasing on the average. This reminds me of the time when Michael Michelas, who was working with me on the White House staff, came in and said he just made the remarkable conclusion, having looked at some numbers, that by 1984 the President was going to have to be a scientist! And I asked him how he arrived at that conclusion, and he showed me a graph he had drawn with two curves on it; one was the GNP and the other was the cost of research and development in the country. The GNP was doubling at about half the rate of the cost of R&D and these two crossed in 1984. I finally got him to admit

that he fudged the numbers a little bit to get them to
cross; if he had not, it might have been 1985 or 1986 or
even 1987. So it was perfectly obvious that things were
going to change in our business, and that I was probably
the last science advisor who was going to be able to live
in an uninhibited budget environment, in the sense that
we could run a free-flowing R&D establishment, that is,
that the natural development of things as people did research, got new ideas, wanted new equipment, and saw new
opportunities, trained young people in this society could
be supported. This had been true for quite a while in the
Defense Department; it was true at that stage in the NIH
(National Institutes of Health) budgets, whose budgets
were growing very rapidly; it was not quite so true in the
NSF (National Science Foundation) budget. But the fact
of the matter was that the federal R&D expenditures were
then going up at 15 percent a year. I doubt that the best
year of the GNP growth ever approximated that in this
country. As a matter of fact, we began to wonder how we
might put some brakes on the R&D growth, how we might
learn how to be more selective, and how we might think
about directing some of the activities into more productive uses.

In the decisions that President Kennedy eventually made
about the space program, he was very conscious of the fact
that this was not a wholly productive use of resources.
His decision was obviously a political one. He came to
the conclusion that the nation could not afford to run
second to the Soviet Union in space. We had created a

psychological situation that was terribly costly to the
United States that had to be reversed. But about once a
week he would say to me, "Can't you think of something
that we can do with that money here on earth that would
be more productive and still have the same impact on the
international scene in demonstrating that in fact we are
not a second-rate nation compared to the Soviet Union in
science and engineering?" And we looked at a great many
things, but we ultimately became convinced that the fact
of the matter was that the space activities and, particularly, the large boosters and the satellites and so on
were so closely linked with the defense activities in
people's minds that there was nothing else that we could
do with the comparable expenditures that could possibly
offset the political liability that the space program created for us. We, I think, very reluctantly came to the
conclusion that that was what we had to do.

The President had three choices as he saw it: one was
to quit the space race completely, another was to accept
the sort of second position that Eisenhower had, trying
to tell the world that it did not matter very much, and
the third was to make an all-out effort. Kennedy would,
I think, have been willing to quit had he seen an effective way to do it, but he was not constitutionally prepared to remain in a defensive second position; so ultimately, he made the only decision he could. But the
impact of those discussions, which went on for several
months, did convince us that there were some deeper problems in the society and that we should try to find ways

of directing some technical resources to more productive
domestic uses. It is interesting to note that at that
time we began to worry about two things which are still
very important. One was planning for conversion: to make
plans that would enable us to steer some R&D activities
into more immediate domestic problems of cities, education, and so on. We did try to begin some activities in
these fields, and we began many studies about them, but
their limited usefulness is demonstrated by the present
situation. We doubtless developed some understanding but
we obviously did not acquire plans that have been useful
to the nation. The second worry arose because we recognized a trend that looked serious then, and looks more
serious now: namely, a great many of our more mature industries were not using technology or R&D to advance their
product quality, their efficiency, and/or their opportunities to the degree that we thought was possible or desirable. For example, in the shipbuilding industry it was
very clear that a major use could be made of automatic
control. But we never got anywhere promoting this idea.
Interestingly enough we were thwarted in these activities
by a combination of industry and union resistance. Neither the unions nor the industries were very anxious to
see this kind of innovation promoted, and they lobbied
very hard against it in the Congress, and by and large
our efforts to develop R&D activities in these fields
were not very successful. In 1962 and 1963 Herbert Hol-
loman and I tried to stimulate civilian R&D activities
through the Department of Commerce. Herb has gone back

to some of our numbers and tried to make some estimates
of whether if had we been able to stimulate the greater
employment of technology that we tried to do would the
manpower problems that we have today still exist in those
fields. It is obviously very dangerous to draw many conclusions, but the numbers are interesting. If one com-
pares the use of technologists, scientists, and engineers
in the American civilian industry with that of Europe or
Japan, for example, we find about a 30 percent lower manpower per dollar output in this country as compared to
those countries. It is also in terms of salaries that the
normal trend in this country for those categories of people is about 30 percent higher. One could ask the question, how many people would be employed in those industries if that 30 percent had gone into hiring people
instead of raising salaries? We have estimated that the
number might amount to as many as 100,000, which interestingly enough is near the estimated figure of the unemployment that exists today. None of this, of course, gives
you any indication of how to correct the situation, and I
hope that maybe this conference will have some ideas.

From the point of view of the Institute, a conference of
this kind is not wholly altruistic. We are desperately in
need of some judgments about the future to guide our own
evolution. We are experiencing reduction in federal support for graduate students; many fellowships have been
eliminated. The argument is that the federal support,
federal encouragement for graduate student education,
stemmed from the fact that the government recognized that

it was a big consumer of technical manpower and was causing shortages in these fields and therefore had a responsibility to add to the numbers. Now that there is no
shortage and the government has quit being a consumer, it
should correct the situation and stop encouraging production, at least its support of production of scientists
and engineers, so that fellowship programs are being cut.
Coincidentally, and I think even more seriously, the Wood-
row Wilson Fellowships in the social sciences, which were
supported by the Ford Foundation, have been cut. This has
created an even more drastic problem in the social sciences. Every institution like ours is now faced with the
choice of either finding additional support for graduate
students or seeing the numbers decrease. If one believed
that there was going to be a long-term decrease in the
demand, in the needs of society, or the opportunities for
people, it obviously would be wise, nationwide, to cut
down the production. If, on the other hand, this is just
a fluctuation, then both from the point of view of the
health of our institution and opportunities for youngsters coming along, we ought to try to find the resources
for students who are not now being supported by the previous sponsors. At the moment we are trying to find new
ways of supporting students. We are not convinced that
there is a major and permanent new trend in society, de-
emphasizing technology, so we are stretching our resources and stopping other things we might be doing in
order to find ways to support graduate students both in
the sciences and in the social sciences.

Also from our point of view, even if there is going to
be a decrease in the total demands for scientists and engineers in the country, we have to make a judgment about
whether it is wise for us to join in a 10 or 20 or 30 percent reduction in the graduate output or whether institutions like ours should try to maintain their output in
view of the fact that we do believe in our superior quality. The total graduate student output of the Institute
is a substantial fraction of the total output of the country, so we do have an important decision to make here.

The questions of science and technology in our society
are obviously very deep ones. And as the SST vote shows,
the nation is wrestling with the question of whether or
not it should allow the unabated and uncontrolled development of all new technology. Many of us who have been
watching intently the evolution of our society have felt
that this was a process that had to be stopped, that we
have to develop meaningful ways of making judgments and
allocations. But the fact of the matter is that we do
not yet have processes which are really very sensible for
doing this. It is clear to me that the continued healthy
evolution of our country, of the world, to a more decent
society does require the continued assistance of people
with technical skills. But it is also clear that, unless
we learn how to control both what we do and the consequences of some of the things we do, we shall have both
great advances and great difficulties. And one of the
problems that I hope we shall address ourselves at M.I.T.
in the years ahead is how to make this bridge between the

social problems and the technological opportunities, how
to create a responsible society that still allows us to
be a relatively diverse pluralistic society, with many
opportunities for experimentation and entrepreneurship.
I think that the kind of discussions that will go on here
may give us some guidance in this.

*Mr. Secor D. Browne, chairman of the Civil Aeronautics
Board, discussed some of the interactions of Washington
politics with the employment market for engineers. He
did not see a bright future.*

Secor D. Browne: I would like to make my remarks brief and
turn the floor over to you for such discussion as you may
wish to have. I have thought about this meeting more than
any that I have been to in recent months. It is quite
easy for me to talk in my field, which is civil aviation,
and the appurtenances to it, such as airports, air traffic
control, supersonic transport, routes, rights, but what
you are considering today has troubled me greatly and is
vital to the system and our country. The implications of
the problems for those of us who are engineers or scientists or people in the technical spectrum of our country
are tremendous.

I have a few thoughts that I hope will be helpful to you.
I was here last week for a luncheon attended by Senator
Brooke and other political figures. It was a small luncheon. The heads of some of our more important industries
were here, and it was not exactly a very cheery luncheon.

One of the things that disturbed me was the question of
geography. The business editor of the *Boston Globe* said
that Massachusetts has lost over 100,000 jobs in the last
couple of years, and whereas he agreed that things would
come back they might not come back to Massachusetts.
There are a variety of reasons for that. At least for the
time being, the day for the large government bundle will
be over. There will not be a big enough package any more
to put in any one place to get any political lift out of
it.

Massachusetts's appeal as a place to put a center in for
any political gain or any conspicuous achievement has lost
a lot of interest or a lot of plausibility. So Massachusetts may not be favored in any distribution of large
lumps. If the work is going out in small lumps, it is
pretty hard to control any flow to any one particular area.
I should like to point out that I have nothing to do with
the Department of Transportation or Defense or anybody
else that gives out money in large lumps. I suggest that
large lumps of money may not of themselves come to Massachusetts in the future. Whereas the economy of the nation
as a whole will in my judgment recover, it may not all
come back here. Also the economic climate for a manufacturer is not the greatest. Taxwise, Massachusetts is very
discouraging to a manufacturer. Such things as strike
benefits, they are fine if you pass them here, but they
could well drive people away from the state. All these
things enter into the whole problem of what I call "geography."

I think the job future of the engineer and the scientist
is a problem of the individual. There is some talk in the
government, whether it be from the administration or individual senators, of retraining. I think again we have
to ask, retraining for what? It is all very well to talk
about pollution and training to fight pollution, but that
is sort of an "un-thing." You can train people to design
mufflers for cars, you can train them to design quieter
engines, you can train them to learn the chemistry of
cleaning up atmosphere, or water or whatever, but you do
not train them to fight sin.

There is considerable gloom forecast for the future of
engineering and science. I am not sure that is right. A
senior officer of a very large engineering company based
here in Boston tells me they were having a hard time finding engineers. The kind of engineers they are having a
hard time finding are people who can design sewer systems,
steam systems, power distribution networks, and other less
glamorous or perhaps less inspired fields of technology.
Again I think it comes back to us as individuals to see
what we will do next. I think we need to take the widest
possible view of our own future, to regard the problem as
an individual one, to understand that whatever education
we had was only the beginning.

When we talk about continuing education, that is something very close to my interests. I do not normally admit it, but I have professional engineering licenses in
two states and belong to all the proper marching and chow-
der societies. I have only one academic degree, and that

is in the History and Literature of England in the seven-
teenth century. I am talking about me only because I
think it might be helpful to you. I graduated in 1938,
and there were not many job opportunities, and I went to
work as a draftsman. Fortunately, I got interested in air
conditioning and instrumentation and went on in the general field of electronics and instruments and nuts and bolts,
and eventually airplanes. What I knew in that area had
to be beaten into my rather thick skull by very dedicated
people, dedicated to keep the job I was working on from
being a bloody collapse. The same way with the languages,
they were important. They were important to the job I was
trying to do; I was always fascinated by international
business negotiation. The languages are, by the way,
French, Italian, Russian, and Japanese. The latter two
are not easy. I started learning Japanese in 1963. I
have a pattern. I do not want to bore you with it but it
cost about $1400 in cash out of pocket and God knows how
many hours, and how many Japanese foreign students here
being taken off to McLean for rest and relaxation. My
point is simply that you are the individual who must look
after you. If you are going to be reconverted or redi-
rected, you are going to have to do it, and you probably
can.

Question: You are the expert on the SST, and we've all
read the newspapers about Senator Proxmire's opposition.
Would you care to comment on the possibility that he will
stop any government support of the V-STOL?

Secor D. Browne: Why Senator Proxmire went after the supersonic transport I suspect does not have a great deal to
do with the supersonic transport itself but is an extension of his concern with the so-called military-industrial
complex. I think his concern has now extended to government design of anything, for, if you wish, this fear that
industry will get something for nothing out of the government. So I suspect he will go after any V-STOL program
on the same basis. In my judgment, he overlooks some
pretty important things. As many of us in the room know,
the engine always comes first. Once you have the engine,
you wrap an airplane around it. The whole chain of engine
and then airframe development has always rested on government R&D, on government funding. In recent years this
kind of development effort has been lacking. I'm not
talking about aerospace or anything else but commercial
transport airplanes. They no longer rest on a base of
military R&D. Therefore if there is or was to be an SST,
there was a need for the government or for the community
as a whole to put up the R&D muscle to make it possible.
That's all that was behind the SST. I suspect that, similarly, if there is to be a successful STOL vehicle, or
V-STOL, it's going to involve the community as a whole
providing some sort of research funding. I'm not aware
of any expensive government effort in the short-haul aircraft field.

Question: Would you care to comment on as to why Senator

Proxmire waited until practically all the money had been
spent before he marshaled his forces for this?

Secor D. Browne: Well, in fairness to Senator Proxmire,
he started a long time ago, and it wasn't Senator Proxmire
that killed the SST; it was the current *mal du siècle*, a
kind of general disenchantment with technology, with the
whole society. I think Senator Proxmire and others have
merely moved on a wave that is, I think, the chief disease
of our time. Actually Senator Proxmire started a long
time ago and nobody listened. Until, all of a sudden this
whole wave moved along, as though we all ought to go back
to the caves, we ought to be clean and sit in our bear-
skins, scratching because they shut all the soap factories. I'm not against the environment; I just want to
live in it.

Question: Who in the country, now, if we're going to throw
bricks at Senator Proxmire, and I have no wits for it, but
to whom do we send a bouquet? To whom do we look to for
leadership?

Secor D. Browne: Well, if I understand what you're saying,
is, who's going to lead the scientist or the engineer out
of the wilderness in which he finds himself as a result
of the technological climate we've been in? The era of
the very large project, be it military or space, has probably disappeared, at least for the time being. Pollution,

which is offered by some politicians as an almost balancing size project area, in my judgment isn't. Fighting
pollution means dividing the problem into the constituent
parts and dealing with them as each of us is able to the
best of our ability and our profession. I happen to be,
although temporarily distracted, very interested in aircraft noise, and very much interested in, among other
things, the emanations from jet engines, which are un-
sightly even if, in my judgment, not harmful in the extent that they are put into our atmosphere. We each have
our small area that we work. Now, I doubt that the government is going to be able to marshal all these talents
into one specific project called Pollution, which is like
going to the moon.

Chapter 2

THE EFFECT OF CHANGING FEDERAL SPENDING
ON EMPLOYMENT OPPORTUNITIES

To present a broad picture of the effect of federal spend-
ing on the job market, the subject was discussed from sev-
eral points of view. The subject was opened by Dr. M.
Louise Curley, vice president of the investment counsel
firm of Scudder, Stevens and Clark, with a discussion of
the long-term economic outlook.

M. Louise Curley: I have chosen to talk about economic
trends very broadly. So let me begin with a quote from
the Spanish philosopher, Miguel de Unamuno y Jugo. Some
50 years ago he wrote, "If what we call the problem of
life, the problem of bread, were once solved the earth
would be turned into a hell by the emergence in a more
violent form of the struggle for survival."

I am rather fond of this quote and often think that it
describes the contemporary scene very well. But there is
something else about it. Is it saying anything more than
that as we learn to solve one problem another more difficult one emerges? Perhaps all it says is that one generation's hell is the previous one's paradise. The human
condition is much like that of Sisyphus, who eternally
pushes his rock up the hill, only to have it come tumbling
down once he gets close to the top.

What, you may well ask, has this got to do with the
long-term economic outlook? To me it suggests that the

economic problems of today are far greater than they were
10 years ago, and will be far greater 10 years hence than
they are now, bad as we think they are now. At the same
time, our capabilities of solving these problems are
greater today than they were 10 years ago, and they could
be greater 10 years hence.

You will note, I hope, that although I said that the
problems will be greater and the capabilities of solving
them could be greater, I have not said that the capabilities of solving the problems would necessarily be up to
the complexity of the problems. We shall still be pushing
that rock up the hill in years hence. What I am hinting
at is that the picture of the seventies, which the economists can now show you, may be paradise to you but may be
hell to your children.

The predictions of gross national product (GNP) for
1960 made in 1950 and those for 1970 made in 1960 turned
out to be fairly close to the mark in general broad out-
line. So what they measured was not really what the pre-
dictors meant. The forecaster in 1950 did not foresee
Sputnik in 1957 and what it did to the educational and
cultural scene. Nor did the forecaster in 1960 foresee
what the emphasis in science and technology engendered by
Sputnik would mean in terms of the environment by 1970.
It is not at all certain that the forecaster of 1960 had
absorbed the meaning of the 1954 Supreme Court decision
on desegregation. And it is obvious that the forecaster
of 1960 did not foresee the Vietnam war and the reaction
to it.

If we define the problem of life, that is, the real economic problem, as Unamuno did with the problem of bread,
that problem for the United States is solved, or at least
it is solvable within the state of the art of economics.
But we no longer define the economic problem as the problem of bread, clothing, shelter, mobility, and so forth.
The change in our definition of the economic problem is
evident from the following two quotes from the important
legislation from the past 20 or so years.

First the Employment Act of 1946:

"The Congress hereby declares that it is the continuing
policy and responsibility of the Federal Government to use
all practical means consistent with its needs and obli-
gations and other essential considerations of national
policy, to promote maximum employment, production and
purchasing power."

Some 22 years later in the National Environmental Policy
Act of 1969 we find this statement:

"The Congress recognizing the profound impact of man's
activity on the interrelations of all components of the
natural environment, particularly the profound influences
of population growth, high density urbanization, industrial expansion, resource exploitation, and new and expanding technological advances and recognizing further the
critical importance of restoring and maintaining environmental quality to the overall welfare and development of

man, declares that it is the continuing policy of the Federal Government in cooperation with state and local governments and other concerned public and private organizations, to use all practical means and measures, including financial and technical assistance, in a manner calculated to foster and promote the general welfare, to create and maintain conditions under which men and nature can exist in productive harmony and fulfill the social, economic and other requirements of present and future generations of Americans."

A rather tall order for us.

Most of the economic models that economists today use to study the economy and to predict its course under different policy assumptions are outgrowths of models developed about the time of the Employment Act of 1946. Incidentally, it was at this university that Dr. Lawrence Klein, who is today one of the foremost econometricians, began to build his first econometric model. Our data on the economy, what we call "national accounts," are conceptually the same as they were 25 years ago. It is only in the past few years that there have been serious proposals and attempts to broaden the concepts. You may have heard of movements to develop social indicators or social reports. To me this development is only a recognition of the changing concept of the economic problem. More and more of life's problems are coming into the economic realm. We have fewer and fewer free goods and more and more goods that enter into the realm of exchange. To mention the

more obvious—clean air and water are no longer free goods.
One might even say that women are no longer free goods.
There is nothing very spectacular about the broadening of
the economic product if one takes a very long view. Many
items in our national accounts in recent years would not
have entered into the realm of economic accounting in the
distant past. A homely example, but a pertinent one in
view of the concern over the disposal of industrial waste,
is the disposal of human waste. It seems I have read that
there were at most 20 bathrooms in all of Paris in the
early eighteenth century. It should be pointed out that
the broadening of the economic products, as I have talked
about it, is not the same thing as the increase in newly
invented or developed goods and services. I am talking
about things that we have taken for granted in the past
as free goods. There is great concern that the broadening
of economic products in this sense will mean lower standards of living. Obviously, if we have to pay for things
that were formerly free, we are worse off. But this view
neglects the fact that not all people are equally well off.
Those who want free clean air and water, by cutting back
on production and population growth, are all too often
those who have all the goods they want.

By broadening the economic product and bringing into the
marketplace many of the factors that we have formerly considered free goods, we may well achieve a higher standard
of living. And, if Kenneth Boulding is right, we might
even make some advance in forming moral judgments. It may
be useful to quote here from Boulding's eloquent address

to the American Economic Association in December 1968. He
touches many of the subjects that we have heard mentioned
earlier this morning.

"Even though economic measurement may be abused, its effect on the formation of moral judgments is great, and on
the whole, I believe beneficial. The whole idea of cost-
benefit analysis, for instance, in terms of monetary units,
say 'real' dollars of constant purchasing power, is of
enormous importance in the evaluation of social choices
and even of social institutions. We can grant, of course,
that the 'real' dollar, which is oddly enough a strictly
imaginary one, is a dangerously imperfect measure of the
quality of human life and human values. Nevertheless, it
is a useful first approximation and in these matters of
evaluation of difficult choices, it is extremely useful to
have a first approximation that we can then modify. Without this, indeed, all evaluation is random selection by
wild hunches. It is true of course that cost-benefit analysis of all sorts of things, whether of water projects, or
other pork barrel items, or in more recent years weapons
systems, can be manipulated to meet the previous prejudices
of people who are trying to influence the decisions. Nevertheless, the fundamental principle that we should count
all costs, whether easily countable or not, and evaluate
all rewards, however hard they are to evaluate, is one
which emerges squarely out of economics and which is at
least a preliminary guideline in the formation of the moral judgment in what might be called the 'economic ethic.'"

Having gone on at great lengths about what economists can do and how they can help in broad problems, let me tell you what they cannot do. They cannot tell you precisely what the economy is going to be like in the seventies, and this is, I know, exactly what you want to know. Like everyone else these days, the economists play the scenario game. Given certain ground rules, they can develop a reasonable plot.

One of the best models I know for playing this game is the one developed by Lawrence Klein, whom I mentioned earlier, and Ross Preston at the Wharton School of the University of Pennsylvania. The Wharton "annual industry model," as it is called, is a large-scale econometric model that projects 10 years ahead, year by year, with the details of gross national product, income, monetary conditions, industry output, employment, and prices. The model is now being used to project the economic environment for the decade of the seventies. And one of the scenarios is the peace and welfare scene. It assumes the winding down and the ending of the Vietnam war and no further wars in the decade. The general direction and interest of the federal government is assumed to turn toward domestic issues of pollution, the reconstruction of cities, and the revitalization of the economic and social environment. In a sense, trying to implement what the National Environment Policy Act has directed us to do. The potential real growth of the economy, which is made up of the labor force and productivity, balances out against the probable demands to produce a doubling of GNP in this decade. The

performance matches the experience of the sixties when GNP
rose from $500 billion to $1 trillion. This means that
by 1980 current dollar GNP will be $2 trillion. Through-
out the decade, the unemployment rate hovers about 4 1/2
percent and the rate of inflation is kept below 3 percent
for most of the period. The federal government achieves
a balanced budget by 1975, and in the last half of the
decade slight surpluses begin to appear. Monetary policy
throughout the decade fosters an expansion in bank credit
which provides a healthy environment for residential capital formation and business fixed capital formation. By
1975, 2.2 million housing starts will be achieved and by
1980, 2.6 million. Relatively stable prices throughout
the decade with no extraordinary excessive increases in
effective demands produce a moderately low level of interest rates by 1973 and interest rate stability for the re-
mainder of the decade. A healthy, real growth of approximately 4.1 percent per year throughout the decade
produces an expansion in corporate profits in current
levels, perhaps $85 billion, to levels approaching $160
billion by 1980. All sectors of the economy participate
in this growth including manufacturing, communication, and
contract construction. The forecast suggests a high ratio of investment to gross national product, which in
turn suggests that a peace-and-welfare-oriented economy
will continue not only to rely heavily on science and
technology but also perhaps to increase its reliance.

   While I could add to the details of this scenario, I
think the broad outlines are sufficient. As I noted ear-

lier, we economists can predict a picture which may appear
to be paradise right now. To make it come out to any near
paradise, not only economists but also scientists in every
field will have to work together. And most important of
all, we as a nation will have to think seriously of the
kind of world we want. We can get what we want if we try.

*Following Dr. Curley's broad look at economic trends,
Professor Lester C. Thurow, a professor of both management and economics at M.I.T., first gave a review of the
effect of the economy on employment of scientists and engineers for the past decade and then went on to give his
picture of the near future.*

Lester C. Thurow: Let me start by talking about how we got
where we are, and then look forward a little bit. In some
sense, if you are looking at the current unemployment
problem among engineers and scientists you do not say that
the current problem is peculiar; you say that 1961 was peculiar, because unemployment rates among professional and
technical workers at the moment are not noticeably different from what they were back in the 1958 recession. Just
about the same ball game is being played over again, although professionals are a much bigger proportion of the
labor force now than they were back in 1958. From the
time of the Korean War till the mid-1960s, two events were
going on. The first event was that post-Korea the military budget did not go down, but there were very rapid
shifts into what I am going to call high-technology de-

fense in the area of strategic deterrents. This was the
Dulles doctrine: wrap up conventional armed forces, forget
about them, and go all to big bombs and missiles. That
meant a very rapid increase in defense expenditure for
high-technology defense, even though the budget was not
changing you were essentially abandoning conventional warfare. At about the time President Kennedy came in, it was
decided that in the defense budget some of this needed to
be turned around, that we had abandoned too much conventional defense. But at that time the space budget took
off and picked up the slack. And so for about a 10-year
period we saw a very rapid escalation and high-technology
defense in space. Now in mid-1965, unfortunately from the
point of view of science and technology (and any other
point of view) Vietnam started. Vietnam was for all practical purposes a conventional war, which meant one had to
escalate conventional warfare expenditures and, if possible, had to cut back on high-technology strategic expenditures. Very shortly thereafter we made it to the moon.
The whole rationale for space exploration was to make it
to the moon, and if you win a race, you do not run the
race over again. You go home and look at your medals and
trophies that you have won. So given the basis upon which
the space race was started, I think it was completely logical to stop the space race when we had won it.

Such expenditure shifts were compounded by general economic policies. We have a recession going on, unemployment rates are generally in excess of 6 percent. Some
groups (teenagers) have 30 percent rates, but engineers

and technical people have 3 percent rates. They are obviously not the group that has been hurt the most; they
are obviously not the group that should be worried about
the most in a recessionary context. It is 1961 that was
peculiar, in that recession engineers and technology flew
right through it and did not know that the rest of society
was experiencing a 7 percent unemployment rate because
they had these two things going for them: the shift to
high-technology defense and the space budget. I think
that Dr. Wiesner is absolutely right. One of the things
that happened was that wages for science and engineers
escalated completely out of line, compared to everybody
else. If you went back to the early postwar period, an engineering or a scientific graduate B.A. did not receive a
very big premium over a liberal arts B.A. By the time the
early 1960s were coming along, the scientific graduate was
receiving a 50 to 100 percent premium over that liberal
arts B.A. I would be willing to bet that by the time the
mid-1970s come along, he no longer has a premium. Fair
or unfair, it is the product of the relative demands that
have been built into the system. I think if we are looking at the moment, we have to make the distinction between
two things: How do you cure the problem of finding jobs
for engineers and what can you say about the long-run demand for engineers? I think those are two very different
things, because I would be willing to bet that if you had
a full employment economy at the moment, with an unemployment rate of 3 1/2 to 4 percent, you would not have the
phenomenon of unemployed engineers. They would have in-

teresting jobs doing some things. They might not be working in their special fields and doing their engineering
and scientific specialities, but they would not have a
problem finding a job. They would be moving into a variety of management opportunities and other things, and so
if you really think of the question of how do we find jobs
for engineers that they would find satisfying, without
worrying about whether they function as engineers or scientists, I think that is a trivial problem that is basically related to the state of the economy.

In the short run you simply ask yourself, "Where will
the economy go, and is the government making the policies
necessary to bring the economy where it ought to be?"
Those questions depend on your political preferences. The
current recession is to a great extent deliberate, in the
sense that it was deliberately started as a technique for
stopping inflation. It got a little out of hand, and the
unemployment rates are a little higher than the policy
makers in Washington wanted, but if you listen to them
talk in the back corridors it was not noticeably higher
than what they wanted or at least some of them wanted.
Then in the short run we ask ourselves, "Where is the economy going?" I am usually more pessimistic than my col-
league Professor Samuelson on these things. I still think
we shall have a 6 percent unemployment rate by the end of
1971, the current year we are in. And that is despite the
first quarter that was announced with much fanfare, because interestingly enough if you subtract automobiles out
of that quarter you still have an economy with a negative

rate of growth. This economy is going downhill, not up-
hill. What we are doing is catching up from a strike, and
the administration has put a very rosy picture on a catch-
up from that strike to make you think that you are in a
boom, when there is no such thing going on. So in the
short run I am very pessimistic about the problems of jobs
for engineers. There is a recession going on, with a 6
percent unemployment rate, and as long as the unemployment
rate is generally over 6 there is no possibility of absorbing engineers and scientists into the general economy.
That is not to say that people who are out of work should
not be looking for work, but it is to say that the general
problem is not going to be solved. That problem can be
solved only when we solve the general problem of unemployment for everybody and decide that stopping inflation by
creating unemployment is not the way to stop inflation.

Let us shift now to the other problem for the demand of
engineers, not jobs for engineers but demand for engineers
and scientists in their speciality and look ahead in the
future and say what you can see coming out. If you really
look at this from the economic point of view, there is
nothing conceivable in the civilian sector of the economy
that has the engineering demand, per dollar, that space and
defense do. There is just no such project. Imagine a civilian project (for example, a housing project) equivalent
to $80 billion per year—the defense budget. It would not
hire nearly the number of engineers that $80 billion in
defense hires. Interestingly enough, the defense budget
has not gone down. It went up to about $85 billion, then

went down to $84, and has held at about $84 billion. When
you are talking about shifts in defense, keep that in the
back of your mind. The budget just stopped rising; it did
not start falling. In some sense it shows how much the
engineering and scientific community depended upon increases in the defense budget, not just a stable defense
budget.

Let us now look at civilian engineering demands. In
general, there will be less demand for scientists and engineers per dollar of GNP. That is reasonably clear. I
also agree completely with Sapolsky that there is very
much less agreement on the civilian goals and that there
are many domestic opponents. I once spent a year of my
life working for the Council of Economic Advisors and
worked on some joint efforts in the Bureau of the Budget.
And I was always shocked at the differences between handling of defense budget and space budgets and civilian
budgets. Typically the federal budget would say $8 bil-
lion for a strategic deterrent. Then you would turn over
to the civilian side of the budget and the level of detail
would be much greater. It would say: "Three packs of pencils 41 cents, Hamilton Tick station, Hamilton, Montana."
Essentially, Congress had given carte blanche to the defense establishment to decide how the money ought to be
spent within broad totals. On the civilian side they gave
nobody carte blanche. They wanted to know exactly how
many dollars were going to be spent where. There were no
capabilities for the guy running the Hamilton Tick station
even to move money between rabbits and pencils. He was

told how many rabbits he was going to have and how many pencils he was going to have. Now that difference between defense-space type budgets and civilian budgets is not an accident. There are lots of people who know exactly how they want every nickel spent on the civilian side, and they are all geared up and have been geared up for years to make sure they get every nickel spent exactly the way they want those nickels spent. If you look at the civilian projects, you not only see there is less engineering and scientific demand per dollar in general but also that it is a very different type of engineering and scientific demand.

First I should say that many of the problems we regard as most important have no engineering and scientific demand at all. The whole problem of poverty and equal opportunity, as far as anyone can see, has a zero scientific and technological demand, though there are many people who would maintain that they are our most important domestic problems. Other things like highways and transportation could have a big science and engineering demand. On the other hand, there are solutions to that problem that have no scientific or engineering demands like simply observing the fact that the real problem you have is a peak load problem. Maybe the way to solve the transportation problem is to put regulations on everybody so that we spread out our rush hours. If we worked around the clock, we would have lots of transportation of every type you can think of. There would be no crowds on the expressway. There would be no crowds on the subways. And you do not

need to invest a nickel in technology or construction.
All you do is to put regulations on people as to when they
can go to work. That is an option to solving that problem. You may not like it, but it is an option that requires no expenditures of funds of almost any sort except
a bureaucracy to regulate when we come to work and when
we are allowed to go shopping. The same thing can be seen
in the pollution and health field. In many of these cases,
where there is a technological component, it is not what
I define as high technology. I would call it low technology. It is not doing something we have not done before
but learning to do something cheaply. That is really the
name of the game in pollution and to some extent in transportation. It is not doing new things, it is doing things
cheaper. That is very different from space and defense.
The idea of having the cheapest A bomb in the world is
ridiculous. Nobody wants the cheapest A bomb in the
world. You want the A bomb with the biggest blast or that
can go the fastest, but nobody has ever heard of the cheapest A bomb. But in the civilian field, the whole premium
is on the cheapest this or that. The same thing applies
to housing. Nobody sits down and says he wants the greatest house in the world; he says he wants the cheapest
house in the world. That is what Operation Breakthrough
is designed for. It is to get cheap housing, not to get
good housing, not the fanciest housing, not the housing
with the most electrical hardware; it is to get the cheapest possible housing. Now there can be a great deal of
technology in that, but I think that is a very different

type of technology than we have been doing. M.I.T. runs
in the same race that everyone else runs in. We are
geared up to do high technology, while in general the civilian programs, even when they do demand technology, demand low technology. It is not the kind of thing that
typically the minds that are in this room or across the
street have been interested in doing in the past. It may
be terribly profitable to do, but it does not have the
same kind of intellectual challenge that going to the moon
has, or splitting the atom, or something like that.

If you look at the industrial demands for technology, it
is clear that there is something very strange going on.
There are many historical reasons for it; some industries
do research and development and some do not. In general
there is no good economic reason for that difference. The
electronic industry has done much research and development
because of government involvement. The agriculture industry has done lots of research and development because the
government completely socialized research and development
in that industry where you have state agricultural colleges, state experimental farms, and state extension services. You discover new things, you run a pilot farm to
prove that it works, and then you hire a guy to go out and
persuade every farmer to use it. But then you have big
industries like automobiles, steel, and things like that.
For all practical purposes they hire almost no engineers
and scientists and do almost no research and development.
There is no good reason why research and development
should have zero payoff in those industries. People have

suggested in steel that there is no research and development because the people running the industry are all lawyers. They could not understand it anyway, so why should
they allow it. They would not believe research if they
did see it. There are many industries which in some potential sense could be hiring research and development
technology, and in some presumed sense need it, since they
are being run out of business by other people who have it,
but for one reason or another have never engaged in the
practice.

Now I do not know what the solution to that problem is,
but I think there is something there. All you can say in
this civilian field is that if you look at the existing
problems it seems as though many of them have no technical components and many of them have low-technology
technical components. All of them are interested in cheap
solutions rather than doing things well. There may be a
lightning strike, there may be something equivalent to
Sputnik in the civilian field, somebody may do something
equivalent in splitting the atom, and we shall all say
technology is the answer to these problems. But at the
moment, just based on your current economic information,
it does not seem to me that if you were rationally sitting
down to attack domestic problems, you would say from
an economic point of view that you would expect technology
to answer the problems. There is a real question here;
let us say that you knew that you had a technology that
could solve the cheap housing problem. But let us say
that institutionally, given a million employers and con-

struction unions who are noticeably reticent to accept new
technology, you could not use it. Would it pay to go off)
and develop something you cannot use?

In summary, what I would say is there are really two
problems: first is the unemployment problem. On a technical level how we solve the unemployment problem is a trivial problem of having the right economic policies. Those
policies exist, and the people who run the government know
them. They may have different sets of value judgments.
Their set of value judgments puts a very high premium on
stopping inflation. They are willing to tolerate quite a
bit of unemployment to stop that inflation. If those
preferences change, they could cure unemployment very rapidly. All the instruments exist, but those preferences
have not changed as far as I can see, so we are going to
tolerate a deliberately high rate of unemployment for the
foreseeable future.

In some sense I am glad engineers and scientists are
unemployed, and I shall tell you why. It is not that I
like unemployed people. It is simply the fact that the
way these policies were traditionally run in the past, and
the way they were run in the 1961 recession attacked inflation by creating unemployment only for the people at
the bottom of the totem pole. I think that is horribly
unfair. If we are going to fight inflation by creating
unemployment, in some sense we should spread it across the
population. Unemployed engineers are one way to spread it
across the population. We should be spreading it among
college teachers and everybody else too. But the idea of

concentrating it at the bottom, I find economically not too useful, and, as an individual, I find it morally reprehensible. If I have to take unemployment as a given, I should like to see many more of the 6 percent unemployed concentrated among those people who are relatively well off, and that includes professional and technical workers. In terms of the long-run demand, and by long-run demand I mean 5 years, I think there may be much in demand for scientists and engineers out of the defense budget, because I think we may be going back to a pre-Vietnam cycle. The Department of Defense and the defense establishment are strong enough to defend their $84 billion. At the moment they are not strong enough to get more, but they are strong enough to keep anybody from getting his hunk of the pie. Given their $84 billion per year, they may move very strongly toward high-technology strategic deterrents once again on the grounds that we cannot fight guerrilla warfare, so let us get rid of the Green Berets and all these kinds of people and use that money for high technology. Vietnam was costing $30 billion per year. When we stop Vietnam, that gives an extra $30 billion to throw into strategic warfare. So there are going to be increasing demands for scientists and engineers, I would think, inside of the defense budget. The $84 billion is going to be increasingly moved toward high technology, and we are going to back out of conventional warfare once again. Probably by 1980 somebody will decide conventional warfare is a good thing, and we shall go through the cycle once more. But I think we are definitely in that kind of a

cycle. So that is a favorable development in terms of
employment of scientists and engineers. I do think, however, that on the civilian side it is a very different
type of ball game. You cannot look to civilian programs
and civilian priorities for engendering large future increases in the demands for scientists and engineers.

*To shift the emphasis from the strictly economic factors
affecting the employment of scientists and engineers, Professor Harvey M. Sapolsky turned his attention to the results of political decisions on jobs in technical fields.
Dr. Sapolsky is an associate professor of political science at M.I.T.*

Harvey M. Sapolsky: My task today is to provide some estimate of the political factors that will affect the future
for technologists. A concern for the political variable
is quite appropriate in a seminar of this type because
government decision making plays a dominant role in determining the opportunities for technology and technologists.
As you are well aware, the government is the prime consumer and prime supporter of technology in the nation. It
was the governmental decisions in the postwar years that
built up the nation's technological base, and most likely
it will be governmental decisions that will determine
whether or not the base will expand, be maintained, or
contract. The government's interest in technology, as you
are also well aware, was an interest motivated largely by
national security concerns. We are told, however, that

priorities are changing. The question to ask then is:
How will the national interest in technology be affected
by the changing national priorities?

What is needed is an accurate political forecast, probably one tied to budgets, showing how many dollars will be
allocated in each policy category. Unfortunately, political science is not yet a science. And the political world
is full of surprises that make accurate forecasting quite
difficult, perhaps even impossible.

We have talked already about some of these surprises.
If we had a meeting like this 15 years ago, we, of course,
would not have known about Sputnik; we also would not have
known about the Cuban missile crisis, the assassination
of a President, the initiation of a long war, the retirement of an incumbent President, and the resurrection of a
defeated political leader. No matter how good our estimate of the total economic picture of the country was, we
would have still missed the good part of the governmental
mix, the money the government allocated among the various
policy area alternatives. And all this makes it very
very difficult to describe how the future will affect
technology and technologists.

The problem of political predictions reminds me of a
story about a noted political scientist who was an expert
in Soviet affairs and Kremlin decision making. He failed,
however, to predict the downfall of Khrushchev, and the
day after it happened he was chided by his colleagues in
other disciplines for having been unable to predict such
an important Soviet political event. He had an answer for

them, though. He said, "Even Khrushchev did not know that
he was going to be overturned."

Given my temerity in making political forecasts, what I
should like to do today is to describe some basic political conditions that will affect decision making in defense
and nondefense areas and to assess the efficacies of certain strategies that some of the participants in these
policy areas are likely to take. In doing so, I shall
limit my remarks to trends in the near future. In that
way I shall be subject to being trapped by fewer surprises
than if I took a longer point of view. It is a rather
modest undertaking, but the only one that is possible, I
believe.

Let me begin with defense, or more precisely the aerospace policy area. In this policy area, the recent ABM
and SST decisions both mark what I think is the same major
political watershed, even though the decisions have gone
in different directions. Prior to these decisions, aerospace allocations were the result of a closed bureaucratic
politics, which took place within government, which was
sustained by a broad national consensus providing a certain large number of dollars to defense activities each
year, and which was based on a belief that technology was
vital for the national defense. The myths of powerful
lobbies notwithstanding, each major project decision was
a political struggle within government, but except for occasional changes in the dollar ceilings, it was politics
little affected by the general political process. Today,
after the controversy over the ABM and SST, every aero-

space project has become vulnerable to challenge. The
B-1, the F-14, the F-15, the space shuttle, are all multimillion-dollar projects, and I believe that each one of
them will come up against some sort of serious challenge.
Not only will there be the traditional debate over the
size of the defense budget, but there will be debate over
the desirability of particular projects. This type of debate has not occurred in the past as often as it will in
the future.

Consider the public discussion of overruns and schedule
slippages in defense contracts, for example. These problems were with us 10 years ago but were viewed quite dif-
ferently then. In the early 1960s there was a great clam-
or about overruns and schedule slippages, and we saw them
then as a product of bureaucratic inefficiency. What we
wanted to do was centralize the Department of Defense and
improve its decision-making capabilities so we could buy
more with the dollars we were allocating for defense. We
have the same problems today, but view them quite differ-
ently. The overruns are about the same today in percentage terms as they were in the early 1960s and late 1950s,
but we have a different attitude toward them. Now it is
said they are the product of a centralized conspiratorial
Defense Department, and now the desire is to eliminate the
overruns so we can spend less money on defense. Politics
goes through fads and fashions. Sputnik started one fashion, the ABM and the SST will, I think, start another one
in the opposite policy direction.

There is also a moralistic tinge to our politics. We

like to conceive of disputes in terms of the good guys
versus the bad guys; we like crusades and crusaders. In
New York City politics the candidates for office still run
against the bosses. The last live boss was walking the
streets of New York about 15 years ago; there has not been
one seen since. But in every election the candidates
claim they are running against the bosses. I think that
in the future many of the candidates for national office
are going to be running against the military-industrial
state in a moralistic crusade. If politics turns in this
direction, certain major projects that employ many engineers and scientists are in obvious danger. It matters
not that we can dredge up quotes from the early 1960s supporting the consensus that gave us the military-industrial
state of the political leaders who are going to be leading
the crusade. It is going to be the platform on which to
run for political office just as asking for more dollars
for defense (and defense technology) was once a platform
of those with political ambitions.

What is the administration's or aerospace industries'
strategy? I think it can be discerned. Despite the warn-
ings about new Soviet threats that appear every once in
a while, it is basically to avoid a struggle, to offer "a
low profile." I think that is the basic governmental policy in this area, and that means talking about contract
reforms. If you are worried about overruns, if you are
worried about schedule slippages, then they will give you
another Defense Department reorganization. Or better
still, they will break up the contracts into very small

packages. We just came through a period of total package
procurement which led to rather disastrous overruns, not
necessarily in percentage terms but in terms of scale.
The hope in breaking up the contracts into much smaller
packages is that you will not be able to see the totals.
And they will also go back to cost-plus fixed-fee types of
contracts instead of the incentive contracting, which
again show overruns and which make the overruns clearer
than in the case of cost-plus fixed-fee arrangements. Despite the fact that the Defense Department is very much
concerned about maintaining the industrial base, I do not
believe this strategy will be much help in keeping projects going. It is a losing strategy, even though in an
election year there is a natural reluctance to put a lot
of people out of work. The reason I say this is that I
believe people will be taking the pledge against the military-industrial state in the 1972 election just the way
most took the pledge against alcohol during the 1920s.

   What about shifting priorities? It is already happening.
I believe the administration likes to think it is happening more than some of you may think it is happening, but
the allocations are moving toward nondefense parts of the
federal budget. I am not, however, optimistic about the
prospects for technology and technologists in this budget-
ing shift. The nondefense policy areas are quite different political ball games. I think a concern with the environment, with transportation, with housing, welfare, and
medical delivery with medical services will not bring

large opportunities for technology and technologists. At
least not opportunities in the kind of organizational
framework or at the kind of scale you are used to in the
defense area. There will be a lot going on, but I think
there will not be many large-scale projects of the type
you are used to seeing.

Let me try to contrast the difference between defense
and nondefense areas. Unlike in the defense area, in the
nondefense area there is no consensus of what constitutes
the policy problem. In the defense area, it was clear
that we had an enemy. Whether or not the enemy was real
or whether or not the enemy's threat was as large as we
thought it was at any given moment is not the point.
There was, at least, a common enemy. In the nondefense
areas, there is no agreement on what constitutes the problem. Consider, for example, the urban crisis. Everybody
is dissatisfied with something, but the dissatisfaction
is very different for different people. Some of us worry
about crime in the streets or people moving into the
neighborhood. Others of us are worried about delivery of
urban services and transportation and all sorts of other
things upon which we find it hard to agree. We can all
be dissatisfied, but it is certain that we are not dissatisfied about the same things. More importantly, I
think, we can contrast defense and nondefense areas in
terms of the fact that there is no consensus that technology is the relevant solution or the best solution available for any of these problems. I am not saying that it

is not a solution or it is not the best solution; but people do not perceive it as the best solution or even a good
solution.

Let us go down the list of the various problems that we
all face, the great crises of the world. First environmental crisis. I am sure my fellow panelists will tell us
that there are many ways to solve the environmental questions besides technology. We can have tax reforms of various kinds or incentive schemes that would change the be-
havior of people toward the desecration of the environment.
Or if we take housing next, we may want to consider technological innovations in housing, but we can also try to
build more of the same type of housing we already have.
I think there will be many people who would like to see
more of the same and would be satisfied with it. Or if we
are concerned with welfare and poverty problems, we can
mail people checks instead of providing them services.
And there are many people in favor of that approach. Or
in delivery of medical services, we can conduct more research, or we can start up neighborhood health clinics and
train more doctors. These are all sorts of alternatives,
and I think the technologically oriented ones are the ones
that are probably last on most people's lists. Not on our
lists necessarily, but on most other people's lists.
There has been no domestic equivalent of the atomic bomb
or radar that convinces everybody that scientists and technologists should be consulted in these kinds of problems.

Unlike in defense, a success by the technologists in nondefense policy areas can hurt people who vote. The Rus-

sians did not vote in our elections during the 1950s and
1960s, but obviously any kind of improvement in weapon
systems was more to their disadvantage than it was to people in our society. But when we move into domestic areas,
as Dr. Wiesner mentioned, we discover that there are powerful lobbies, lobbies that are in fact more powerful than
the military-industrial state lobbies. The planning for
military-related projects has been a rather closed system,
involving only a few favorably disposed groups. In planning for technological projects in the domestic area you
find, however, construction unions, the welfare professionals, educationalists, the highway builders, and all sorts
of other groups that are ready and able to defend their
turf. They will fight any attempt to take away a share of
the allocations that they believe should go to their own
programs rather than let it move toward the technologists.
Budget allocations are quite a zero-sum game, but I think
it will be perceived that way by those who have stakes in
the domestic policy areas.

Finally, unlike defense, there is no hierarchical organization to control projects. At a conference like this
it is commonplace to talk about dispersal of buyers and the
fragmentation of decision makers in the nondefense areas.
There is general agreement that it would be best to
centralize all of this and place in the hands of one buyer
or a few buyers the responsibility for making rational,
system-wide decisions. In the defense area there are
a small number of large buyers, monopolists is the word
economists use, and they are able to control almost an en-

tire system. We like to believe they do a great deal of
planning for entire systems, but I think if you looked
carefully at particular projects you will find that they
really suboptimized. The Navy, for example, is concerned
about the Navy's missiles, and the Air Force is concerned
about the Air Force's missiles. But nevertheless, they
can at least worry about the missiles and the missiles
systems. But when we get into the nondefense area, there
are all sorts of other people involved and all sorts of
decision makers. We have local government, county government, regional government, we have private groups, and
every one of them shares in the decision making. The federal government itself is fragmented into numerous sub-
units. But even if the federal government were to be centralized into a few large domestic policy units, there
would be the fragmentation at other levels of government
with which to contend. And the social trends are working
against centralization. With increased affluence, increased education, and increased social awareness, it appears that the citizens demand more, not less, participation. Increases in participation, in turn, increase
governmental fragmentation. Recall that attempts to implement centralized decisions in education, fluoridation, and
urban renewal have met the resistance of local initiative.
I think attempts to plan new cities, to build new transportation systems, and to provide comprehensive health
care will meet resistance, too. Democracy requires decen-
tralization and participation. Perhaps the scientists and
technologists who are accustomed to large-scale defense

programs will find that democracy fits very well with
their visions of what society should do in nondefense policy areas.

What I am saying is that a strategy directed toward
gaining a share of the dollars being allocated to solving
domestic problems and toward establishing large-scale programs in nondefense technologies is not likely to be very
successful in the near future. Of course, I am concerned
only with the near future. Justice and truth will triumph
in the end. You have to eat though before then. I am not
saying that there will not be more money for R&D in these
areas. Each one of the domestic technology programs has
recently received a larger budget. But each of the defense programs that I have mentioned previously was in the
$100-million to $400-million range, and that is just the
initial funding. They are likely to total $10 billion
each if they were to be completed. Although there will
be many increases and the percentage increases will be
quite high, nondefense projects are not likely to reach
soon the scale available in the defense area.

Is there a solution? I doubt it. I really do not have
one, but I could perhaps mention briefly what kind of political strategy might gain money to demonstrate the skill
of the scientists and technologists in the social policy
areas. It has to do with the conversion process. I do
not really think that it should be called conversion; I
would have a different label on it. What you need to do
is open up a different political arena for scientists and
technologists: not one part of those that exist in the ur-

ban, environmental, or transportation areas where there
are groups already well entrenched and ready to defend
themselves. You could talk in terms of conservation of
national defense resources. Maybe this is a cynical approach, but we occasionally do the right things for the
wrong reasons, perhaps the SST decision falls in this category. You could talk in terms of maintaining the industrial reserve or maintaining large-scale, highly skilled
systems groups to be used to protect against defense surprises. The nation occasionally experiences such surprises, and I think the public will believe that they are
possible. Then perhaps the resources will be made available on the scale needed to provide some major demonstrations. One could be in air traffic control, not because
air traffic control rates a higher priority than say the
urban problem, but rather because it will provide an ac-
ceptable use of the skills of the people who are there to
protect us against surprises. I am not ready to push this
suggestion very hard, however, because there are problems.
Most particularly, it is not clear that the demonstrations
will work, that the skills of military technologists are
transferable.

A fairly detailed discussion of the present economic situation as it related to the difficult job market for scientists and engineers was presented by Dr. Paul A. Samuelson, professor of economics at M.I.T. and the first Nobel
Laureate in the field of economics. He first presented a
list of ten factors that worked against scientists and en-

gineers trying to change their careers at the present time and then discussed the future trends in the light of these unfavorable factors.

Paul A. Samuelson: This discussion has proved the theorem that if you scratch a Wall Street vice president you find a philosopher, and if you scratch two academic ivory tower professors, you find practical men ready to pour cold water on the audience. I too will be throwing some more cold water in my remarks, but maybe blood, sweat, and tears is what you came to hear. Let me summarize what it is I heard, and also give some other considerations that occurred to me.

I want to quote the opening lines of my textbook back in 1948. It was a quotation from the Dean of the Harvard Law School, presumably Roscoe Pound, who said as he addressed the freshman class each year: "Gentlemen, look at the person on your left and look at the person on your right because next year one of you won't be here." Well, as scientists and engineers with jobs at the moment, I suggest that you look at the man on your left and on your right because one of you next year may not be a scientist or engineer according to the census classification. I realize that Professor Thurow, who has been described correctly as the wave of the future, assures you that you will find a job as a franchiser of Kentucky Fried Chicken or at least you will if President Nixon gets the message and starts listening to the wave of the future. But that process of finding a new niche can be a very uncomfortable one.

Now for the cold water. It seems to me that the typical
person hanging on precariously to a job in the field of
science and engineering has about nine or ten strikes
against him at the present time. Let me enumerate what
they are. First and very important, the aerospace program
is winding down. That is obvious and has been discussed.
Second, and it is not the same thing, there is a wind-down
to the war: too slow for many of us, but definitely a
wind-down, particularly in terms of the percentage of the
GNP. There is no necessary reason, of course, why those
should coincide. Then there is the recent recession. I
agree completely with Professor Thurow's remarks that anyone who looks at the headlines and thinks that we are back
on the road to a full recovery in a very rapid time is not
an expert.

Then there is a fourth wind-down, which is related to
some of the others, but is not obvious on the surface.
There is a wind-down to government support for research
in general. That is just a fact, but it need not have
been that way. An enormous amount of government support
to research in this country has come through the back door
of the Pentagon. Many a fellow who could not get tenure
as assistant professor at M.I.T.—and some who did get it—
could go to Route 128 and start a company of his own, win-
ning a Defense Department contract even for rather pure
research. And if he was between production contracts, he
could get a sustaining contract explicitly for research.
But recently there has been a real shift in government

support of research. Again there is no reason why all
this should have coincided.

Let me illustrate. I spoke to a suburban neighbor of
mine. He told me that he is a consultant to a pollution
firm. He reports it is harder today to get a government
subsidy to try out the removing of sulfur by a particular
process from a public utility stack than it was when we
were all straining to get to the moon. Let me continue
with this. We have McLean Hospital in the suburbs here;
it is a great mental hospital. A psychiatrist whom I met
on the tennis court told me that the best treatment for
mental disease can be found in the Boston area. And he
said that government-subsidized programs had begun to be
set up all over the country to train people to give that
same kind of mental care. Now that has been cut out.
There is no reason why at the same time that we are cutting down on the war we should be cutting down on such
programs, but it does affect the supply of and demand for
people in science and engineering.

Fifth, nobody has yet mentioned competition from abroad.
The Japanese are ever present in the minds of our electrical engineering graduates of recent years. The chairman
of our Electrical Engineering Department tells me that the
last automated television line has been dropped by GE.
They cannot compete with the Japanese. He was complaining
that, because of space and because of the war, we have
been sending all our trained people to high-technology
esoteric science in electrical engineering. Nobody knows

how to design an ordinary assembly line for television
sets anymore. So just as the textile and shoe industries
in New England are complaining bitterly about the foreign
imports, the next big lobby is going to be in electronics.
I have singled out the Japanese, but they are simply the
most outstanding and obvious example of what we are also
getting from the comeback of science and technology in
Western Europe. I speak as a professional economist when
I say that what complicates the problem is that the American dollar is an overrated dollar. The parity between
the dollar and the yen, the dollar and the mark, is wrong
and it makes for lots of imports of textiles, shoes, and
electronic equipment. If that is corrected, as perhaps it
will be after a crisis or so, these particular industries
will get some more protection—and the kind of protection
economists approve of, as against quotas and the kind that
the Mills bill tried to foist upon our economy. (I should
not say "foist" because the grass roots strength for protection is very strong in this country. It is a difficult
battle to keep down the protectionist.) Well, that might
improve the situation, but it would improve it only relatively because the trend is for more competition from
abroad, and this affects the demand for engineers in America. We were once so much ahead of the world that we
earned economic rent; that is no longer the case.

The sixth strike against you is rather technical, but
I shall try to state it and then define it so at least
you get the idea. You are victims of what we call the ac-

celeration principle in economic analysis. According to
this principle, the demand for many items depends upon the
rate of *growth* of demand and not upon the *level* of that
demand. Breakfast food sales, for example, depend upon
the level of demand. But if you take the demand for machine tools or the demand for engineers, that depends upon
the velocity of something, plus the fact that we need many
pilots or engineers—it takes engineers to train engineers.
And so the shortage is accentuated because you have to
keep feeding back into the pipeline as teachers of engineers, and that gives you less engineers for the final
product. That is just lovely until it catches up with you,
and you cease to have the exponential growth. The minute
you begin a decline in the velocity, even though the absolute growth still is positive, you have a colossal fall in
these industries subject to the acceleration principle.
The Cartter report was a report on the supply and demand
for teachers with Ph.D.'s, done several years ago by Chan-
cellor Cartter, who is now at NYU but was then at the Car-
negie Foundation. He estimated that by the early 1970s
there would be a crisis because the number of trained
Ph.D.'s was going to cross the demand for Ph.D.'s, and
that crisis, I can assure you, is on us in practically
every field. The result is: just when people are getting
thrown out of work on Route 128, they cannot go back to
teaching science in a junior college. I have noticed that
in some other countries where there is beginning to be a
little wind-down in the demand for science and engineers

in industry, there is an efficacious program to train them as teachers because the acceleration principle, the Cartter point, has not yet arrived.

Seventh, I see a definite antiscience mood in the country. This is not all completely against the balance of supply and demand. Do any of you remember the alleged fact that, after World War I, when there was a great killing off of men in the armies of the world, the number of male births went up relative to the number of female births? This was statistically significant, and the explanation people gave was that Mother Nature's wisdom was restoring the balance! Well, maybe Mother Nature is working again because, and you must remember this speaker is not a "wave of the future," we all know that students are not much interested in working in hard science and engineering anymore. Maybe that is nature's way of helping to solve the problem: just when the country needs less scientists and wants less scientists, they are less willing to be scientists. For example, the chemistry enrollment at Harvard is down to half of what it was—the staff is perhaps twice as large as it was 12 years ago, but the enrollment is down by half. The number of freshman coming in to be scientists shot up after Sputnik, because there was always a tremendous tradition in college, but this mix is changing. I looked at the largest eight fields of concentration in Radcliffe and Harvard—last year and 10 years ago—and the composition is drastically changing. People are moving away from everything analytic. Social relations is by far the biggest subject at Radcliffe.

Economics, alas, is one of the harder social sciences (and
I use it in the technical sense), and it is down but still
in the first eight. There is no mathematics or science in
the first eight at Radcliffe. There is, I think, biology
at Harvard in the first eight fields of concentration. So
that is going to have an effect upon the future supply and
demand, but not fast enough for you. I think President
Wiesner has a real problem in working out what the function of M.I.T. should be, and how to adjust M.I.T. to the
changing mix both of students' desires and of ways to use
our people.

Point number eight is again related to Japanese competition. It is possible that with mass education the privi-
leged position of educated people is being undermined.
Back before World War II it used to be my great privilege
and pleasure to sit about once every 4 or 5 weeks on a
Monday night with President Conant of Harvard. He then
had a bee in his bonnet. He thought that we were going to
have an intellectual proletariat, too many college students: the pattern that existed allegedly in Japan, of
college graduates who run little book shops and turn radi-
cal, or the Budapest pattern where when the first snow
comes all the Ph.D.'s leave the coffee house and apply
for a shovel and a paying job. That was the vision Conant
envisaged for the United States. And he said that what we
ought to have was vocational training, not higher education.

Well, how wrong can a man be? There never was a more
gross error if he was projecting for the period from 1939

to, let us say, 1965. The American system just had a colossal appetite for high-IQ, highly trained people. But
his long-run vision was more nearly correct than his short-
run vision. The war moved the mix toward certain peculiar
high intellectual traits. I agree completely with Professor Thurow that if you do what we call a Leontief input-
output study, and take the final dollar of each different
thing and trace it through for what kind of employment it
gives to copper, for what kind of employment it gives to
different kinds of labor, and so on, you could not imagine
a more favorable mix than the high-technology mix of the
combined aerospace program and the defense program. We
all know that. You have all been in the field. I knew a
mathematician in another institution, a brilliant fellow,
who went literally crazy. Yet for 2 or 3 or 4 years
thereafter, project after project was saying "let's put
him on the payroll." "So and so would like to go to a
scientific meeting in London; do you want to put it on
this budget or that budget?" There was so much money in
some of these areas that there was a great deal of fat
along with the muscle. Well, those days are gone and now
it is not the question of cutting out fat; it is the question of cutting out muscle. There is finally the problem.

  And one must add the problem—not a new one—of the lifetime dynamics of the engineer. When the premium developed
in the field of engineering and science over liberal arts
graduates, it was somewhat deceptive. A liberal arts student would get, let us say, a $7000 offer, and a science

graduate at the same level would get an $11,000 offer; and
he would be besieged at every convention to come down to
Orlando, Florida, or to San Diego for all the good life
and so forth, and he got promoted. But after about 5
years something happened, namely they wanted the new science graduate. There was a faster obsolescence on the job
and a slower lifetime profile of promotion and earnings
than in many other fields. Unless you did what you used
to do all the time in the 1920s and the 1930s—let us take
the 1920s because that was high-employment time—when engineers went out of engineering and became businessmen.
(That is the solution that I think that Professor Thurow
is counseling many of you to do in the period that is
ahead.) Now this may have something to do with the rapid-
ity of obsolescence of knowledge acquired and the obsoles-
cent deterioration due to aging, so that at 30 an engineer
is an old engineer. For a mathematical logician the age
is even younger—at 23 those fellows are used up, they become deans. Historians, in contrast, ripen in judgment
for much longer. So this particular lifetime problem com-
pounds the obsolescence effect.

Now, let me say that I agree with Thurow that the present recession is contrived in order to fight inflation,
not out of wickedness or sadism. I agree that the thing
got out of hand, and, as a result of the speaking out of
the electorate in November, we have still another new
Nixon. We have many new Nixons; this one is an expansion-
ist, a spender. We welcome him to the club, but he must

work his passage; acceptance comes not from mere talk and blown-up estimates. If he does, the recession will end and more jobs of some kind will be available.

But I still want to point out that there is a lot of heartache in being shaken from your lifework. Somebody on Route 128 who thought he was set for life—making $25,000 and expecting, if he kept his nose clean, that in 20 years he would retire with a higher salary and with a decent pension—suddenly finds he is out on the street, out of a job. I appeared on a television program with some of those people and it was heartrending. Many of these people had sent out three hundred resumes. They were trained people; as I looked at these men I thought that any bank with any sense ought to grab some of them. For one thing, they had a tremendous capacity for dealing with adversity—something that not every person has.

Why is it such a problem if an engineer gets put out of work, I mean a well-paid scientist engineer in the high-technology complex? If I may say so, it would not be such a problem for a woman. If a woman is out of work, there is no problem in this country. If a black is out of work, there is no problem. If you are unskilled, there is no problem. If you are a ditch digger, you are no better at 26 than you were at 25, and you are worse at 32 than you were at 25. It is a sad fact (Professor Robert Hall of our department has gathered some data on this) that there is only one group in our community who advances with age in status and pay after say the age of 25. These are the white males. If a woman loses her job, well she never had

a good job anyway. Dr. Curley is one of the rarest sights
you will ever see in the world, a woman with a good job.
Among the graduates of the Harvard class of 1937, the lowest man who will report in to an alumni association is
making $20,000 a year, and they go up $80,000 and $100,000,
and the median is probably $39,000 or $45,000. If you
know anything about income distribution, you know that
this is the fantastic height of the pyramid. If you look
at the Radcliffe class of 1937—I assure you a more highly
select group in terms of intellect than the 1937 Harvard
class because that was before the days of meritocracy at
Harvard—the highest graduate is getting $19,000 a year,
and there are an unbelievable number of them earning
$9500. And it is not because they are mothers with seven
children doing a little part-time work and who left the
labor force. This is what librarians and assistant personnel officers make, and this also applies in secondary
school teaching, which in the past has been a lousy profession in terms of pay for men and has always been "a
magnificent job opportunity" for women.

Well, if you never had a good job it does not matter
when you lose it, because you then go and find another job
like that. But white men, and particularly beyond the age
of 35, have got a tremendous economic advantage in their
job. Now maybe you are not worth it, and maybe it is all
an elaborate miscalculation, but you had it; and the people who are lucky enough to be in the breakfast food business continue to go up the scale and continue to get their
raises with age. When you get shaken by any outside event

in the professional classes like that, you will find another job; but unless you are a very rare bird, you will
find a worse job in terms of perquisites and in terms of
pay. So it is no joke.

My final query is this. Why do we run the system in
such a way that people have to play Russian roulette with
their careers? At the age of sixteen you have to decide
whether you will be a chemical engineer. You train yourself (expensively) for 8, 10, 12 more years. Then you
have a career for the next 40 years in that line. Think
what a prophet you have to be to guess right. People ask
me about the pricing of stocks; that is nothing to the
problem of how you invest in your own career. You *have*
to speculate. Just as stocks can go up or go down and you
can make a mistake, so it is with your career. Now suppose I made a mistake, and I should have been a plumber,
but by miscalculation I became a professor. I was lucky.
There was not anything else to do, and I probably do not
have the capabilities for anything else. But let us take
the people who were sucked into the military-scientific-
technology complex by post-Sputnik. I think the government has a responsibility to them. We told them how much
they were needed in that line and brought them out to
Route 128, then we fired them with one year of severance
pay at an age where they cannot find an equivalent job.
This is dirty pool.

Now, let me bring to your attention an alternative system, the Japanese system. In Japan you work your head off
to get into the University of Tokyo, like working to get

into M.I.T. or the other elite schools. If you get into
the University of Tokyo, you can get a top job with one
of the large companies. When you get a job with one of
these large companies, you are in the company for life.
You would never switch from Westinghouse to General Electric, from General Electric to Itek, from Itek to Ramo-
Wooldridge. If the demand for their product goes down,
they still have to support you. The problem of reconverting you is thrown on the industries, because they do not
want to support you in idleness. They have to retrain you
for other purposes.

Why should not our defense establishment somehow insist
upon (within the same plants) companies reconverting the
scientists to another use? It is, of course, very hard to
reconvert within the area of science for all the reasons
that have been mentioned. Let me call to your attention
this fact: our Instrumentation Laboratory, the Draper
Laboratory, is agreed by all to be one of the most magnificent technical work teams of the ages. And when the climate of opinion changed—of public opinion, of student
opinion, and of faculty opinion—the Instrumentation Laboratory became a cancer on the body of M.I.T. which had to
be thrown off. President Johnson came before a packed
faculty meeting and he said, "Give me the chance, give me
one year to convert this great laboratory to functions of
peace." He was given that chance, and President Johnson,
who is a very clever and very energetic man, could not
even make a start on doing it. There should be a social
responsibility to prevent such cannibalism—that I think

is particularly strong in the scientific and engineering
professions—on a lifetime basis.

I shall finally finish, agreeing a little bit with Lester Thurow, by saying that if there has to be some unemployment it could not happen to a nicer bunch of guys than
you fellows, and let me say why. Unemployment in the last
slowdown or two seemed to be something that happened only
in the ghetto. It did not happen to nice people like you
and me. My wife had triplets, and when I mentioned this
at a faculty tea one woman moved away from me and she said
that sort of thing does not happen to people like us.
Well it did, and so did unemployment happen to engineers
and scientists on Route 128 and in the suburbs. This has
hope for greater political action because the poor are
really anonymous. That is one of the things about the
poor; they are shut up in places of their own, and they
really do not know how to speak and are never heard. People like you *can* kick and protest and put pressure upon
Congress to have something done about it; and if you do,
I think we shall have a better-run system.

*After the formal presentation of these papers Professor
Franco Modigliani, who was acting as moderator for the
discussion, joined in answering questions from the audience. Dr. Modigliani is both a professor of economics and
a professor of finance at M.I.T.*

Franco Modigliani: I should like to make a brief comment
on this and a related subject. The whole question is what

is behind unemployment and who gets unemployed and for
what reasons. There is some disagreement about the likely
rate of unemployment by the end of the year: some analysts
are thinking it will be around 5 and some around 6 percent.
I should like to point out that this difference about the
rate of unemployment really says very little about job opportunities and unemployment for a class of people like
engineers. Indeed, one important reason why there is some
difference in the rate of unemployment projections is the
fact that unemployment is hard to forecast because it is
the difference between two numbers: labor force on the one
hand and employment on the other. And the labor force is
hard to forecast for various reasons, among which is the
fact that the labor force responds to unemployment itself.
In other words, when employment goes up by a hundred, unemployment does not go down by a hundred because some new
people come into the labor force, and, therefore, the unemployment goes down by less. Thus, despite some apparent
differences there is, I think, substantial agreement that
there is ahead of us a very sluggish economy.

  I would completely agree with Samuelson that the forecasts on the whole are pessimistic in terms of what it
means for you.

  This does lead me to a comment in connection with what
Thurow said; I agree completely with the various approaches
he mentioned. But I think he left one out that might be
important, although there is some difference of opinion
within the profession as to how important. What I am re-
ferring to are essentially manpower programs. One way to

cut the unemployment for a given level of employment opportunities, or jobs to be filled, consists in endeavoring
to reduce the flow through the market, resulting from the
flow of accessions and separations.

For a given constant level of employment, terminations
of jobs, through fires and quits, are of course offset by
new hires. Nonetheless, these flows are a major source
of unemployment. Indeed, as should be easy for an engineer to see, the level of unemployment may be thought of
as the product of the flow through the market times the
average search time—that is, the length of time it takes
on the average for an unemployed to find a job. At the
present time, the magnitude of these flows in the American
economy is rather staggering; available data suggest that
the monthly flow is typically of the order of 3 percent
of the number of people employed. This implies a turnover
rate of over 1/3 per year, or equivalently that the average tenure of a job is below 3 years. You will probably
find these figures surprising because most of you are used
to careers in which you get into a job and you keep it
forever. But a lot of this turnover is due to other kinds
of people, like the women Paul Samuelson was talking about,
for whom termination of the current employment is a frequent occurrence.

Manpower programs could make a contribution to reducing
unemployment and, at the same time, vacancies, both by
reducing the flow and by shortening search time. What
causes the large flow referred to earlier? It comes, in
part, from the fact that we have a dynamic economy in

which some firms are gaining and some firms are losing
shares even though the total is constant. Some people get
thrown out of jobs and some new jobs are opened. This
source of flow is hard to reduce as long as we want to
maintain a dynamic economy, though something could be done
by appropriate choices of stabilization policies. Another
source of the flow, however, comes from poor matching between job and jobholder, which results in voluntary quits
and fires. A better matching system may reduce this kind
of flow through the markets. Also the search time can be
reduced by a better method of gathering and distributing
information that would enable people more quickly to find
out what jobs are available and where they are available.
To some extent training programs could reduce the length
of search by providing people who can fit the vacancies
that exist. In the past, relatively little effort has
been devoted to designing and funding these kinds of programs. I personally feel this whole area of manpower
programs deserves a great deal more attention.

Paul A. Samuelson: I think that a good deal of the advance of our living standards is due to technological
change but it's hard to relate as closely as that to scientific training or expenditure on science. But over a
longer period of time it seems reasonable that that's the
case. In a way, Americans have a special stake in this
because if you ask, "What are we good at?," let's say in
international trade, we have in the past been good at new
things. The moment a thing becomes standardized DuPont

can't do it as against a sweatshop. We have always to be
finding new things. Similarly with respect to technology,
America was ahead, and we export new things until the
others catch on. But there is a trouble with that. If we
have the advantage of fertile Iowa farmland and somebody
else doesn't, then that goes on permanently and trade is
mutually profitable because of our comparative advantage.
But if your comparative advantage is really in ingenuity,
new things, you are always running just in order to stand
still. Now I suspect that our technology is slipping away.
We have an expression in economics for this: when we discuss different interest rate markets, we say money mingles;
well, knowledge mingles too. You can't keep technology
your own monopoly, and one of the big events, I believe,
of that last 20 years, and I don't know that anyone could
have predicted it, is that the United States, which has
always been the leader, is slipping; the gap between us
and the rest of the world has been steadily narrowed by
the miracles abroad. I have, for example, just jotted
down some numbers that were estimated of the rates of
growth for the next 10 years, in real terms, in real output, for the seven principal countries of the world. This
was done in Paris by the OECD (Organization for Economic
Co-operation and Development), which we belong to. The
group as a whole, the seven principal countries, will grow
by 90 percent in real terms with no inflation counted in.
But of course, only one country is going to grow by more
than 90 percent—that's Japan. It's going to grow by 160
percent. You would never guess what the second country in

growth would be. The second country is decadent France—
79 percent. Decadent Italy—72 percent; Canada—67 percent; and I think that if we corrected that per capita it
wouldn't be all that different. The United States—58
percent. West Germany, and this is a surprise, 57 percent as against our 58 percent—who could believe that?
Well, we still have manpower growing. We still have a
past baby boom feeding the labor markets, which is why the
$28.5 billion of the first quarter, after being purified
of the strike rebound, isn't even up to the power of the
increase in our labor force. The United Kingdom, which,
of course, has neither technology nor baby boom, is going
to grow by only 37 percent.

Well now, despite the American challenge in all those
books you read about the colossus that all the Europeans
talk about, the fact of life is that everybody else is,
relatively speaking, catching up with us. It is partly
our Marshall Plan, but not all. Just as when rubber plants
went from Brazil, because they couldn't keep the monopoly,
to Malaya, Brazil ceased to be a viable rubber producer.
So this catching-up process is going on. It needn't, of
course, impoverish us. It simply means that there are going to be more affluent people like us. But it will impoverish certain industries that depend upon keeping ahead.
Furthermore, I think that if there is a truly antiscien-
tific mood in the country, and all the kids want to write
poetry, this won't show itself in the 1970 decade but it
will show itself in the trend we are talking about now in
1990 to 2000.

Question: Do you draw the inference then that lack of input and engineers into the system will one day show itself
up as a reduction in the growth rate of the United States?

Paul A. Samuelson: Yes, and it will show itself as a
change in the geographic world division of labor, because
affluence hits hardest where it hits first. For example,
the United Kingdom had its watershed in 1870; before that
it was the workshop of the world, but it earlier seemed
to run out of its élan in the area that we are talking
about—technology—but maybe not in the field of literature. And maybe something like that is going on with the
United States. I don't deplore it; people don't live for
growth, if they are going to be happy. The only thing I'm
not sure of, and here I depart from the text of our discussion, are we happy? If you go to Harvard Square, go
and look at the faces, are the guinea pigs happy?

Comment: I want to make two observations without analysis
or comment. First, in relation to living with inflation,
I have at home a German postage stamp, a 200 million mark
stamp, government surcharged before it could be issued to
200 billion marks. This came from the period when the
German workman was being paid three times a day so that
his wife could quickly go and spend it before the mark de-
clined in value. The second comment might perhaps shed a
little ray of light in relation to Japanese competition.
I had occasion to price some printed circuit boards in
Japan. I found out that the Japanese are now getting a

good deal of this sort of semiskilled work done in Korea
and Hong Kong because they can't afford Japanese labor!

Question: Professor Thurow mentioned during the speech
that he did not think it ethical for unemployment to be
concentrated among the poor and he felt that there was a
certain amount of justice in unemployment being spread
among those who used to be wealthy as well. I would like
him to comment on the hypothesis that having full employment of the people who have reached a high level of training, such as M.I.T. graduates and graduates from other institutions of higher learning, assures that we will have
a plentiful supply of people who, through this training,
can enhance productivity, and whether perhaps a fairer division might not be better achieved by giving people schol-
arship grants.

Lester C. Thurow: I think that one of the terrible things
we do when we discuss inflation is always to debate it in
terms of polar extremes. We talk about a zero rate versus
Germany with 8 million a month, or whatever. That's an
interesting debate but incredibly irrelevant. The real
debate is what are the pros and cons of a 5 percent rate
of inflation, and many of the things that are an objection
to a 800 million rate are not objections at a 5 percent
rate, so I think you need to bring the discussion back and
talk in the real world because there is very little evidence that if a 4 percent rate of unemployment was associated with a 5 percent rate of inflation the 5 percent

would accelerate. Your second point essentially had to
do with a meritocracy argument. We worked hard and therefore we shouldn't be unemployed while other people who are
unemployed didn't work hard, and so it's more fair that
they should be unemployed. I find it hard to swallow that
kind of an argument, and even on a technical level it isn't
obvious that it is true. You know, it takes a long time
to be an electrician or a plumber. You've got to be ap-
prenticed for just about as long as it takes to get a
Ph.D., and you invest just about as much because you get
low wages during that apprenticeship period. Electricians
and plumbers have skills that are different from mine but
in some sense require just as much blood, sweat, and tears
on their part as my skills do as an economics Ph.D. I
cannot find any axiom that says that I worked hard, therefore I shouldn't be unemployed, while all these other
people who haven't worked hard ought to be unemployed.

Franco Modigliani: I think it's a little strange that you
should consider electricians among the low-paid industries
(laughter) because at this time this class of people who
go through this long training belong indeed to the high-
paid occupations.

Lester C. Thurow: They are not low-paid, but they're subject to unemployment.

Franco Modigliani: Yes, to some extent, although I would
not think of this group as one that typically bears the

brunt of cyclical changes in employment. But, let me come
back to the previous comment from the floor and Thurow's
reply to see if I can clear up some misunderstanding. The
speaker was really talking about the economic costs to society of the incidence of unemployment. He was suggesting
that since people who have more training are more productive, the unemployment of highly skilled personnel has
larger opportunity costs to society. This may have some
validity, but Thurow's argument was not an economic one
but essentially a political one. The political argument
is that in the past there has been a considerable tendency
on the part of people in the higher-income brackets to pay
little attention to the unemployment problem. They had
the idea that all people who are unemployed are those who
don't want to work. Anybody who wants to work can really
find a job, so never mind this unemployment. When it hits
you, you realize that it is not true, that a person who is
not employed may very well be trying desperately to find
a job, and it's just very hard to find one. And in this
sense then, I think he might become more conscious of
what it means to be unemployed.

Lester C. Thurow: I agree with you. I was at the Department of Agriculture recently, discussing the family assistance plan that is the welfare plan, and somebody asked
the question, "How much would farm output go down if you
had a $2400 minimum wage?" One of the agricultural econ-
omists immediately spoke up and said let's assume that
every one of those guys quits working who now lives on

a farm and makes less than $2400; you wouldn't even notice
the difference because all of our farm output is produced
on big farms. It doesn't have anything to do with those
guys making less than $2400.

Comment: I submit that your thesis is wrong that we should
spread this unemployment around because there's a little
bit of fire built into our social system in that the guy
who normally makes $90 or $100 a week has a potential unemployment compensation of say $85 a week and it may be
highly desirable to be unemployed, but for the man used to
earning $20,000, $85 a week is a tremendous problem.

Franco Modigliani: I would like to ask Professor Sapolsky
to comment on Thurow's view, which Samuelson has agreed
to, to some extent, that the Defense Department may be expected to move back in the near future toward essentially
high-technology kind of expenditure, reducing expenditure
on hardware and increasing expenditure on technological-
rich or engineer-rich dollars.

Harvey M. Sapolsky: I believe it is only partly correct.
To be sure, when wars wind down, the percentage of the military budget devoted to sophisticated weapons usually goes
up. The move toward a volunteer army, however, is likely
to absorb a very large part of the defense budget at whatever level it is maintained. The level is probably going
to go down somewhat and I don't think that there will be
a major shift to advanced weapons in the mix given the

cost of a volunteer army. They have removed 1 million
people from the defense payrolls, the civil service and
military payrolls, in the last 2 or 3 years and yet the
dollar amount went up 5 percent for personnel costs because of the wage increases for military and civilian personnel.

I have a question for Professor Samuelson. At the end
of my talk, I was hinting, and not saying it too loudly,
that perhaps we need a WPA for scientists and engineers
and perhaps they could get themselves organized to pressure for a WPA. We are now suggesting something along the
same lines in terms of having scientists and engineers
being maintained in their employment and that companies
have some sort of responsibility to retrain them. Is
there any possibility of retraining them to do something
else, but also keeping a kind of an agricultural soil bank
in scientists and engineers?

Paul A. Samuelson: Well, I was touching on that sort of
issue. I mentioned that I was on a television program
with some unemployed Route 128 people, and I tried to
think of what would actually help those people. The only
thing I could think of was really putting pressure on government to keep spending. The WPA comes to mind. The
SST, of course, is another case in point. I'll tell you
a story about the SST which I think is appropriate. On
the day of the vote in the Senate on the SST, I had a
phone call from a friend of mine in Washington who was
fighting the SST very hard. And he said to me, "One of

the senators is on the fence about this. This is what
bothers him. Will we lose some work teams in being, if
we don't fund this continued prototype and, he said, do
you think that Dr. Wiesner would call the senator and give
him his opinion on that subject?" I talked to Wiesner on
the phone, and I simply repeated the conversation to him,
and Wiesner said, "Well, I could call him up but I'm not
sure whether it would help the cause or hurt the cause,"
because he said, "I think there is merit in that argument—
we will lose some teams in the aeronautical field," and
then he said, and this is something that will interest the
economists, "to keep those work teams in being is about
five times as expensive as to build the prototype because
most of the expenditure on the prototype is for an end
product that you don't want." There ought to be some way
in between producing pyramids that we don't want in order
to keep up our skills and letting those work teams go.
So I guess you'll get more jobs with a WPA because the
dollars per job of the WPA "make work" in engineering are
much greater in the short run than just waiting for a full
employment policy to filter down to the engineers, incidentally which may not filter down at all in the form of
engineering jobs. I don't think it's easy to have WPA
programs, but I do much applaud President Nixon's change
of mind in which he produced $42 million for retraining
purposes and similar matters. I think that that will do
more concretely for the lives of the unemployed Route 128
people within the next 6 to 12 months than will any other
policy.

Lester C. Thurow: If you think about the Japanese example, you essentially have a private WPA in the sense of everybody having tenure like a professor, and that tenure does not just extend to high technologists, it extends to every worker in the firm. It has an interesting by-product. On the surface, an economist would tell you it was inefficient because people don't move between firms, and they don't do lots of things, but the one thing it seems to produce is that if you have a guaranteed lifetime job you have no resistance to technical change. You don't have all these work rule fights that you typically have in American companies where everyone is fighting to keep his job and worried if a machine comes in "I'll be out of work and on the street." It may very well be that from an economist's point of view this kind of lifetime tenure is very inefficient in any short-run period but terribly efficient in the long run because you get rid of the obstacles to technical progress that we have in this country. In the construction industry, as I was mentioning earlier, if you had the greatest idea in the world you wouldn't be able to use it. But if every construction worker had a guaranteed job and he knew that adopting a new technique would not mean throwing him out of work, he might be willing to use it, but not now in the United States, where he shows up in a hiring hall every morning and his job is on the line every morning. He doesn't even have a 1-year tenure, he has a 1-day-at-a-time tenure.

Franco Modigliani: One important feature that goes togeth-

er with the Japanese tenure scheme is the very low age of
retirement, which is an option the firm has. Essentially
you have a system of retirement at something like 55, so
that, if by that time you are outdated, the company has an
option of terminating its responsibility to provide you
with employment. You may have all kinds of retirement
provisions, but the responsibility for employment ceases.

Question: It seems to me, Professor Thurow, at one point
you said that there was a mechanism or way for economic
systems to slow down inflation without buying unemployment.
If I could take that back with me, I'd feel that the week-
end was really worthwhile.

Lester C. Thurow: It is clear that if you look at the current instruments possessed by government there is no such
mechanism. Is it worth going to the trouble to create
other instruments for stopping inflation? Should we use
wage-price controls or really vigorous antitrust-type policies against both unions and company? You know the kind
of thing where you don't break General Motors up into
three corporations, you break them up into a hundred corporations. I don't think we are going to have vigorous
enough antitrust laws of that kind, so I suggest another
option. You know there is a very famous passage in Saint
Augustine's *The City of God* where they are debating moral
problems. If the infidels are coming and a group of nuns
are going to get raped, have they committed a sin if they
slightly enjoy getting raped? He comes to the conclusion

that they really haven't committed a sin under these cir-
cumstances. Similarly I suggest that perhaps what we are
going to have to do is learn to live with a 5 percent rate
of inflation and not get so uptight. Inflation is an interesting thing if you're talking about a 5 percent rate.
It doesn't make the total size of the pie smaller; it just
changes its division, and there are hosts of devices that
we can think about to prevent changes in the division of
the pie from coming about. It is very hard to figure out
whom inflation hurts because it is vertically equalizing.
In a period of full employment and inflation, the poor
catch up with the rich, so to speak. If you can take two
people with the same income before an inflationary period,
they'll have different incomes after inflation. One interesting thing is that we always say we are fighting inflation to protect the widows and orphans. But some widows and orphans are rich and some are poor. And maybe we
can think about protecting the poor widows and orphans and
not worry about the wealthy ones. That may be the real
ball park we have to think about. If in order to have
full employment we have to tolerate a 5 percent inflation,
let's tolerate it.

Chapter 3

FORECAST OF OVERALL NEEDS IN THE COMING DECADE

As background for the general discussion of career planning, it seemed important to spend some time reviewing trends in the employment picture and trying to forecast what might lie ahead. To do this, Professor Charles A. Myers, a professor of management at M.I.T. and director of the Industrial Relations Section of the Sloan School of Management, had asked several experts in the manpower field to present their views. These speakers were Mr. John D. Alden, executive secretary of the Engineering Manpower Commission of the Engineers Joint Council of New York City; Professor Paul Penfield, Jr., of the Department of Electrical Engineering at M.I.T., who had served as chairman of an Economic Analysis Committee of the Boston Section of the IEEE; and Professor Lee Grodzins, a physics professor from M.I.T. who served as the chairman of the Economic Concerns Committee of the American Physical Society.

<u>Charles A. Myers</u>: We do not know how many engineers and scientists are really out of work in this country. For example, one unofficial government estimate was the following: of the nation's 1.2 million scientists and engineers, some 50,000 to 65,000, or about 5 percent, are unemployed. This figure is not high compared with the present nationwide average rate of 5.8. At the same time, *Business Week*, reporting just recently, used the figure

(whether they drew it out of the air I do not know) of
100,000, which represents a much higher unemployment rate.

Some of you may have received the National Science Foundation's National Register of Scientific and Professional
Personnel. The NSF sent out a card to everyone on the
Register, asking in effect: "Have you been employed in the
present place where you are for a certain period of time?
If so, ignore the rest. If not, are you unemployed?"
If you are unemployed, it asks a lot more questions. Now
for that group I presume we have a relatively valid figure, but that does not take into account, of course, the
fact that many people are not on this Register. (Subse-
quently the NSF reported lower unemployment rates for scientists and engineers on its Register than the estimates
I cited.)

I should like to say something about the level of employment of scientists and engineers in defense-related
activities. There are some studies by the Bureau of Labor
Statistics, for example, which indicate that 20 percent
of the nation's engineers were in defense-related jobs in
the middle of 1968, and we know what has happened since
then. At that time defense and space occupied the talent
of 59 percent of the nation's aeronautical engineers; 22
percent of its electrical engineers; 45 percent of the
nation's metallurgical, industrial, and chemical engineers; and 40 percent of the nation's physicists.

What about the future prospects? You may have seen reports based on the Bureau of Labor Statistics long-range
projections for 1968 to 1980. This is what the BLS fore-

casts for college-educated workers 1968 to 1980. Estimated 1968 employment of engineers was 1,100,000. Projected 1980 requirements are 1,500,000 or a 40 percent increase. For physicists, on which we will hear more in
detail on the Ph.D. group from Professor Grodzins, 45,000
in 1968, 75,000 required in 1980—a 63.9 percent increase.
There are similar estimates for life scientists, and so on.

  The only trouble here is that these are based on assumptions about the state of the economy over time that you
heard questioned at this meeting. For example, the forecast reflects the Bureau of Labor's basic model of the
economy in 1980, and most econometric models as far ahead
as that have a great deal of error in them. They assume
the following: the institutional framework of the economy
will not change radically through the 1970s; there will be
full employment in 1980, with an unemployment rate of 3
to 4 percent; the international climate will be improved;
defense spending will be reduced from the levels of the
Vietnam conflict; fiscal and monetary policies and an active manpower program will achieve a satisfactory balance
between the low unemployment rate and relative price stability; and all levels of government will unite to meet a
wide variety of domestic requirements—the Congress will
channel more funds to state and local governments for
these purposes. Other assumptions are that occupational
status will have the same effects in causing workers to
enter specific occupations as in the past; trends in the
proportion of college-age population will continue; and
so on. All I want to stress is that any projections so

far ahead are based on fairly specific assumptions that
may not be borne out, although we hope that they will be.

John D. Alden: We are here today because the engineering
profession recognizes that it has an employment problem
and all of us are involved with it one way or the other.
I realize that people are not statistics. Each of us is
an individual, and we all probably have different problems.
Nevertheless, from my position, what I have to say primarily deals with statistics, averages, medians, and means,
and I do not want to give the impression that I am unaware
of the individual problems that are involved. Many of you
think that the problems we have now are new. I do not
think they are. I am reminded of a personal experience
just 6 years ago, if you will forgive the reference. It
was before I was hired as a "manpower expert." Then, I
was just an engineer at a dead end in his personal career,
looking for a job. I had submitted my application for
retirement from the navy after 22 years of active duty—
the date was set—I was a lame duck. I had résumés out
to over a hundred companies seeking job opportunities, and
I was not hearing from any. You may recall that the period was one of defense cutbacks and contract cancellations,
just before the outbreak of the Vietnamese situation. Remember the cancellation of the Dyna-Soar contract and certain other long-forgotten missile contracts? At any rate,
to me the situation looked like this: Who would want a
fellow pushing 45 years of age whose experience bore little
resemblance to the education that was attested to by his

degrees (one of which was in electrical engineering from
M.I.T.), whose skills lay in areas of military applications
where contract cancellations were taking place and budget
cutbacks were in vogue, whose technical knowledge was ob-
solescent and rusty in comparison to the 30,000 or so new
graduates? But things changed. So fact number one, in my
view, is that the present employment problem for engineers
is not really new. It has some new elements, to be sure.
But it is also a replay to some extent of the events which
took place in 1964. Before that we had similar episodes
in the late forties and in the fifties.

The second point I should like to make has already been
made, and I shall not dwell on it. The engineering employment problem and the scientific employment problem are
by no means the same thing. Their relationship is not as
close as is implied by the juxtaposition of the terms
"science and technology" or "engineers and scientists,"
which you so often read in the press and published statistics. Dr. Allan M. Cartter presented a very lucid analysis
of the scientific problem in his article "Scientific Manpower for 1970 to 1985," which is in the 9 April 1971 issue of *Science*, and which he gave as an address at the
AAAS meeting in Chicago in December 1970. Dr. Grodzins
was on the panel, and I was on the panel. We all talked
about this problem. As Dr. Cartter and Dr. Grodzins have
pointed out, and I defer to their superior judgment in
this case, the scientific manpower problem is focused on
the Ph.D., whereas the engineering profession is largely
still a bachelor's and master's degree field. Only about

8 percent of all the employed college graduate engineers
hold a Ph.D.   I am perfectly willing to accept the findings of Dr. Cartter, Dr. Wallace R. Brode, and other people who show that we have a current oversupply of Ph.D.'s.
To a considerable extent, newly graduating Ph.D. engineers
will share the problems of other Ph.D.'s in the field.
But I want to reiterate, this is not the crux of the engineering employment problem that we have today.

Now, just what is this problem?   There is no doubt at
all in anyone's mind that many engineers have been hit by
massive aerospace and defense cutbacks.   There are many
engineers with impeccable credentials who are out of work
and who are having great difficulty in finding employment.
Incredible as it may seem, however, the federal government
does not know how many engineers are in this predicament;
nor does it know their characteristics in terms of age,
geographical distribution, level of education, or specialized abilities acquired through education or experience.
We encounter statements, sometimes made with a great air
of authority, that there are 35,000 or 50,000 unemployed
engineers.   All are guesses or estimates, some more educated than others, but all based on incomplete statistics,
imprecise definitions of the term "engineer," and other
dubious factors that could be explored at great detail.
The very fact that there are so many different estimates
floating around, all purporting to be authoritative, is, I
think, evidence enough that the hard figures are lacking.
As a matter of fact, the National Science Foundation just
a week ago yesterday authorized the Engineers' Joint Coun-

cil to launch a survey of the engineering profession, as
exemplified by members of engineering societies, to find
out their current employment status versus that of a year
ago. They are letting us go to a sample of 100,000 engineers. This will be a parallel to the survey of 350,000
scientists, whose questionnaire Professor Myers talked
about, and the results are supposed to be statistically
comparable in terms of the questions that are being asked.
I am glad to say that the Engineers' survey will go into
somewhat greater depth in exploring the underemployment
situation among engineers rather than simply looking at
out-and-out unemployment. The National Science Foundation
expects to have the results tabulated and analyzed by late
August or September, I believe. Until we have some authoritative data on unemployment and underemployment, we are
really operating on rather shaky ground when we try to
develop programs or prescribe what should be done to correct the problem.

I might also point out that we have very limited and
poor information on demand. Where are the job openings
right now, and what will be needed 1 year, 2 years, or 5
years from now? Before we can prescribe what is to be
done to correct the problem, we have to know what the problem is. We also have to know in what areas we need to retrain or redirect our engineers, and we are lacking both
of those vital parts.

The indications that we do have are rather conflicting,
and I shall give you a few of them. On one hand, you have
seen a veritable barrage of press stories portraying the

plight of unemployed engineers, the one who wore a Santa
Claus suit last December, the ones pounding the streets
on Long Island, and the ones on the West Coast. Friends
of mine are driving cabs, so I know it is a real problem.
But when you analyze these stories, surprisingly enough,
sometimes they are not even talking about real engineers.
Quite often the people whose difficulties they cite are
people who drifted into the technical world from a basic
science background or are upgraded technicians who became
"engineers" in their companies by dint of long experience
in some specialized technical field, and the need for that
particular field has ceased to exist. But whether these
people are engineers, is, I think, a matter of definition
and one that we should take into consideration. According
to the Labor Department, the unemployment rate among engineers in recent months has ranged from 2.2 percent up to
about 3 percent. I am not quite sure what they are reporting it as right now. The point is that this rate is
based only on those who have applied for unemployment insurance or who have registered as being unemployed. Furthermore, a former engineer driving a cab is not an unemployed engineer, he is an employed taxi driver. I am
reluctant to repeat Labor Department statistics on the
engineering unemployment rate because I know enough about
them to recognize that they do not define the problem from
the point of view of the people within the profession.

On the other hand, total national unemployment, as you
all know, is now 6 percent. Therefore, according to the
Labor Department figures and, I think, the statements of

the other speakers, the raw unemployment rate for engineers
is certainly not worse than it is in any other occupation.
That makes it rather hard for us to go down to Washington
and claim priority of funds. The only recent survey that
I know about with what I consider good statistical validity was conducted by the American Institute of Chemical
Engineers in January and February of this year among a
sample of its own membership. This showed as a national
figure an unemployment rate of 1.7 percent—unemployed and
seeking a job. But the rates were twice or almost twice
that in three areas: the Mountain states, New England, and
the West Coast states. Chemical engineers are evidently
in better shape than other disciplines, and if the unemployment rate among electrical engineers is really 10 percent or higher, you can see that right within the engineering profession we have some extremes. I think this is
very true and something we always have to keep in mind,
that engineering is not a monolithic profession. We have
innumerable varieties or specializations and applications,
and the problems are not the same in all of them, let
alone being the same as they are in the science and Ph.D.
areas. We have good evidence that last year's engineering
and technology graduates did not have undue difficulty in
finding jobs. Even this year, according to the March figures put out by the College Placement Council, salary offers to prospective engineering graduates are still increasing over last year, although not by as much, and they
continue to lead almost all other fields of college graduates in actual dollars. There is no evidence then that

a surplus of engineers has led employers to drastic cost
cutting, at least in terms of their recruitment in the new
graduate field.

This leads me back to the central question that I think
I was supposed to talk about: What is the real demand for
engineers, now and in the future? Demand, I think, is the
most elusive concept in the whole field of manpower planning and forecasting. How does one measure it? What is
it? What determines it? Obviously, there are psychological factors involved such as employers' expectations of
business trends. The types of basic assumptions that have
to be made in any long-range economic forecast or estimate
are involved here. Obviously, too, Congress and the President can influence demand very suddenly and dramatically
by terminating major projects such as the SST, which over-
night put 8000 engineers out of work, or terminating the
Florida Ship Canal, or many other projects that you can
think of, or, in a more basic sense, by what we call
changing national priorities. It is almost impossible to
predict the political winds that influence the demand for
engineers in practically any major technological venture
that this country might undertake. One popular index of
so-called "demand" is based on the number of lines of recruiting ads in various journals. Another is based on the
ratio of applicants to openings listed with the U.S. Employment Service. These so-called "indices" show all
kinds of wild fluctuations and draw headlines that in 1
year are translated into great euphoria and the next year
into terrible pessimism. They have serious deficiencies

as true indicators of demand because the fact is that engineering employment as reported from year to year by the Labor Department has continued to increase steadily and consistently, despite the upward and downward swings of advertising, college recruiting activity, job vacancies, or anything else that you can put your finger on.

There are basically two ways of projecting future manpower demand that I am familiar with that have some fundamental basis. One is the Labor Department method, which is essentially long-range economic forecasting, in which such factors as the ratio of engineers to total employers in each industry or the ratio of engineers to gross national product dollars are used to give a long-range type of projection. The current Labor Department projection is that engineering employment is expected to grow from 1,100,000 in 1968 to 1,500,000 in 1975. This is stated in terms of an annual average demand of 53,000 engineers per year for the period under discussion. Unfortunately, as we all know, 1970 and 1971 were years that were by no means average in demand. There is certainly no evidence that 53,000 engineers per year were needed in those 2 years. On the other hand, as recently as a year ago, the Labor Department's projection was that the average annual need was 65,000 engineers. Our analysis of the situation in mid-1970 was sufficiently alarming that the president of the Engineers Joint Council went to the Secretary of Labor recommending that engineering be removed from the list of national manpower shortage occupations, an action that the Secretary finally took. The net result of this

action was to require that immigrants have a promised job
before being admitted to the United States.

Now, how do we relate Labor Department's long-range analysis to the immediate hiring plans of employers? The device we at EJC have used is to survey a sample of employers
and ask them to relate this year's planned hires to last
year's actual hires and then by applying the proper weight-
ing factors to blow this up into a national total. This
gives percentages up or down, but it does not clearly establish a base line in terms of national employment totals.
There are many factors making that difficult. In my own
analysis last year, I put various factors together and
arrived at an estimate of 45,000 engineers as being the
demand for 1970 and 41,000 for 1971, compared to the long-
range Labor Department estimate of 65,000 a year for the
same period. Today, if I had to redo that analysis, I
would say that my estimate for 1971 was probably, if anything, optimistic. This is because the employers whom I
asked then what their anticipations were have themselves
become pessimistic and have reduced their expectations,
as far as I have been able to ascertain from the few that
I have talked with. A survey of employers conducted by
the College Placement Council just last fall indicated
that the new graduate hires for this year would be 27 percent lower than they were in 1970. If this accurately
represents the total national hiring picture, I would estimate that the demand for new engineers in 1971 would be
down to about 33,000.

Just how alarming is that number? In order to evaluate
it, you have to look at the relationship between demand
and supply in the engineering field in recent years. The
fact is that the supply of new engineers has never since
the 1950s been sufficient to meet the stated demand. Since,
in economic terms, supply and demand have to reach equilibrium, employers either have had to reduce their expectations to fit the supply or have had to increase the supply of so-called engineers through various manpower
utilization devices. In practice, they have done both.
The tremendous input of nonengineering graduates into the
engineering work force in recent years, which now amounts
to about two-fifths of the Labor Department's total figures is, I think, ample proof that we had a chronic shortage situation in the supply of engineers in the past. But
looking at it from another point of view, a demand of
65,000 engineers a year, or 53,000, or even 45,000 bears
no realistic resemblance to the actual supply that has
been or will be available. The fact that employers have
now lowered their expectations to a level of about 33,000
for this year should be measured not against the inflated
demand levels of the past but against a realistic supply
estimate of the engineers who will be available this year,
about 33,000. As several of the other speakers have
pointed out, what this really means is that the employment
problem is not being inflicted upon the new graduate in
engineering; the brunt is being borne by the older person
who is displaced. This is what I said was not really new.

It has been with us before. It is a problem that has
tended to be concealed, and therefore we have not faced it
squarely in the past.

So, what do I think the problem really is? First, I
think several things that it is not. In contrast to of-
ficial government statements, I do not think it is due
primarily or simply to aerospace and defense cutbacks.
People close to the employment picture in all industries
have identified many other factors from overcapacity in
the petrochemical industry to foreign competition in consumer electronics, from effects of the economic slowdown
in all areas to increased need for engineering manpower
in the mining industry and electric utilities. There is
no lack of demand in those last two areas. The fact is
that engineers are so widely diversified and so widely
dispersed throughout all areas of employment that no single industry, not even aerospace or defense, is able to
swing total national employment statistics by more than a
few percentage points. I also take exception to those
very high estimates of the defense employment of engineers
that have been cited recently. I think you have to go
back and ask the economists what percentage defense spending is of the gross national product in order to get at a
better estimate, because the question on which those manpower statistics are based was not "Are you working full
time in defense and aerospace?" but "Did any part of your
salary come from defense and aerospace work?" Naturally,
many engineers work for diversified companies that have
one or two government contracts, but this does not mean

that they are all working for the government. So, again,
you must look at what is in back of the statistics.

As I see today's problems, they really lie more within
the nature of technology itself and in the structure (or
lack of same) of the engineering profession than they do
in outside influences. The problems are not new. We have
been able to sweep them back under the rug every time they
have showed themselves in the past because we have had new
prosperity or a new outbreak of international conflict
that covered up the problem.

These are what I consider to be the real problems.

Number one, technological change leading to forced manpower obsolescence over a time cycle that is now much
shorter than the average engineer's working career span.
This is a fact of modern life, and I do not think we are
equipped to deal with it.

The second problem is the absence of effective professional antidotes to this technological obsolescence and of
safeguards for protecting the professional victims of it.
Here I shall simply mention that there have been widely
expressed needs for such things as job banks, retraining
programs, practical continuing education schemes, portable
pensions—the type of thing that people seem to feel a
need of to protect themselves against this fact of technological obsolescence. It is not the new graduate engineer that is suffering, he is not technologically obsolete.
It is the older ones who find themselves locked out of the
present-day job market.

The third problem is a vacuum in national manpower plan-

ning. Sometimes you will find this referred to as a lack
of a national manpower policy. I do not think we shall
ever have anything as clear-cut as a national manpower
policy, but I think there is a very definite absence of
technological manpower input in our major national decisions. My organization, EJC, has felt the need of this
for a good many years. It is not a new problem either.

The fourth aspect of the problem is that we have an engineering profession here in America whose voice cannot
make itself heard over the hue and cry of the press and
politics, whose fragmented structure and internally diver-
gent interests effectively drown out the signals that we
are trying to get through a blanket of random noise.

In the medium to long range, I have no doubt that the
nation will continue to need the numbers of engineers that
we can realistically expect to graduate from our colleges.
Basic demand factors are built into the national economy,
population structure, economic system, and our way of life.
They are things that simply cannot change radically over-
night. But until we as a nation can learn to anticipate
and control the unhealthy fluctuations in the supply-and-
demand cycle, which seem to produce large numbers of graduates in years of slack demand and small numbers of graduates when the demand is already high, I am afraid we must
expect to suffer the continued deleterious effect of these
cycles on the engineering profession.

Paul Penfield, Jr.: I have been involved in manpower
studies because I am an officer of the IEEE in the Boston

section, and we have been trying to find out what is going
on and what could go on under better conditions and what
we might do to make the conditions better. I do not have
a great deal of optimism that I can share with you today.
I want to say, first of all, that engineers are different
from physicists, especially from Ph.D. physicists. The
employment situation is not, I feel, as bad for engineers
as it is for some scientists and probably especially physicists.

When I first became interested in this some months ago,
I met and talked to several people who were unemployed.
Virtually all of them now have jobs, and it is a new crop
of people who are unemployed. It is not so much that
there are individuals who are unemployed for years at a
time; a more accurate characterization is that there is a
continual churning: the identity of the unemployed people
keeps changing. There is, nevertheless, a much higher
rate now than there has been in past years.

Figure 3.1 shows some statistics, plotted as a function
of time during the past decade. These include the U.S.
population of about 200 million and a labor force of about
80 million. The professional and technical labor force,
of which scientists and engineers are a portion, is rising
at a much more rapid rate than the U.S. population. Furthermore, the category of engineers alone is rising even
faster than that. Obviously this cannot go on forever because if it did, in the next century there would be more
engineers than people. Something has got to give somewhere, that is obvious, but what is not so obvious is ex-

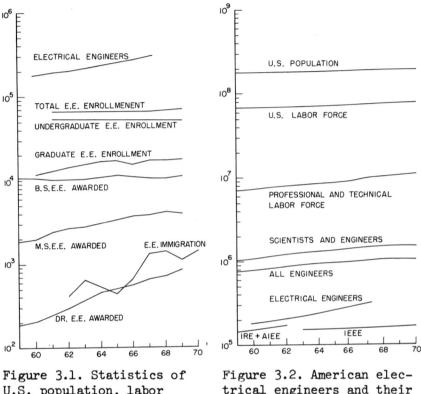

Figure 3.1. Statistics of U.S. population, labor force, and technical personnel.

Figure 3.2. American electrical engineers and their degrees.

actly when. I should just point out several things about the employment pattern of engineers. The dominant employment is in industry. Among those both in industry and not in industry, a substantial fraction is in defense work. The number of engineers in universities is rather low.   In summary, the vast majority work for industry, a few for the federal government, and a few for state governments.

Let me tell you next about electrical engineers (Figure

3.2). One surprising thing to me is that electrical engineers are important. Because 1 out of every 250 workers in America is an electrical engineer. This was amazing to me. Take 250 workers at random, and you will get an average of 1 electrical engineer! About 20 percent of their salaries is ultimately paid for by the Defense Department. The number of electrical engineers in universities is very small, only a few thousand—an insignificant part of the total.

Undergraduate electrical engineering enrollment (Figure 3.2) has remained roughly constant over the past 10 years, and the number of B.S. degrees has remained roughly constant. That is about 10,000 per year (30,000 or 40,000 per year for all engineers). The number of master's degrees has been rising sharply, and the number of doctor's degrees has gone up all out of proportion. Obviously this cannot continue; otherwise soon there will be more doctorate engineers than bachelors. As the total number of E.E.'s increases, the production of electrical engineers at the bachelor's level stays roughly the same. If you try to account for the rise in electrical engineers by integrating the curve, which in principle you should be able to do, you find that the numbers do not really agree. First of all, there is the immigration of electrical engineers, which accounts for part of the difference, and second, there is the upgrading of technicians to do actual electrical engineering work. These numbers about electrical engineers reflect people who do not necessarily have a degree and are not necessarily graduate engineers but

they do engineering work and are regarded as such.   A
large part of the increase is due to people who were promoted from the technician's level.

 You could naturally ask, where are electrical engineers
employed and whom do they work for?   Well, they work all
over, but one of the major employers is the electronics
industry.   The electronics market (Figure 3.3), if you are
interested in that, is about 2.5 percent of the GNP of the
United States, about a $25 billion market, of which sales
to the government represent the lion's share.   Electronics
sales to the government are leveling off or declining, and

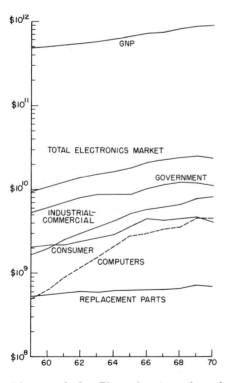

Figure 3.3. The electronics industry.

we expect in future years that this situation will continue. The industrial and commercial sales, however, continue
to rise, mainly because this category includes computers
and industrial controls. This very healthy market will
continue to rise. The consumer portion has taken a nose
dive between 1969 and 1970. There are severe pressures
from abroad, as you all know if you have tried to buy an
American-made tape recorder. Most consumer electronics
products are both designed abroad and made abroad. So the
point is that the competition from abroad in consumer electronics items is very stiff, and most United States firms,
as we all know, are moving their operations offshore. The
federal portion of the electronics market is almost exclu-
sively due to the Department of Defense. The NASA portion
peaked out in 1966 and is now on its way down (Figure 3.4).
However, it is small compared to the Defense Department
sales. To show what the Defense Department is doing, let
us look at the latest figures (Figure 3.5). As the gross
national product continues to increase, of course, the
federal money continues to increase. The Defense Department budget is beginning to go down, as we all know, and
is continuing to go down in 1971 and 1972. The part which
really affects the electronics industry is the procurement, and that portion of the procurement due to electronics, aircraft, and missiles. Not all of that is electronics, but that is the portion which the electronics market
feels the most.

I should like to say just a word now, after setting the
stage here and try to describe just how bad things are

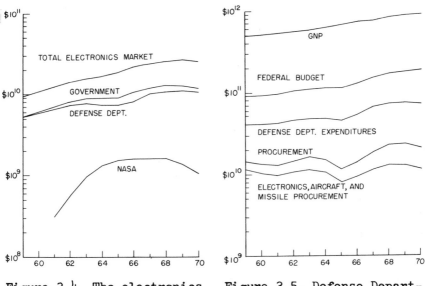

Figure 3.4. The electronics market and the government share.

Figure 3.5. Defense Department expenditures.

now. The Boston section of IEEE ran a questionnaire in
our monthly magazine asking people to send back a postcard
and check off various boxes, for example, are you employed? We found that well over 10 percent, and closer to 15
percent, were either unemployed or underemployed, at least
they claimed they were underemployed. (We did not have a
box for overemployment.) The Route 128 Job Center, which,
I think, all of you probably know about, since it has been
set up—and it is only a few months—has handled 3600
cases. It has managed to match up about 60 people to jobs.
This does not sound like a tremendous thing, but they keep
saying, "Oh, there's a long lead time here. Don't get
discouraged because we've only 60 so far. We've a lot

more in the mill." The figure 3600 for professional and
technical types of people I think is significant, because
if we extrapolate that throughout the country this means
that there are something in the neighborhood of 80,000 to
90,000, of a category that could have used the Route 128
Job Center, unemployed right now. And this is to my way
of thinking almost an 8 percent unemployment rate among
scientists and engineers.

I said I did not see any short-term solution, but I just
want to end on a note of optimism. The scuttlebutt in the
electronics industry is that you can see the bottom. We
are not there yet. It is in the future. It is somewhere
in the summer, maybe in the fall, but top management in
many cases is now in the process of deciding exactly how
they are going to spend money, substantial chunks of money
that is, in the late fall and winter of 1971. This is
true of several companies where I have talked to people
who are involved with this. They feel that things are
going to be looking up come later fall and early winter,
and they want to have their plans laid as to how to take
advantage of it. There are several other firms that are
introducing new products; they feel that right now is an
excellent time to introduce new products because there is
a surge that is going to start taking place in 6 to 8
months. Now it is very hard to pin something like this
down; nevertheless, I think it is a note of optimism we
ought to keep in mind before we all get too pessimistic.
It may not apply to any of us individually, and in fact
there are probably people sitting right here in this room

who will never do engineering again because they cannot
wait until December 1971 to get a job. There are many
people who will get completely out of the engineering
field, but, statistically speaking, in the long term I
think there is more hope than is indicated by the present
pessimism.

Lee Grodzins: Before discussing the manpower crisis for
physicists, permit me to comment on the meaning of unemployment figures for engineers and scientists. Contrary
to the views of some of the earlier speakers, I do not
find it useful to compare such figures with those for nonprofessionals as though they scale with a common measure.
To be sure, unemployment figures have the defined common
denominator that the unemployed are not earning wages, but
the interpretation of these figures had better reflect the
great distinction in employment patterns between professionals and nonprofessionals if the conclusions are to be
meaningful.

   Others have referred to the disparity between the training time of professionals and nonprofessionals, the differences in their economic burdens, the unequal consequences of their unemployment for the nation's future
productivity. I would stress other differences.

   Scientists have a different base point for full employment than do nonprofessional workers, and the causes of
high unemployment rates are generally quite different for
the two groups. Consider the former. Full employment in
the United States is taken to be a 3 percent unemployment

rate; the average worker is unemployed for about 1 month
out of every 3 years, a not unreasonable figure if only
because the nonprofessional does not usually look for work
until after he becomes unemployed. For scientists, on the
other hand, demand traditionally exceeded supply, and scientists were rarely unemployed between jobs. From 1958
until 1960, for example, the U.S. universities fell 20 percent short of graduating enough Ph.D.'s to fill the job
openings for physicists; openings that were filled by scientists from abroad and by engineers taking jobs as physicists. For physics, as for most sciences, full employment
was in effect a negative unemployment rate, and a 5 percent unemployment rate required a 25 percent swing in the
job market. On the other hand, a 5 percent unemployment
rate for nonprofessionals signifies a 2 percent swing.
Thus unemployment rates reflect different magnitudes in
the changes of the job market.

As to the causes of unemployment, consider the following
elementary distinction. Substantial increases in unemployment for the entire labor force must reflect a decrease
in the number of jobs, not an increase in the labor force
itself, which is growing by no more than a few percent per
year. For the scientific portion of the labor force the
situation is quite different. Their labor pool has been
increasing by about 10 percent per year (by almost twice
that figure in some fields of science), so that a station-
ary job market automatically results in a rapidly growing
unemployment rate. If the present scientific job market
is stable for the next 5 years, neither increasing nor de-

creasing, then it is easy to predict, on the basis of the
number of scientists now in school, that nearly 50 percent
of the trained scientists in the country will not be employed in their scientific capacity. The unemployment rate
for scientists can then be far higher than for the entire
labor force.

The foregoing digression is not uncoupled from the body
of this talk, which summarizes the findings of the Economic
Concerns Committee of the American Physical Society. The
distinctive features of the manpower problems for physicists are a necessary input to the interpretation of the
many surveys that have been carried out by the committee.[1]
I shall summarize these findings as well as those of an
unpublished survey of the manpower problems for physicists
in the Boston area, a survey that ended in June 1971.

One important piece of background to the manpower discussion, already alluded to, is shown graphically in Figure 3.6. The doctoral production rates in U.S. universities
show a growth of 7 percent per year from 1920 until the
late 1930s and a 10 percent growth rate in recent decades.
There was a dip in Ph.D. production during World War II
which was almost exactly offset by the bulge in production
just after the war. The Ph.D. production rates for some
fields were considerably higher than for all sciences, and
there was a wide dispersion in the growth rates among the
subfields of a given discipline. For example, the Ph.D.

----

1. "The Manpower Crisis in Physics," L. Grodzins, Bull.
Am. Phys. Soc., 16, 737 (1971).

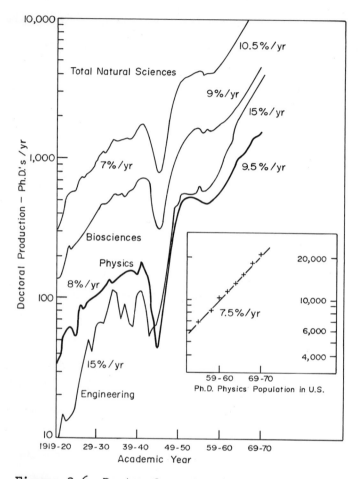

Figure 3.6. Doctoral production in the U.S. for selected fields. The approximate percentage growth per year during certain rising times is indicated beside the curves. The inset shows the growth of the Ph.D. physics population as determined from the American Scientific Manpower (ASM) series. The Ph.D. personnel in those series have been multiplied by a factor of 1.25 to account for incomplete returns of the National Register.

production rate for microbiology has been growing at nearly
20 percent per year, versus about 9 percent per year for
all biosciences.

The Ph.D. production rates of Figure 3.6 are generally
several percentage points higher than the growth rates of
the fields themselves since some of the new graduates replace those who die or retire, some are foreign nationals
who return home, and some leave their field after gradua-
tion, never making direct use of their training. (The
growth in the physics community is shown in the inset of
Figure 3.6.) Nevertheless, the growth rates of the scientific community have been many times faster than of the
labor force as a whole. It has also been considerably
greater than the growth rate of the gross national product.

Figures 3.7 and 3.8 depict the fluxes in physics employment during 1967 and 1970, respectively. In 1970 there
were about 20,000 Ph.D. physicists versus about 15,000
3 years earlier. The patterns of employment remained about
the same: 50 percent in universities, and 25 percent each
in industry and in government laboratories. In both years
the fluxes in employment were substantial. Even when there
was almost no net increase in the number of jobs, as in
1970, there was almost a 10 percent turnover in jobs. This
job mobility accounts for the fact that even in bad times
the new graduates can find jobs, but they do so at the expense of experienced men being displaced out of the field.

In 1967 the U.S. universities did not graduate enough
Ph.D. physicists to fill the evident need as measured by
the increase in the number of filled jobs for physicists.

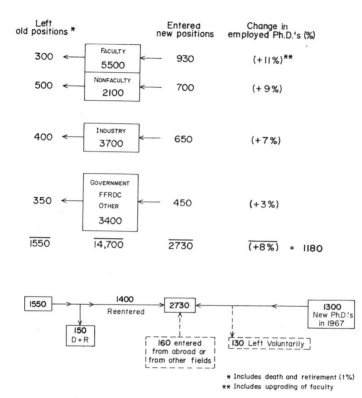

Figure 3.7. The flux of Ph.D. employment in 1967. The values in the faculty sector were obtained from direct counts of physics faculty directories together with the following assumption regarding Ph.D.'s in the various types of faculty. All faculty who entered or left Ph.D.-granting schools were assumed to have a Ph.D. In the B.S.- and M.S.-granting schools, ranks below assistant professor were ignored; all who entered or left with the rank above assistant professor were assumed to have a Ph.D.; only 25 percent of those who left with the rank of assistant professor but all who entered with that rank were assumed to have Ph.D.'s. The changes in employment for the other sectors were determined as the averages from 1964 to 1968 according to the ASM series. Other figures are explained in the text. (See Reference 1.) FFRDC means federally funded research and development corporations.

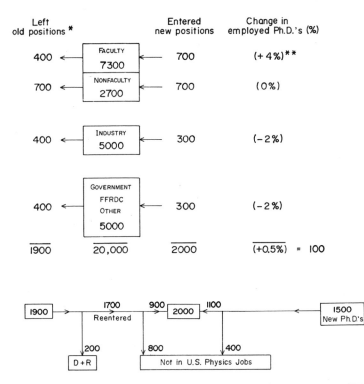

Figure 3.8. The flux of Ph.D. employment in 1970. The remarks on faculty figures under Figure 3.7 apply here. The
changes in employment in the other sectors were estimated
from surveys and from information supplied by the funding
agencies as described in the text. (See Reference 1.)

We have been able to show that this so-called shortfall
was made up by foreign scientists coming to the U.S. (the
brain drain) and by scientists trained in other areas
taking jobs in physics.

By 1970 the situation had turned about. There was almost
no net increase in the Ph.D. physics labor market that year

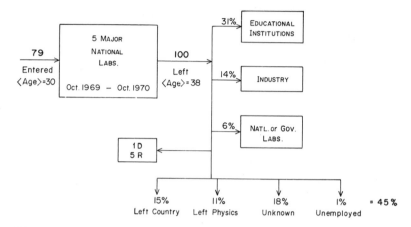

Figure 3.9. The employment status of Ph.D. physicists who left Argonne, Brookhaven, Livermore, Los Alamos, and Oak Ridge National Laboratories between October 1969 and October 1970.   (See Reference 1.)

over the previous year. Industry as well as government laboratories contracted their scientific staffs. For many reasons the fresh Ph.D. fared better in the job market than did those older physicists who had to find a job. (Much of the detailed exposition of the employment flux is presented in Reference 1.) Figure 3.9 is representative of several surveys of prestigious laboratories. It shows the employment patterns of those Ph.D.'s who left five major National Laboratories (Argonne, Brookhaven, Los Alamos, Livermore, and Oak Ridge) during the year between October 1969 and October 1970. Those who left the laboratories were considerably older than those who were hired, and there was a net decrease in personnel. Also, 15 percent of those who left the laboratories also left the country: most of this group were foreign nationals. Another large group took po-

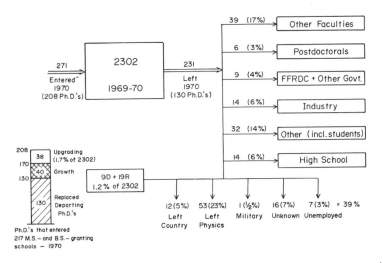

Figure 3.10. Migration of physics faculties from (a) 150 colleges granting up to a B.S. in physics and (b) 67 colleges granting up to an M.S. in physics. These are the complete results from about one-third of all the B.S.-granting departments in the country and about one-half of all the M.S.-granting departments. About 40 percent of those who left the college departments are not now employed effectively as physicists in this country.

sitions that did not make use of their physics training. More than 15 percent were unemployed when they left the laboratories (these are grouped in the category of unknown, their status at the time of the survey.)

Figure 3.10 is from a more recent survey[2] of the migration of physics faculties in schools that do not grant a Ph.D. in physics but do award up to a B.S. or up to an M.S. degree in physics. This figure is included to illustrate several points. The flux of employment is also high

----

2. "Migration of Faculty in Colleges of the U.S.," L. Grodzins and J. Viola, to be published.

in this sector in which physicists do little research: there was a 10 percent turnover in faculty even though there was less than a 2 percent net increase. Then too, there was an obvious upgrading in the educational level of the faculty: the proportion who had Ph.D.'s was higher for the group that entered than it was for the group that left. Also, relatively fewer of those who left their faculties went abroad, but a sizable proportion (23 percent) changed fields, mainly into other branches of science.

The patterns illustrated by Figures 3.9 and 3.10 are repeated in other surveys. The more prestigious the laboratory of last employment, the more likely the scientist is to stay in physics, though many go abroad to do so. Also, and understandably, in these times of Ph.D. surpluses there is an increased preference for Ph.D.'s when a job is filled.

The census-type analysis of Figures 3.9 and 3.10 made it possible to obtain a reasonably clear picture of how the physicists in government and universities met the labor crisis. Little insight, however, was obtained about what was happening in industry. To fill this gap, we carried out an extensive survey, during the spring of 1971, of physicists in the greater Boston area. The results obtained from a mailing to 2600 physicists showed that industrial physicists had a much more difficult time in the job market than did physicists from other sectors. The following is a summary.[3]

---

3. "Employment Study of Physicists in the Greater Boston

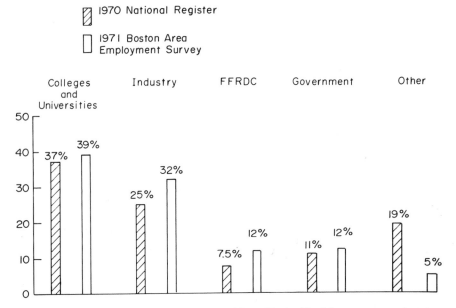

Figure 3.11. A comparison of the distribution among types of employers for physicists in the Boston area (white) and in the entire country (black), Ph.D.'s and non-Ph.D.'s.

1. Sixty percent of the unemployed physicists in the Boston area had their last job in industry, which employs but 25 percent of the physicists in the area. (The distribution of all physicists as well as the distribution of only the Ph.D. physicists in the Boston area is remarkably similar to that in the nation as a whole: see Figure 3.11.)

Area, 1971." To be published. There was a 65 percent return from the 2600 questionnaires mailed. Table 3.1 (see p. 116) was compiled when about 50 percent of the questionnaires had been analyzed. A follow-up study failed to determine the extent of bias in the results from the 35 percent nonreturns.

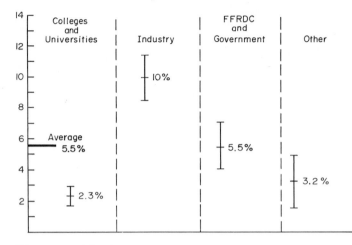

Figure 3.12. Unemployment percentages versus employment sector for all physicists in the Boston area.

2. The percentage unemployed in each sector is shown in Figure 3.12. Unemployment in industry is 10 percent, in federally funded laboratories, 5.5 percent, in universities, 2.3 percent. One out of every five has been unemployed for more than 1 year. One out of two has been unemployed for more than 6 months.

3. Many now employed were unemployed for extensive periods prior to taking a job. The average time of unemployment was 6 months.

4. The raw unemployment values of Figure 3.12 do not give a complete measure of the problem. Not only did a large percentage of the previously unemployed take a job that underemployed their talents but so too did a significant number of those who changed jobs without ever being unemployed. Presumably this latter group did not have the

resources to sustain themselves while looking for more appropriate employment.

The sum of all percentages for presently unemployed, plus
presently employed but recently unemployed, plus underemployed but never unemployed is as follows:

Industry: 10% + 10% + 8% = 28%. Federally funded and
government laboratories: 5.6% + 3.5% + 5.6% = 14.7%. Universities: 2.3% + 3.5% + 4.5% = 10.3%.

5. Employment difficulties are much greater for the older
physicist. Of course, relatively fewer older physicists
change jobs, but when they have to they encounter severe
problems in finding another. This point is illustrated in
Table 3.1, which gives unemployment figures versus age.
Also in this table we have attempted to examine the difficulty in finding work by concentrating only on those who
sought a job in the 2 years prior to the survey.

The overall turnover in the Boston area was high, about
15 percent per year. The 30 percent per year turnover for
physicists under 29 is surely due in part from the survey
being in an area of many universities, but the high value
may also reflect the vulnerability of this group in the job
market. The 15 percent turnover for physicists over 50,
which took place in the 2-year span covered by the question,
undoubtedly reflects the closing of the NASA Electronics
Center as well as smaller physics laboratories in industry.

Of the group that sought work since 1969, 19 percent were
still unemployed in the spring of 1971. Age was a decisive
factor. Seven out of every twelve physicists older than
50 who left a job in the 2-year span were still unem-

Table 3.1. Unemployment as a Function of Number Changing Positions

1	2	3	4	5	6	7	8
Age	Total* No. in Survey	No. Needing a Job in 1969-1970	% Looking for a Job in 1969-1970 $\frac{\text{Column 3}}{\text{Column 2}}$	No. Now Unemployed	Ratio $\frac{\text{Column 5}}{\text{Column 3}}$	No. Now Unemployed or Unemployed in 1969-1970	Ratio Unemployed $\frac{\text{Column 7}}{\text{Column 3}}$
20-29	245	149	61%	19	13%	32	21%
30-38	396	146	37%	21	14%	47	32%
39-49	443	110	25%	26	24%	47	43%
50-65	161	24	15%	14	58%	19	79%
All	1245	429	34%	80	19%	145	34%

*Students were omitted from this table.

ployed at the time of the survey. Only one in five maintained uninterrupted employment while changing jobs.

The picture that emerges from these many surveys of the
scientific community shows how the various sectors re-
sponded to the economic pressures against their personnel
and laboratories.

Universities, which must maintain a level of teaching
staff, can in times of stress operate at a financial loss.
Their personnel suffered less than government laboratories,
all of which slowed the pace of research in order to maintain some operation. Industry, however, could not operate
in the red for long, and many companies dispensed with research activities.

The recession in employment is particularly hard on
younger men who have the lowest "seniority." About 50 percent of the natural scientists are in "permanent" positions; their jobs are not jeopardized by the buffeting of
economic recessions or government funding. These are scientists with tenure positions at universities and colleges
and with senior scientist positions in the large government laboratories and the large, stable industrial laboratories. During hard times this group acts as a fixed
cost (and generally a high cost), exerting a powerful leverage against the vulnerable. For example, consider a
university department with 50 percent of its faculty with
tenure. The latter consume nearly 70 percent of the total
salary paid to the faculty. Thus to effect a 10 percent
saving in a given year without reducing salaries, the number of younger faculty must be reduced by a third.

The leverage is generally greater for research-oriented departments, since most of the salary for tenured faculty comes from the institution, while the junior faculty derives most of its salary from the research contracts. In one department that we examined where 60 percent of the faculty was tenured, the junior faculty received only 20 percent of the university-paid salary. The leverage was thus a factor of 5 to 1.

We emphasize that an amplified economic pressure against the vulnerable is not confined to universities, nor is it confined to the younger scientists. As we indicated before, for example, an entire research laboratory of a company may be in jeopardy in an economic squeeze where the immediate health of the company takes priority over future growth.

Finally, we emphasize that the result of the crisis appears only partly in unemployment. To salvage their careers, scientists who must find a job are going abroad, working on problems for which they are overtrained, taking positions at the periphery of science. But an increasing number are leaving science altogether.

While it is not the purpose of this talk to examine the future employment patterns for physics, a few comments seem in order.

A study of trends in graduate enrollment shows that for physics the Ph.D. production rate is now at its maximum. In the next years we can be reasonably sure that the Ph.D. rate will fall from the present 1500 per year to about 1000 per year in 1976. An examination of the probable de-

mand for physicists indicates that in 1976 there is very
likely to be an overall demand for about as many graduates
as will need a job. (This would require a growth of about
3 percent in jobs during 1976.) Even so we will face two
dilemmas.

First, it is unlikely that the Ph.D.'s graduating in 1976
will be trained for the jobs which will become available.
For example, we expect that at least one-third of the
Ph.D.'s will do their thesis in either elementary particle
physics or in nuclear physics. It is not obvious that
either field will grow at all that year. Second, and more
important, is that an equilibrium in the growths of the
job and labor pools during 1976 leaves unresolved the log-
jam of Ph.D.'s who have been displaced out of their field
in the intervening years. This group of as many as 5000
physicists must be absorbed into the scientific community
(or at least into jobs in which they feel satisfied) if
the oversupply of scientists is not to confront and con-
found us throughout this decade.

We cannot predict the number of Ph.D. graduates much beyond 1976. From that time the question of supply is open.
We do, however, know something about the need for physicists during the 1970s and 1980s. Allan Cartter has pointed[4]
out that not only the growth of the total faculty but the
growth of the individual departments are coupled primarily
to the growth in the total student enrollments. The growth

----

4. Allan M. Cartter, "Scientific Manpower Trends for 1970-
1985," Science, 172, 139 (1971).

of the individual departments depends, in general, only
weakly on the need to teach the specialists their advanced
subjects. We have verified that this is approximately satisfied for physics. Thus if patterns of science teaching
do not change dramatically in the coming decades, demographic data together with gross trends in higher education
allow a reasonable prediction of the need for physics
teachers in the colleges and universities of the U.S. for
the next 20 years. The analysis shows that physics faculties, in keeping with faculties in all other branches of
sciences, will require a decreasing growth during the next
15 years. In the middle 1980s, total college enrollment
will begin to decline, so that there will be a decreasing
absolute need for physics faculties in the late 1980s.
Thus one of the main impulses for higher education—the
need to train people to teach an ever-increasing student
body—is spending its force. The consequences for physics,
as for all fields with a significant employment in education, will be fundamental. The present crisis, which has
been caused primarily by an economic recession and di-
minished growths in government funding, has forced us to
a realization of the nearness of the basic crisis in science education. We must learn to make effective use of a
labor force that is educated beyond the narrow needs of
available jobs. And we must at the same time reevaluate
the educational system to understand what we are educating
our students for.

Most of the discussion following these papers centered around employment problems of men from 35 to 40 years of age who for one reason or another were seeking new jobs. It was pointed out by a number of the discussants that the plight of this age group was not adequately represented by statistical studies of average manpower trends and forecasts.

Charles A. Myers: Professor Grodzins has asked to make a clarifying comment.

Lee Grodzins: I've often wondered how the supply and demand for scientists balances in detail. The statisticians tell us that if we have 30,000 new openings for engineers and there are 30,000 new engineers on the labor market then the engineering manpower equation balances. But 30,000 engineers do not match up so readily with 30,000 jobs. For example, what if all of the jobs are for civil engineers and all of the graduates are electrical engineers? I've looked at this question for physicists. For the last four or five years—and for the foreseeable future—the demand for elementary particle physicists has grown but slowly and has not come close to keeping pace with the potential growth of 20 percent per year from new graduates. In the meanwhile the demand in several less popular subfields was far greater than the supply. There still are not enough acoustical engineers to fill the demand, and optics and plasma physics are keeping pace with the supply. (Saturation is appearing in these areas primarily because of immigration from other physicists trained in other areas of physics. There are other ways in which supply and demand mismatch. Many jobs are available only if the right man is there to fill it. Several recent M.I.T. graduates-- including one in elementary particle physics--received more than a half-dozen unsolicited offers of jobs while other graduates received none.

Question: I'd like to ask Professor Grodzins about his statement "the crunch was on the middle-aged citizen" and relate that to two or three factors in the industry. First of all, the federal prohibition against discrimination be- cause of age, and second, because of the concept of tenure, which is orally stated throughout much of the industrial employment of physicists for years, except there's no written contract. And third, the statement concerning re- tirement plans, which again accumulates the impression that so long as you're a good fellow and maintain your proper professional status, you'll be well taken care of at the end.

Lee Grodzins: Back in December, when we began to collect the statistics which indicated that the younger members— the new Ph.D.'s—were making it into the system but that they were doing so at the expense of an older group which was displaced out of physics in the U.S., we examined the questions. "Is there a direct displacement of an older person by a younger person? Is an older physicist let go and a younger physicist hired in his place?" As far as we can tell there is almost no one-for-one replacement. What seems to happen is typified by the following example from one of the national laboratories where the average age of those who left in 1969-1970 was more than 40 while the average age of those who were hired during the same period was less than 30. And as many people were hired as left. Moreover 80 percent of those who left did so involuntarily; several retired in their fifties. That laboratory had an unbreakable commitment to a large on-going project which was approaching the final construction stages. Congress was backing the multimillion-dollar project heavily, but the budget for the entire laboratory was not increased to keep pace with the project's needs. In order to continue to build the staff on the priority project, the laboratory closed out an unrelated area of physics, letting go physicists with many years' experience in order to hire those who could be directly effective for the big project. Thus laboratories disband one group in order that the others may continue to be healthy. Another factor to which many attest is that in times of economic crisis, laboratories demand that those they hire require little and possibly no retraining. These laboratories want immediate payoff; they cannot afford the luxury of long apprenticeships. They expect that the budget they will have to work with next year will depend more on how well they do this year than it will on how well they expect to do next year.

Question: Professor Myers, could you say anything about opportunities in management?

Charles A. Myers: To answer the question, we need to consider the projections by age group. The demographic picture
for the decade of the seventies indicates that there will
be only a 4 percent increase in the 45 to 64 age group and
a 12 percent increase in the 35 to 44 group, less than for
other age groups. Now in the management field, these are
probably the critical groups. That is, these are the middle
managers, presumably on their way up. Assuming the economy
moves ahead in the next year or two, the opportunity for
people in management in this age group will be increasing.
We see in the Sloan School of Management fewer job offers
than we've had before, but the demand seems to be enough
so that most master's people are placed. (All but one found
jobs by summer 1971.) If you look at the number of people
in the management field, subdivided by managers, officials,
and proprietors (so this would include single proprietor-
ships), the total employment in 1968 was 7.5 million. This
is much greater than the total number of those employed as
engineers. And the projections, with all the limitations
that Mr. Alden and I mentioned earlier, are for 9.5 million by 1980.

Now it's a fact, and Mr. Alden has made this point, that
there are many engineers already in management. This is
what we see, for example, in the people who come to the
Sloan School for master's degrees, or in our long-standing
Sloan Fellowship Program that brings middle managers, nom-
inated by their companies or their organizations (we get
quite a few from government, including NASA) to come to
the Sloan School for one full year's study for a master's

degree. Many of these Sloan Fellows made the shift from an engineering specialty to project management and then into other branches of management. This shift may be possible for other engineers, as managerial positions develop in the public sector, also.

While I'm commenting on this, I am reminded of John W. Gardner, who wrote the book *Excellence*, quoted by Professor Grodzins in the foreword to his paper. Gardner said, "There's a great emphasis in our society, but not enough, on self-development." And the fact that displaced engineers have to be retrained, as some agencies of government are proposing, suggests that they can't retrain or redevelop themselves. I think that there is considerable self-development going on. Those who fail to do that fall by the wayside.

One of our graduate students in economics did a study several years ago of engineers and scientists who were laid off by eight Route 128 firms in 1966 when there were defense cutbacks. Briefly, he found that those who were laid off tended to have their degrees 10 years ago or more, tended not to have kept abreast of their field, and their earlier engineering degrees were weak in math and physics relative to the newer degrees. And so they were the ones whose capacity to be transferred to other work was less than those who were retrained. This shows a lack of attention to self-development, which is an opportunity for people in every field. Ours is a very flexible labor force, but it depends a great deal on self-development rather than waiting for federal programs that aren't going to be enough.

John D. Alden: I don't want to preempt questions from the
audience, but can I answer that one and also Professor
Grodzins's first question, if you don't mind? In the matter
of retraining, I just want to step up in defense of the individuals, to some extent. I think many of us have attempted to keep abreast of things and retrain ourselves and
do a lot of self-development, but we can't always guess the
right areas. Just again to cite a personal example, while
I was in the navy I kept retraining myself. I went to many
courses on things like nuclear weapons effects, and new
shipbuilding techniques, but then the navy decided they
didn't need me as an admiral. I then took a course in commercial law, and one in economics as part of an effort to
retrain myself for civilian life. Then I got hired as a
"manpower expert," so I didn't need those things. I think
many engineers have kept themselves abreast of their fields,
but what good will it do you when the jobs cease to exist?
What good will tenure do for professors when colleges close
their doors, as some of them may do?

You may have done everything right from the professional
point of view, but all of a sudden your specialty has been
foreclosed and you realize that you took the wrong road a
long time back. I think that individual engineers do deserve plenty of sympathy, and I think the profession ought
to be finding some way to help them, not only to retrain
or keep themselves abreast but to try to guide them out of
these dead ends.

As for the question with regard to management, I have

some interesting statistics that I'd like to give you from
a survey that will be published in about two weeks. The
relationship between engineering and management has always
been one of my pet subjects. We finally got the right questions in a survey a couple of years ago and ascertained the
levels of managerial or supervisory responsibility of a
large sample of engineering society members. Here's what
came out. The lowest level was those who had no supervisory
responsibilities, 18 percent of all respondents. The age
group into which they fell primarily was 25 to 29. Those
with indirect or staff supervision were 18 percent. Those
who were supervisors of teams or units, which was the
smallest group that I was able to identify, 12 percent.
(These terms are rather imprecise, but I used terms that
I knew were fairly common.) The two previous groups, interestingly enough, fell into the same modal age bracket,
30 to 34. The next higher level was project or section
management; 22 percent of the respondents said they were
managers of that size group, and their modal age spread
was 40 to 44. The next category was manager of a major department or program, 20 percent. And, finally, general
management of an organization, 10 percent. The modal age
spread for those two highest groups was 45 to 49. If that
doesn't show that the normal progression of engineering
work leads into management, I don't know what it does show.
But the demand figures that I cited earlier don't have any
allowance at all for engineers going into management work,
and the Labor Department classifies managers in a completely

different occupational group. So I always feel that we have
this hedge available that if we aren't needed as engineers
there's a tremendous need for managers.

Finally, I want to answer Professor Grodzins's question
on how do we match these individual specialties to demand,
and obviously, there is no good answer to that. I think it
is particularly a problem for advanced degree people because they are inherently more specialized in the Ph.D.
programs. The master's programs I consider more of a broadening education on top of an engineering degree, and they
seem to be quite in demand among industrial employers.
The solution, if I could call it such, at least the direction in which I think we've got to go, is more toward flexibility in education, and I think that the engineering programs are doing this willy-nilly. Most schools no longer
designate an engineering specialty in the first two years.
You're just a general engineering student for two years.
So, you've advanced as far as that before you have to spe-
cialize. And I think delaying the point of no return is
probably the direction to go. I think that the educators,
although they don't like outsiders to tell them this, must
accept more feedback from industry and from employers and
not just educate the type of people they think ought to be
needed, without determining whether they really will be in
demand. I think perhaps another solution is to have more
people return for graduate work after they've worked in industry.

Interestingly enough, this same survey that I mentioned

shows that a rather high percentage of engineers with advanced degrees did get them after having worked. They were
not in a direct program from freshman to Ph.D., but rather
they broke their education. Many of them came back on the
company payroll or under company sponsorship to get an advanced degree in a field where they knew they had a job.
Engineers with advanced degrees have tended much more toward that pattern, I think, than has been the case in other
fields. I really want to say that the solution to all this
is certainly not to cut off freshman enrollments; yet that's
the only solution that I hear advocated.

Question to John D. Alden: You spoke about a net demand of
33,000 in the current picture. From statistics from the
National Science Foundation, I thought, from 1968 to 1969,
the actual employment changed from 1,543,000 to 1,555,000,
or a 12,000 increase in scientists and engineers and an
estimated reduction to about 1,550,000 in 1970. Now, previously we did have an average growth rate of 53,000 per
year, but in the last two years it's gone to zero, and is
slightly negative, in actual employment figures. Now, I
wonder where your 33,000 comes from?

John D. Alden: Well, they've done something I don't like
to do, combined engineers and scientists. I don't know
whether the decline is in one or the other because that
aggregated type of figure doesn't tell you. The estimate
that I came up with of 33,000 was simply based on this. I
know that last year's graduating class, which was approxi-

mately 40,000, ended up either being placed in jobs, or
going to graduate school, or going into the military. We
have a fair notion of where they went. As very few were
left without jobs, so we had full employment. Now if, as
the College Placement Council survey indicates, employers
have reduced their hiring plans by 27 percent this year
compared to last, and last year they thought they were going to hire more than they actually did, I roughly get
down to about 30,000 or 33,000. That figure just came from
that type of simple arithmetic. It's really not based on
any profound analysis. The results this June will show
whether we actually end up placing all of our new graduates
or not. We may very well not, for the first time in quite
a few years.

Paul Penfield, Jr.: I think the matter of whether or not
we place all our new graduates is probably irrelevant. (Of
course, it's not irrelevant to the placement officers or
to the new graduates themselves.) Lee Grodzins pointed out
very well what happens in his area, and I think it's the
same in the engineering field, namely, that the companies
are hiring new graduates in one door and at the same time
they're letting go the men who are 35 and 40 out the other
door. It's a little misleading to try to say that just because we placed all our graduates that there is that demand for 30,000 or 40,000, without taking a look at the
figures that would reflect how many people are simultane-
ously being let out the other door.

Question: I have another point, I find that total employment of scientists and engineers increases somewhat more
rapidly than the gross national product, but in the last
10 years the curves in the graphs are almost identical.
Have we reached a saturation?

Lee Grodzins: The point is well taken. The growth in science funds is now matching and is indeed less than the
growth of the gross national product; up until a few years
ago science funding was growing faster. Thus there is certainly a pragmatic saturation. I fail to see, however, why
the saturation should come when it did. Should the ratio
of funds for science to the GNP be 1/2 percent, 2 percent,
or 10 percent? The population of physicists in the U.S. is
not large, about 0.01 percent of the total. Is that too
many? Too many for what? The Bureau of Labor Statistics
makes projections based on various simpleminded extrapola-
tions. I doubt if these prognostications have much validity.
We have yet to see a close examination of the future needs
of the nation for scientists. Nor has there been to my
knowledge a serious examination of how much of the GNP
should be spent on basic science, on applied science, on
the various subfields of science, and so on. Until such
studies are made, then any relationship between the funds
spent for a discipline and the GNP is a description of the
past which may have little relationship to the events of
the future.

Comment: I submit that we have some history over the last
5 to 10 years that indicates that the actual employment of
scientists and engineers is directly related to gross national product in that we can expect this relationship to
exist for the next 2 to 3 years and all we have to do is
watch real gross national product and we will see what
the employment opportunities are for scientists and engineers.

Charles A. Myers: That's in the aggregate. That was the
point I think that Thurow made this morning. That if we
get from the present 6 percent unemployment to what Mr.
Nixon has projected for what he calls the third quarter of
1972, euphemistically, that would be an increase in total
aggregate employment affecting engineering and science
manpower along with most other occupation groups. If we
can get down to 3 or 4 percent, there'll be more scientists
and engineers employed, but they don't necessarily get employed in the same things they were employed in before.
And I think what we've heard today is that in aerospace
or missiles, Professor Samuelson's point on the concur-
rence of several things at the same time is what has created the current problem. But if the recession is ended,
then at least one of those problems is solved, and I think
we've heard today about the flexibility of the labor force
in the scientific and technical field, the emphasis Mr.
Alden has placed on desirability of more general and flex-

ible type of engineering education is somewhat related to
that. But I'm more hopeful about the mobility of scientific
and engineering manpower. If this group isn't mobile, what
do you think is true of people with many fewer skills and
less general and high talented education? So, I guess my
long-run view is more optimistic. In fact, If I can sum up
this panel, I think it is a little more optimistic than the
morning panel. And maybe that's the note to end on.

Chapter 4

CHANGING CAREERS IN ELECTRONICS, AEROSPACE, AND
REPROGRAPHY

*The employment situation in the fields of electronics,
aerospace, and reprography were introduced by three experts in these fields: John Blair, director of research for
the Raytheon Manufacturing Co.; Wallace E. Vander Velde,
professor of aeronautics and astronautics at M.I.T.; and
Daniel F. Fairbanks, manager of the Research Division of
the Dennison Manufacturing Company.*

John Blair: Let us first look at the federal budget which
for 1972 was proposed by President Nixon to be at the
$229.2 billion level. Historically over the past 10 years
the budget has been on the average about 20 percent of the
gross national product, as shown in Figure 4.1.

Figure 4.2 shows the partitioning of income and the partitioning of outlays, and I would like to call attention
to the right-hand circle, in particular to the two major

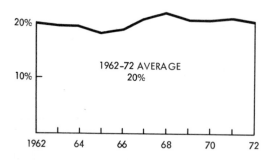

Figure 4.1. Federal outlays as a function of gross national
product.

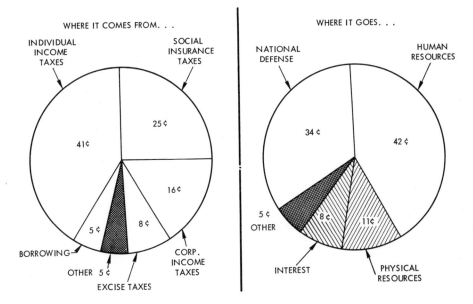

Figure 4.2. The partitioning of the budget dollar.

segments. National defense, 34 percent; human resources,
42 percent. This information is from the Office of Management and Budget as are some of the following charts.

It is interesting to show in detail the allocation of the
budgetary figures. Table 4.1 shows a comparison between
1965 and 1972. The first and the third columns are percentages of the total budget as it is distributed by the
various categories. The second and the fourth column are
actual dollars. From 1965 to 1972 the percentage allocation to national defense clearly decreased. In the area
of human resources, one sees a considerable increase from
1965 to 1972, from about 30 percent to 42 percent and a
correspondingly large increase in the total dollar expenditures. There are some changes, although the figures are

Table 4.1. Budget Outlays, 1965 and 1972

Function	1965 %	1965 $B	1972 %	1972 $B
National Defense	41.9	49.6	33.8	77.5
Human Resources	29.9	35.4	42.0	96.2
Education and manpower	1.9	2.3	3.8	8.8
Health	1.5	1.7	7.0	16.0
Income security	21.7	25.7	26.5	60.7
Veterans benefits and services	4.8	5.7	4.6	10.6
Physical Resources	12.3	14.5	11.1	25.5
Agriculture and rural development	4.1	4.8	2.5	5.8
Natural resources	1.7	2.0	1.9	4.2
Commerce and transportation	6.2	7.4	4.8	10.9
Community development and housing	.2	.3	2.0	4.5
Interest	8.7	10.4	8.6	19.7
Other	9.9	11.6	5.3	12.2
International affairs and finance	3.7	4.3	1.8	4.0
Space research and technology	4.3	5.1	1.4	3.2
General government	1.9	2.2	2.2	5.0
Allowances	–	–	2.6	6.0
Deductions and Unallocable	-2.6	-3.1	-3.4	-7.8
Total	100.0	118.4	100.0	229.3

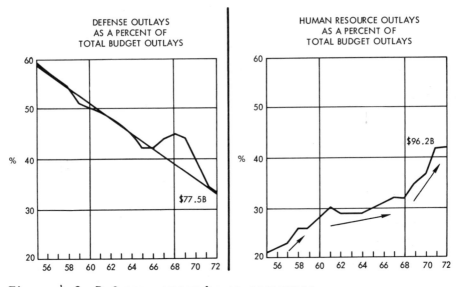

Figure 4.3. Defense versus human resources.

smaller in comparison, in the areas of commerce and transportation. However, the primary impetus in the human resources area, with the largest single growth item in health,
is clearly visible.

Figure 4.3 shows the trend of reordering the nation's
priorities. Going back to 1956 and taking the definition
of the human resources area as detailed in the previous
figure and comparing it with defense outlays, it becomes
clear that the reordering of national priorities has been
going on since about 1955. There is a peak around 1968 in
defense outlays, with a corresponding leveling off in the
human resources growth. This peak corresponds to heavy expenditures resulting from the Vietnam War. By 1972 we are
back again on the trend line.

Table 4.2 shows an additional proposed federal input into

Table 4.2. Revenue Sharing

	$ B
General Revenue Sharing, 1972	5.0
Special Revenue Sharing, 1972	11.4
Elementary and secondary education	3.0
Manpower training	2.0
Transportation	2.6
Urban development	2.0
Rural development	1.0
Law enforcement	.5
"Hold harmless" reserve	.3
Total	$ 16.4

the economy in an area which is largely considered human resources oriented. This is the proposed federal revenue sharing plan. A total of $16.4 billion is to be spent in a dispersed manner by the states, with portions going into education, manpower and training, urban development, law enforcement, and transportation. It is quite apparent that the human resources spending from the federal budget and the revenue sharing expenditures are going to be spent in a highly dispersed manner as opposed to outlays from some of the government agencies such as the Department of Defense. The latter area is essentially a one-customer-oriented situation, whereas in the former one we are moving, and have been moving for some time, toward a dispersed-customer situation. I consider this an important point.

Government Electronics

With this general background I want to turn to projections specific to electronics. Table 4.3 shows such a conservative forecast for government electronics. It considers the period 1970 to 1974, a near-in period. The Department of Defense shows certain percentage growths. In connection with this, I would like to call one fact to your attention. It will be assumed throughout that the inflationary erosion is about 4 1/2 percent a year. During a 4-year period

Table 4.3. Four-year Projection—Government Electronics

Department of Defense	$ Millions 1970	1974	% Growth
Procurement	4,600	6,000	30
RDT&E	2,400	2,800	17
O&M	2,100	2,300	9
Department of Defense Total	9,100	11,100	22
NASA	1,200	1,100	(8)
FAA	115	225	95
Total	10,415	12,425	20

at a rate of 4 1/2 percent per year compounded, this erosion represents 20 percentage points. To obtain real growth,
we have to subtract from the increases this percentage.

If we look at the bottom line, which represents a 20 percent growth in the total government outlays in electronics,
and subtract the 20 percentage points from the total growth,
there is no growth at all. We are holding our own.

What hurts most from the point of view of engineering is
the RDT&E item: research, development, testing and evaluation. Those dollars have the highest engineering content
and the highest number of engineering employment per dollar spent. The growth is 17 percent, so in terms of real
growth this is a 3 percent decline. NASA, of course, with
the 8 percent in parentheses, represents a 28 percent real
decline.[1]

On the other hand, FAA (Federal Aviation Administration)
is going strong. This is very encouraging except for the
fact that the total dollar expenditures are relatively
small and thus are not going to produce a very large impact on the total employment picture. So, it is clear that
in the long-standing reordering of the national priorities
this is what we can expect to happen to a major share of
the electronics industry segment. About $10 billion worth

----

1. At the time of editing, the Department of Defense announced a need for a weapons modernization program. Expenditures connected with this activity will feed heavily
into RDT&E. The space shuttle program was also announced
at this time. This program will create about 20,000 engineering jobs—an illustration of the tremendous swing factor of federal technology expenditures.

of the electronics industry is going to stay practically
still. This of course does not mean stagnation. Increased
competition will shift the market share captured among the
individual industrial units.

But indeed, if there is a reordering of the national
priorities, you would assume that there would be larger
growth in the industrial commercial sector of the electronics industry. Let us see if this conclusion results
from the following.

Commercial and Industrial Electronics

I have divided nongovernment electronics into two major
areas. The first one characterized by mature technology is
shown in Table 4.4. This is the bread and butter of electronics that has been around for a long time and in innovation and growth is rather conservative. Switches, wire
and cable, car radios, discrete devices, and electron tubes
have been around for a long time. If you look at the engineering content of this segment of the industry, it is
relatively low. Just the same, the total figures in 1970,
about $10 billion and the growth to about $14 billion in
1974, is 32 percent, which is above the 20 percent standstill. Now I said that this growth will create jobs for
R&D engineers. To what extent is something I would like to
leave for my conclusions.

Table 4.5 lists the categories in electronics which are
currently new technology, the exciting areas where engineers like to work, and, surprisingly enough, this is also
$10 billion in round figures. Some of the interesting

Table 4.4. Mature Technology

	$ Millions	
	1970	1974
Consumer Electronics	3,900	5,300
Antennas Hardware	427	526
Capacitors	434	541
Connectors	326	464
Electromechanical Devices	540	743
Tubes	1,212	1,402
Ferrite Devices	312	409
Filters	75	119
Loudspeakers	110	133
Magnetic Tape	211	336
Printed Circuit Boards	273	415
Quartz Crystals	49	68
Resistors	349	415
Relays	246	352
Switches	188	297
Transducers	101	143
Wire and Cable	356	440
Power Supplies	84	119
Industrial Electronic Equipment, Conventional	598	896
Discrete Conventional Semiconductors	492	383
Discrete Special Semiconductor Devices	185	252
Rectifiers	120	160
Dictating Devices	107	125
Total	10,695	14,038

items in terms of growth are computers, medical electronics, integrated circuits, pollution monitoring, communications, instrumentation. You can look at some of the dollars associated with these areas. For example, communications is

Table 4.5. New Technology

	$ Millions	
	1970	1974
Monolithic 1C-S Integrated Circuits	431	848
Optoelectronics	38	80
Test and Measuring Instruments	796	1123
Microwave Measuring Instruments	82	131
Medical	374	544
Nuclear	207	309
Computer and Related	4754	7029
Digital Process Control	507	761
Communications	1906	2633
Laser Equipment	68	136
Cable TV Equipment	77	125
Pollution Monitoring	10	23
Total	9,250	13,742

an extremely promising growth area; so are computers and the two instrumentation categories. So are integrated circuits. Pollution monitoring is growing twofold over the 4-year period, but the total dollar volume is small. Medical electronics is growing also, not to the same extent of pollution monitoring, but here you have to be careful just how medical electronics is defined. A very large share of those figures is diagnostic instrumentation that has been around for a long time, such as x rays and x-ray related equipment. The growth in these areas is impressive, but it

is not quite as rapid as the growth in the newer areas of
medical electronic instrumentation.

In summary, I would like to emphasize that growth in new
technology is close to 50 percent over the 4-year period.
Thus there is something to the saying that where you are
investing R&D and where you are exploiting new technologies
are the areas where the opportunities lie. The figures tend
to bear this out.

Conclusions

Now let me summarize in Table 4.6 what I have been saying.
This table is a breakdown of electronics by areas. I put the
federal dollars in for comparison because they are important
and large. Note that due to the inflationary assumption, a
20 percent dollar growth for the 4-year period represents a

Table 4.6. Summary of Real Growth
Inflationary erosion at 4.5 percent per year is 20 percent
for the 4 years considered.

| | $ Millions | | Percent Increase | Percent Real Increase |
	1970	1974		
Federal	10,415	12,425	19	0
Commercial Industrial				
Mature Technology	10,695	14,038	31.3	11.5
New Technology	9,250	13,742	49.0	29.0

Table 4.7. R&D Engineering Employment Growth

	Engineers/ $ Million	Real Increase %	Growth 1970 $M	New R&D Engineers Hired
Federal	–	–		–
Commercial Industrial				
Mature Technology	1	11.5	1220	1200
New Technology	3	29	2700	8000
Total				9200

standstill. So in terms of real increase, mature technology represents an 11 percent growth over the 4 years, and for the new technology area it is 29 percent for the same period.

Table 4.7 shows the impact of growth on R&D engineering employment. It is assumed here that in mature technology the R&D investment is 5 percent and in new technology it is 15 percent. An R&D engineer costs approximately $50,000 per year to a company. Thus for every million dollars' worth of growth in sales, one can add one R&D engineer in mature technology, and three to the new technology area.

The R&D engineering manpower pool growth is thus seen to be 9200 over the 4 years considered.

I will leave to the audience to decide whether this rate

of expansion represents disaster or opportunities in electronics R&D employment.

Wallace E. Vander Velde: The discussion that John Blair
gave of the electronic industry could be repeated almost
word for word in the context of the aerospace industry. It
is no secret to all of you, I am sure, that the largest
customers by far for aerospace R&D effort are the military services, and second to them in recent years has been
NASA, with commercial and general aviation coming behind
that. So the aerospace industry has a very similar outlook, namely, that the areas of large volume cannot be
projected as seeing very large growth in the near future.
There are areas of growth to be sure, but again they are
in areas of smaller volume.

I think there is no question but that the Defense budget
will be under considerable pressure in the foreseeable future. There is some evidence that within the D.O.D. they
will attempt to maintain the R&D portion of their budget
even in the face of a decreasing overall budget. To my
mind, that would be a very sound policy, but we cannot be
sure at this point whether that will happen. Similarly, I
am sure that the NASA budget will be under pressure for
the foreseeable future. During the peak of the Apollo program we were spending $10 million a day in that activity
across the country. That is a hard act to follow. I suspect
that we will not see substantial growth, at least to that
level, in the very near future.

On the other hand, commercial aviation, in terms of passenger miles, has until this recent recession been growing
at the rate of about 20 percent a year, which is very
strong growth indeed. At present, of course, the airlines
are under widely known pressure. Travel is down, and as
they say in the industry, the Boeing 747 flew in on the
wings of a recession. The airlines are now putting out the
capital outlays to buy these magnificent aircraft at a
time when it turned out that their capacity was not really
needed. I am sure many of you have had the experience recently of flying both domestically and overseas on these
big 747's with very light passenger loads. We are going to
see a recovery to a substantial growth picture again in
air transportation, but I cannot see that it will have a
very large impact on engineering requirements in the near
future. The present mood of the country is that we do not
want to go faster, that is to say, supersonically. It is
not at all clear that we are going to need larger aircraft
in the near future. We have the 747, and the wide-bodied
air buses from Lockheed and McDonnell Douglas are coming
into service very soon. These are magnificent aircraft,
and I believe that they will continue to provide the bulk
of the long- and medium-haul large-volume service for the
foreseeable future.

There is, on the other hand, a clear need for a slower
vehicle. That is to say, a slow takeoff and landing-type
vehicle, STOL. I think everyone expects that we will see
the STOL play a much larger role in air transportation in
the future, a vehicle that can get into a city center using

much less real estate and, by virtue of its steep entry and
climb-out patterns, restrict the noise problem to a much
more constrained area. Also, a vehicle that here in the
Boston area could economically make two or three stops
around the Route 128 perimeter, for example, and then without requiring the passengers to change vehicles proceed at
high speed to New York or Washington. This kind of vehicle
is definitely going to be used and is not yet developed.
The base of technology which is required to develop such a
vehicle is not nearly so well in hand as the technology
base which is involved in the standard subsonic jets. So
this constitutes an appreciable challenge for engineering
and development in the near future. But it will not be a
very large activity altogether. The commercial air transport fleet in this country is about 2000 aircraft. There
will be, I am sure, several designs competing for the STOL
market, but you cannot project this as a large-volume requirement for research and engineering development.

Additionally, general aviation is growing very rapidly,
even more rapidly than is commercial aviation. But this
too is a very small percentage of the total market.

We are very pleased to note that, with the coming of the
user tax at airports, the Department of Transportation now
has what will probably be a continuing and secure source
of income allocated specifically to the transportation problem, so that the increasingly obvious difficulties of air
traffic control and other problems can be addressed without the contingency of annual appropriations from Congress.
This is a growing area. The Department of Transportation is

very much interested in the air traffic control situation
and, specifically, as it will apply to the use of STOL vehicles in the total transportation mix. But here again we
are talking about only relatively small numbers.

So the aerospace engineering community is being presented
some of its most exacting and exciting challenges of all
time: the requirement for a quiet and economical transport
aircraft for short-haul intercity service, the need for
systems that will render transportation to earth orbit and
return a routine and less costly operation, the requirement for highly reliable systems for missions of several
years' duration to the outer planets, and the continuing
need for advanced developments to meet military requirements. Highly qualified and creative engineers will be
needed to meet these requirements—but not in as large
numbers as in the recent past. The aerospace industry has
had a severe shaking out, and I believe the worst of that
is over. But it would be unrealistic to suggest that aerospace engineering employment will now climb rapidly to its
previous high level.

Enrollment in aeronautical engineering departments of the
universities across the country is apparently down sharply.
This is an understandable reaction to the headlines we all
read, but it is clearly an overreaction. The requirement
for high technological achievement that has always characterized aerospace engineering will continue into the future.
The usual demands for performance and efficiency are being
joined by new emphases on reliability, environmental im-

pact, and others. A continuing infusion of fresh talent
will be needed to meet these challenges.

Daniel F. Fairbanks: It is a big order to predict the future. There is always the possibility that an unforeseen
or unappreciated factor can be present and there is no better illustration than in the reprography business. Chester
Carlson, who was a patent attorney, chemical engineer, and
who was the inventor of xerography wandered from door to
door for many years. I have heard numbers from thirty to
forty different companies were approached with his possible
patents. Finally he found a small home after mortgaging his
future and his home and everything else with the Battelle
Institute, who wanted half of his proceeds, and finally
with the little Haloid Corporation in Rochester.

I saw my first big Xerox machine about 8 years ago just
after I joined the National Research Corporation, and I
was amazed. I had fussed around with some of the earlier
kinds of office copiers, the dirty, messy ones, the ones
that were all wet and you stained your fingers on them and
things of that sort, and it was a very impressive thing,
but it was only 8 years ago that I saw my first. Actually
Xerox had been started quite a while before that. They had
not really gotten rolling until about the early sixties.
My own company, Dennison, had started with a competitive
process developed by the RCA corporation in 1958, and they
were one of the first ones in the electrograph business.
Well, my illustration here is simply that this unforeseen

coming of electrostatic printing, or photoelectric printing,
revolutionized a business.

In order to get to the aerie heights that you have to be
at in order to see something of the future prospects, you
have to get away from the humdrum day-to-day fight that you
are normally living.

I did do a little surveying and research. I read a couple
of magazine articles. There are many around on the prospects
of the reprography industry. In general, they are in general
agreement. I talked with some of my friends at Dennison, who
seemed to know something, and I read a recent survey, by the
Arthur D. Little Company, Inc. I think this is pretty thin
preparation, actually, for trying to develop a really solid
survey of the prospects. So, be forewarned, I am not trying
to talk as an oracle from Delphi. This is just Cambridge,
Massachusetts, and we are trying to see what might be coming.

What I can do is first to indicate to you what the reprography business is, what technologies are involved in
it, and what the present business forces are and technological possibilities that promise to cause changes. You have
to recognize that the reprography business is not a government contract business. It is a consumer-oriented business,
and we sell to the public, to normal consumers, some of
whom are the government, but not all.

First, to indicate what the business is we might compare
it with two allied ones, the business of photography and
the business of printing. Both of these are pretty old businesses. Mathew Brady was making pictures over a 100 years

ago, and the printing business is an old one. The Gutenberg
Bible sells for a pretty high price today, and that was 400
years ago, and that was just movable type. The Chinese say
they did it before that. So we have got old businesses that
we are comparing. On one side let us put printing and the
regular kind of presses that we use, the letterpresses, the
offset lithographic presses that are used to make calendar
pictures and can labels for vegetables and things of that
sort. Also let us list the letter-set presses, which are
offset again but like a letterpress, and gravure offset
presses, which are used to make the finest kind of printing,
and then the screen processes that are used for a variety
of things including decorating packages. Here we have one
kind of reproduction of images, the printing press type
operation, which usually counts itself in the millions of
copies. On the other side we have photography, which is
represented by Kodak and by Polaroid, and is used usually
to make one or two or a few copies. And in between we have
another kind of thing that we call reprography. Before the
advent of Chester Carlson and Electrofax, this was mostly
things like the hectograph, that tray of gelatin where you
put a master sheet with special dyes, which you could even
make on a typewriter or by using pencils, and then make
copies from it. We still see some of those used in schools.
Then we have the spirit process, which is a mechanized hec-
tography where you turn a crank and the dyes are transferred with alcohol on to the piece of paper. Then we have
the Mimeograph, which came a little later. I think most of
you remember the messy, smudgy mimeograph copies, which

were not typical of what could be done but were very often
what was done. And finally, the offset lithography, the offset lithographic press, which is very much like the printing
press and differs only in the fact that it has become quite
easy to make masters for it. You can make a master photo-
graphically in about 5 minutes and have them clicking off
an offset press down in the stockroom or in the duplicating
room very quickly.

These then are kinds of reprography. This is called duplicating, and it is characterized by the fact that you
have to have a master in every case. You make a master that
is not the original copy. You have to make it with special
inks, or aluminum in the case of offset lithography, or
some kind of special master is used to produce copies, and
in that case it is something like printing except it is
usually set up to be easier.

Actually, before Chester Carlson came along there was a
Thermofax process, which is 3M's system. This is a copying process which depends on being able to illuminate an
original and cause the dark-colored, typewritten copy,
where the image is to become hotter than the white paper
around it because infrared will be absorbed by the black,
come in direct contact with a piece of yellowed, dyed paper.
This heat causes a color change that shows up as an image--
and you can make copies from the original in a Thermofax
machine. It is a fairly old process. It has been a very
stable industry. Today it amounts to $80 million a year
in sales. And it's mostly 3M's.

Then we have the Xerox and the Electrofax processes. Both
of these depend upon having a photoconductive coating. In
the case of the Xerox machine, the photoconductive coating
is on a drum contained inside the machine and is used over
and over again. In the case of the Electrofax paper, the
coating is actually on the paper, zinc oxide is the active
material. It is charged up with a spray from a corona elec-
trostatically, maybe 500 volts, then discharged by illumi-
nation from the original that you are trying to copy,
through a lens, and then developed with little dark particles (these are regular electrostatic particles), and
these are then fixed in place and the copy is delivered out
of the drawer. The Xerox machine develops the copy on the
drum in the same way. You first charge the drum, then you
illuminate it. The charge leaks off in those areas where
light hits it and you then dust the remaining charge with
black particles and transfer them, in the case of Xerox,
to a piece of paper.

So those are the kinds of technology that are involved
in this. The Xerox process probably amounts to about $1
billion worth of sales a year. The Electrofax business is
probably around $400 million a year at the present time.
In contrast then, in terms of copying, we have $80 million
for Thermofax a year, about $1 billion for the Xerox busi-
ness—this is a machine, service, paper, toner, materials,
all that the customer buys, and about $400 million for
Electrofax, giving a total of around $1 1/2 billion. It is
a $1 1/2 billion industry for copying.

The other side of the reprographic industry is duplicat-

ing, and that is about $1 1/2 billion today, too, mostly
in the offset press, offset lithography. So we have a $3
billion reprography industry.

It is hard to estimate comparable numbers for the photography industry, mainly because it is hard to know just
where to draw the line. Do you draw the line at just what
Eastman Kodak and Polaroid make, or do you go into the
service angle of it, or do you talk about delivered photographs from photographic studios? Just talking about the
manufacturers themselves of these raw products that are
used to make pictures, it is about $2 billion. And here
the machines are the cameras, and the supplies are the
photographic films and chemicals and things of that sort.
So $2 billion for photography, $3 billion for reprography,
and printing is much larger. I honestly do not know how to
estimate that. You do not find these numbers often, and
printing will be lost in things like magazines, newspapers,
and things like this. Actually the newspaper is not a printing business, it is an advertising or news business. It uses
only presses and paper and ink and supplies. And the kind of
business that I am talking about stops at that point, where
you are making presses, engineering them, or delivering
paper to them, or delivering inks to them. After that it is
the customer's business. But that is large, I would guess
$10 billion or something of that sort in the printing busi-
ness.

The reprography business itself consists of at least four
items. One is the machine business, manufacturing the Xerox
machine, for example, or the Electrofax machine that does

the automatic handling of the paper and developing of an
image. Two, in the case especially of the Electrofax business, it is the manufacture of the paper, the zinc oxide
coated paper that is used for the process, and the fine-
particled toners that are used to develop it. And then,
finally, service. It is very important to realize that
these copier businesses are highly service oriented. Actually, at Dennison our copier division, which represents
maybe 20 percent of our total, has the highest gross margin
of all, that is the amount of what you get in for sales
separated from what you paid to make a product. It has the
highest gross margin of sales, and yet it has been just
about a break-even thing for several years. It is finally
beginning to look profitable, but it is because of high
service cost that is not covered by the gross margin that
we have problems.

As I said, it is a highly service-oriented industry. You
sell or very often lease the machines and then are responsible for them thereafter. I might say that in other industries like photography and printing, the service aspect
is not as intense, it is not part of the business.

The kind of growth that is going on in the copying and
duplicating business in the last 5 years has been at about
an annual rate of 17 percent a year growth overall through
that period, so it has been a rapid growth industry. The
projection by Arthur D. Little and others for the next 5
years is about a 10 percent growth. The thing seems to be
pretty well saturated, however, and I think the data need
some interpretation. Ten percent per year is just about

what you might expect from inflation. However, I think you have to look a little more closely at the reprographic industry to realize what some of the forces at work have been and how they are probably going to resolve their conflicts in the future. One thing that has been characteristic of the whole field has been the vast number of companies that have jumped in. We remember that during the past 5 years, before the stock market began to fall, it was very easy to get venture capital. An Electrofax machine is a rather simple machine to make engineeringwise; for $500,000 almost anybody could jump in and get into the business. And it was a growth industry and it was easy to get money. As a result of this there must have been thirty to fifty different companies involved making Electrofax machines. Some could distribute them only in the New York City area or something of this sort, but it has been a real wild industry for price-cutting competition. And as long as people are anxious to pump $500,000 into the industry for a venture it is very hard to make money at it. They will keep pumping this money in and, because they are competing so vigorously, they lose their shirts. Now some of the companies that are of better standing than others in the Electrofax business include Charles Broun and Company, Smith-Corona Marchant, Bell & Howell with their Ditto Division, General Aniline & GAF Corporation, Apēco (the American Photocopy Equipment Company), Savin, and Pitney-Bowes, Copystatics, A. B. Dick, Addressograph-Multigraph, Olivetti-Underwood, Remington Rand, and Royfax. These have all had good copiers available.

In addition to that, paper companies have gone into the
manufacture of supplies. These include Scott Paper, Nashua
Corporation, St. Regis, Riegel Paper, Mead Corporation,
West Virginia Pulp and Paper, S. D. Warren, Weyerhaeuser,
and Crown Zellerbach. I think Crown Zellerbach is out of
the business now, but they were in it fairly strongly for
a while. This then represents a very competitive situation.
During this 17 percent growth rate period, we have had a
very competitive thing going on in Electrofax. At the
present time we do not see as many new competitors in the
machine business, and we see paper companies actually get-
ing out of the business. We see some Japanese companies
coming into the machine business, and they are doing a
very nice job, and it could mean that we are not going to
be so much in the machine business any more. Toshiba,
Minolta, Hitachi, and Cannon all have reasonable electrostatic copiers on hand. Still this is what has been going
on in the Electrofax business with the coated sheets of
paper, highly competitive. The toner business has been
good, those are the black particles that are used. Hunt
Chemical, Dennison, Interchemical, and Sun Chemical are a
few of the companies that make toners, but it is been a
fairly smaller group, and it has been quite profitable.

The Xerox Corporation, meanwhile, has ridden along with
no competition because they had some excellent patents.
They have been able to deliver copies on clear bond paper
beautifully, and they had good machine designs, very expensive machine designs, because a Xerox machine necessarily calls for a very fine machining job in order to get

the tolerances that are needed for the transfer process
from the drum. This is about to end. And this is one of the
forces you can see right now. IBM has come in with a transfer machine, over which there is a big suit that probably
will go on for quite a while. And there are other transfer
machines on the horizon possibly. So that Xerox, who has
had approximately 70 percent of the business, will begin
to run into some competition. It is hard to expect them to
drop their prices, and at the present time the Xerox process
generally costs more than the Electrofax process, and this
is the reason for the two processes. The Xerox process tends
to become profitable in the very high volume range where
maybe you are running 100,000 copies a month or something
of that sort on a machine, whereas an electrotype machine
can survive on maybe 500 or a 1000 copies a day.

So that we can see on the horizon the coming of other
companies possibly into the transfer process, competition
for Xerox. We see, I think, a diminution of competition in
the Electrofax business so it will become perhaps a little
more healthy. At the same time Xerox's plans are not to expand in this business. If you have 70 percent of the copying business, you do not try to cost cut because you cannot win there. They definitely have to use their profit
someplace else, and according to their statements they are
attempting to get more into the duplicating business to replace offset duplicating machines. This is the reason for
their high-speed, high-capacity machines. I expect to see
Xerox try to take over some of the offset lithography on
the other $1 1/2 billion's worth of this duplicating business.

Another trend that is coming along—I see two trends so
far—the reduction in the number of companies plus the competition for Xerox. The tendency of Xerox and any other
plain paper transfer system could come along to move into
offset lithography. Another obvious possibility is that of
getting into the photography business, of the copying business running into the photography business. At the present
time it is possible in the laboratory to make perfectly
nice looking black-and-white prints from photographs, and
the Electrofax process, especially, can be used for this.
It is possible in the laboratory to make good color prints
that have one advantage over most of the Kodachromes and
Kodacolors that you see in that they have archival quality.
You can make firmer pigments if you want, rather than having
to depend upon particular dyes that are light sensitive
someplace along the line. And, also the Electrofax process
and the Xerox process now have a process that has an ASA
rating of about 2, speed rating for film, as compared with
something like maybe 20 that you can get with color film
in a movie camera. So that if we had an order-of-magnitude
change, if we could increase the sensitivity of the process
by an order of magnitude, it is perfectly reasonable to expect that this process might possibly begin to become competitive with photography or silver halide photography. I
do not have to talk to you about the diminishing supplies
of silver and all the rest of it for you to recognize that
this is a reasonable thing and we do have archival capability here so that this is not too bad.

There is a good application for Electrofax printouts. One

of the most advantageous things is to get information out
of a computer. One of the real hangups right now is how to
get information out of a high-speed computer when it comes
in great detail without a lot of digestion. The impact
printers that are being used are just too slow, and we need
something else. Now you can display information quite rapidly and well on a television tube and have good response,
and if you can photograph that information as it comes on
the television tube, one image after another, you can get
fast printouts. So there is a possibility here, and many
people, including RCA, are looking forward to this. I would
not say the activity is active or really intense right now
for it seems a little early for some of the developments,
but we are looking forward to that. Of course, RCA has pub-
licized the fact that they are working on a homefax. They
are looking forward to the day 20 or 30 years from now when
you will not be able to get any newspaper boys to deliver
papers and everyone will be spread all over suburbia and
paper deliveries will be terrible. They are looking forward to the day when an Electrofax copy that will be printed
out can be delivered from your television receiver. You will
print the page you want—sports, you just get sports and it
comes rolling out. And this would be an evolution from the
cathode-ray tube printer. These are then possible trends
and things that might come out in the future.

One of the business competition factors is going to be
the Japanese activity. The Japanese make very good machines.
I do not think they are capable of making a good Xerox
machine yet, but they can make a very good Electrofax one.

It is a little simpler machine, and that is why it is
cheaper. And then, of course, another factor is going to
be the worldwide usage rate. Electrofax is still a little
expensive for Europe, it is a little expensive for Japan,
and yet with the prices dropping and the level of the economics of those areas rising, we can expect more.

I think, too, that we expect that the Electrofax producers will be developing cheaper systems and getting
around one of the main bugaboos with the Electrofax system, which has been the slimy coating. Secretaries and
others could feel that they had a coated sheet of paper in
their hand, and they did not like that. I think we will be
seeing some resolution of that problem coming along. And I
think you will see that the dependability of the machines
will increase.

Perhaps I should just summarize to say that in general
we expect to see an average growth rate of 10 percent in
the next 5 years in the business. However, within that general business there are going to be some areas that are going to increase quite rapidly, and there are going to be
some new developments which perhaps are going to be new
growth areas, and I have tried to indicate what some of
these may be. I think many companies will be dropping
out of the Electrofax business in the near future. I think
there are reasonably good opportunities, then, in the re-
prographics business for engineers, chemists, physicists,
people of that type. I think it is probably more so in the
Electrofax business than the Xerox kind of business. The
Xerox Company has done a very good job, and I think they

are just about saturated in their increase in numbers of
engineers and scientists. Many of the Electrofax companies,
on the other hand, have been technologically backward industries. My own company, I think I would have to classify
that way. We have been coming out of the dark ages as far
as modern technology and the application of it to production and service and things of this sort go. I think
there are good opportunities there. The companies are coming to realize that they are in a high-technology business
like the photographic business and are beginning to learn
how to use high-grade production engineers, industrial engineers, and research and development people.

*All three of the speakers were questioned about the em-
ployment market in their particular specialties and commented on the kinds of scientists and engineers who were
being sought in their areas.*

Question: I'd like to ask Professor Vander Velde a question.
You spoke of the STOL development. I wonder what you think
the probability is that the government will in fact support
such development.

Wallace E. Vander Velde: Direct government support for the
development of an aircraft is a very unpopular thing, as
you know. I would like to address this question first by
way of commenting on the SST case, which had some other
problems too, to be sure. It seems to me that we just went
about that in the wrong way. The SST was viewed by people

as being essentially a direct government subsidy to the development of a commercial product, in this case ultimately
to enhance the Boeing Company. And that's an objectionable
activity of government in the minds of many people. On the
other hand, it's been very common in the past to have government support for the development of technologies of various sorts, including such things as communication satellites, all of which then becomes available to industry to
exploit as it can and will. This has been, I think, quite
generally accepted by people. So, with respect to the STOL,
there is work now being done through the government laboratories and sponsored by the various agencies which does
have applicability to the STOL-type aircraft: basic technology development of various sorts, including the complicated aerodynamics of these vehicles, the significant guidance and control requirements, and so on. This is happening
now, and the results of all that will be available, in effect, to subsidize the development of the aircraft. But I
doubt very seriously that we will see the government involved in a program that resembles in any way the form of
the SST program, where essentially a design by a given company was being sponsored.

Question: I would like to ask Professor Vander Velde also
about what he sees as the future of the recovery of ground
transportation and for participation of the aerospace industry in this area; and also the possible complication of
the aerospace industry.

Wallace E. Vander Velde: There's no question but that
ground transportation of a new order is in the picture for
the future, and perhaps even the near future. When every
aerospace company looks at the future and sees the outlook
that I just gave, they all look to see what can they do
next, and everyone sees transportation, including ground
transportation, as one of the few things that looks big
and has a substantial technological content. So we will see
the aerospace companies trying to participate in the development of new forms of ground transportation. It's already
happening, of course. United Aircraft has built a high-
speed train. We'll see a good deal of that, I'm sure. And
there is a substantial technological overlap in connection
with some of these. The tracked air-cushioned vehicle, for
instance, which is one of the very popular ways of supporting a high-speed ground vehicle, is really flying low
if you will.

Question: Dr. Fairbanks, what is the status now of the
Electrox process with the Chester Carlson patents?

Daniel F. Fairbanks: Well, it's still in the courts, as a
matter of fact. The Chester Carlson patents, the early
ones, have been expired quite a while ago. The first one,
I think, was 1944 or someplace back in there. We at Dennison are being sued by Xerox at the present and are coun-
tersuing, asking for triple damages, for monopolistic ten-
dencies in this area right now. The problem is that there
are two patents covering this general area. One is the

Xerox patent, which derives originally from Chester Carlson
and improvements on it, and there is a whole series of hun-
dreds of patents here. One is for the transfer process, the
selenium drum, where you expose on the selenium drum and
transfer the toner on the image and then transfer off on
to a bare piece of paper. The other is the RCA patent, developed by RCA back around 1956 or so, in which zinc oxide
is used as a photoconductor, and other materials can be
used as a photoconductor on a piece of paper, and the electrostatic image is laid on that piece of paper and finally
toned, and that's the final image, there's no transfer in
between. Well Xerox claims that one of their patents, or
a couple of their patents, cover the RCA process. Now these
two giants have not approached each other directly. RCA
doesn't manufacture Electrofax but licenses the patents to
other people, and they go after them and say, "Pay up."
Well, we paid up to RCA because they are the ones who
showed us how to do it originally, gave us the patents.
Xerox meanwhile comes after you in the other direction and
says, "Pay us under our patents," you see, and they both
would like to collect 5 percent royalties. Well, we have
selected RCA. We had been paying them, Smith-Corona Marchant
for instance, selected Xerox, and they've been paying them.
RCA sued Smith-Corona Marchant, and the suit was thrown out
of court. We're still embroiled in the court. It may very
well end up that ours should be thrown out of court, too,
as a matter of fact—that's maybe my company philosophy
here—but it may end up that no one will have an active

patent when we're through on the Electrofax process. This
doesn't affect the Xerox process.

Question: John Blair. In your new technology, I see com-
puter-related parts, do you include all computer hardware?
How do you define the difference between computer software
and computer hardware?

John Blair: Well, this is all computer hardware and software that I was talking about, and this is the main frame
as well as peripherals that is lumped into that total figure that I have shown. If you look at the breakdown, the
biggest piece of the action is in the peripherals in terms
of growth, and that is the area where there is the largest
competition, and in terms of company finances the largest
instability. That area is characterized by small companies,
highly competitive, some of them in terms of sales are investing tremendously large percentages in the hope of rapid
payback, and whether or not they will stay in business is
very much in question.

Question: Mr. Blair, I notice you didn't mention radar. I
wonder if you'd care to say a few words about the future
of radar. Do you see any new uses for it, other than military?

John Blair: Yes. Several of the items in my listings under
the mature technology are involved in the radar field and
that area shows significant growth. If you look at the FAA

growth graph shown on the government figure, which is
roughly about 100 percent growth in terms of electronics
over the next 4 years, I would say that a good portion of
those funds will go into radar or GCA or ILS, ground control landing approach or instrument landing systems, in
this general family which, indeed, draws very heavily on
radar talents. So this is a growth area, primarily government stimulated, surely from the civilian sector of the gov-
vernment, but government stimulated. There are, of course,
other areas such as commercial radars for law enforcement,
marine radars for merchant marine or pleasure boating;
these areas also will enjoy growth but by no means the extent of the growth that the FAA-stimulated area will enjoy.

Question: Do you think this is going to stimulate any hiring from the companies involved in this unless they're
pretty well staffed in those areas already?

John Blair: No, I would probably say that since the radar-
based activities have been primarily government oriented
there's going to be a reshuffling, and I don't expect a
major stimulation.

Question: How do you think the same kind of individuals
that have carried out the military program will be able to
handle some of the other applications more commercially
oriented? Will they be looking for perhaps different kinds
of individuals?

John Blair: Well, it seems that really the hard-core know-how in the radar area has been militarily funded and in technical developments. I think that this is probably the easiest area to make the transition. There is just no manpower pool other than what is in existence in the military area to take care of the technical requirements of the air transportation sector.

Question: I have a question for Mr. Blair. You showed in your mature technologies for commercial application in almost every case an increase in dollar sales forecast for the next 4 years. Isn't there a possibility that Japanese and other foreign sources will reverse that, so that they could go down instead of up?

John Blair: Indeed there is a very strong possibility of this. For example, the first item under mature technology, which is the consumer electronics area, is by and large 40 to 50 percent dominated by imports, and there is a very strong possibility of imports eroding a large portion of this growth.

Question: With respect to the salary levels of aerospace engineers: there have been accusations that these people are receiving much too high salaries in comparison with other industries. Do you expect this to continue?

Wallace E. Vander Velde: I don't have any real store of direct information that deals with this, although I recall

having seen some summaries of data of this sort in the
past. I believe it was true that those industries that
were bidding so strongly for engineering talent during the
last half dozen years or so, which includes aerospace and
electronics, say computers in particular, bid up salaries
to some extent by comparison with the more stable industries that have not had the requirement for growth of their
engineering staff. So I think there has been some differential. And if the natural laws continue to operate, I
would expect to see that differential erode in the near
future.

Question: I'd like to put a question to the members of the
panel that I think may be of interest, and that's a question of hiring policy of perhaps you yourself may do or
you're familiar with in parts of your company. What kind
of people do you tend to be looking for these days in terms
of young people versus old people, or specialization versus
generalists, and maybe we could have some on that if you
could comment?

John Blair: Well, at the present time everything is very
much up in the air, and it's very difficult to make any
sense out of what is going on in terms of hiring or trans-
ferring people around internally to accommodate growth
areas. This is what is being given the highest priority,
and just what is going to happen in terms of hiring in the
future and what mix of people we'd be looking for is perhaps premature to say. But I think there was a reference

to quality especially in terms of hiring young people directly out of schools, and this certainly is going to continue. In general, hiring bachelors' or masters' people
out of universities, there is an unwritten law that we'd
like to get above a certain average, and these averages
are continually increasing.

Daniel F. Fairbanks: I think hiring may be partly a function of the industry that you're in or the particular company that you're in. We've raised our sights a great deal
in the recent years in terms of the quality of the technical person that we are trying to hire. And yet, I think you
have to look at what you mean by quality. Probably it means
one able to work within your own company's environment. And
companies do vary in their environment. At the present time
we're looking for people with at least good master's level
preparation in research and development and perhaps 5 years'
experience, someone who has undergone an internship and
brings experienced knowledge of how to operate within a
company context into the company. This is partly because
as I indicated, I think Dennison had been backward in some
of its technological areas, and we're trying to bring in
people who know how to bring in technology into the company. We're trying to bring in people who, say, are familiar with computer programming. We'd love to have some more
people around who can keep track of our industries. We
have, say, 6000 products, and they've all been kept by
ladies down in the basement someplace who have been keeping the records, and we'd like to computerize that, and

yet we don't have the talent in the company. So we're looking for people who not only know how to operate a computer
but know how to communicate with people and find out the
kind of information they have to find out and get it into
the computer and get a program going and fight top management when top management doesn't know what it's doing. This
is sometimes the case. All these things lead you to an assessment of the person: first of all, good technical background in some area that can work for us, and two, personal
characteristics that allow the person to operate, to take
initiative, to operate perhaps all alone or to gain help
from those he needs the help from rather than being outrun
by other people because very often there's no one to tell
him exactly what to do.

Question: I wonder if I can ask you one other question on
that line. Frequently perhaps people with knowledge of high
technology have come from very research oriented organizations, are you looking for any either experience or knowledge along more business-oriented considerations? The fact
that you have to be profit oriented in very competitive
business, are you looking for any characteristics that
relate to that?

Daniel F. Fairbanks: Not necessarily direct experience that
relates to business but certainly the kinds of wide-going
interests. Take a chemist who comes into the laboratory,
we have such a complicated business in general that if the
man or woman has the ability he very soon will become the

expert at a particular branch of technology. He very often
can cut out a branch of technology that's all his own and
his immediate supervisors won't know it as well as he does.
So we're not looking for a helper but for an authority,
and we're looking for the kind of person who can become an
authority in this area quickly.

John Blair: Can I add to that from the point of view of
electronics? In the new technology area that I discussed
previously, if you look at the makeup of that segment of
the electronics industry, it's teeming with entrepreneurs
and it's teeming with small companies. And if you look at
the progress of an engineer who starts out in research and
development, you will find very rapidly that by necessity
he is going to have to become a marketeer in a short period
of time very shortly after he has developed his product,
and in a sense he's going to move away from being a creative, in the sense of creating hardware, type of individual
into a creative, in the sense of creating business, type
of individual. Engineers in these high-technology areas
are extremely well suited if they have the personal makeup
to be effective marketeers because the markets are highly
specialized and the interfaces carry a great deal of technical content and it's necessary to have an understanding
of not only the product but the technical requirements of
the customers so that the gap can be bridged. So when I
say, and I'd like to put this in an optimistic note, although my former colleagues may resent that I'm campaign-
ing here for engineers to become marketeers, I'd like to

say that when I talk about the growth and the 9000 or so
engineers going into the system, there's going to be a flow
of these who will move into the business end of the operations, and as a result may make available a larger number
of spots than I have projected.

*Martin H. Schrage, Senior Systems Engineer for Computer
Signal Processors, Inc., was acting as chairman of this
session.*

Martin H. Schrage: I'd just like to make one comment along
that line from my own experience. The firm I'm with is a
little over 2 years old and it's a very small firm, about
25 people or so that manufacture some very advanced computer equipment. I have experienced precisely what you describe there. I started off working with Fourier trans-
forms and doing that kind of work, but more and more it's
necessary to go out and sell. Sales activity is so technical that our salesmen really can't handle it themselves,
and so frequently you have to go out, and really the cre-
ativity aspect is in applying the technology you have to
a customer's problems, which many times might require you
to stand at a blackboard and explain the sampling theorem
to them, which is an old homework many years ago for me,
but they really don't understand it, and you have to put
it in terms that they understand and also try to solve the
problems that they have at hand, whether it be the controlling of vibration shake table or measuring of noise
level from a machine or whatever the problem is. I spend

a great deal of my time doing that kind of thing and it's
by necessity in order for our firm to market our products.
And it's actually very interesting. I first started off,
as I say, doing very highly mathematical things, and I did
not foresee myself out there peddling, so to speak. But it
is very interesting, and it's very much a teaching activity.
So, truly it's really kind of interesting, and I've enjoyed
that part of the job.

Comment: I can see an engineer trying to market his product
in a small company, but in a large company the engineer has
plenty of marketing types around so that if you have not
only to create the product but to sell it as well, I think
that's a real loss of the individual's talents.

Daniel F. Fairbanks: I think you're right if the talents
aren't being used at the level that they're needed. We find
in our company that we have both industrial sales and consumer sales, that is to say, the copier would be a consumer-
type sale because normally you are interfacing with secretaries or managers who don't understand the technical properties of the thing, and there you generally don't need an
engineer to interface. But if you get into another kind of
product, for example the crepe paper used for the little
transformers that stand on telephone poles, there the sales
job is to go in and talk to a design engineer at Westinghouse or General Electric, or some place of this sort and
find out what his present technique of design is in manufacture and try to convert him to a different design system.

And this calls for fairly high caliber technical sales.
This particular product was developed originally in our
laboratory about 10 years ago, it was sold by the people
who had developed it for at least 3 years. The company then
decided they could take it over, they gave it to an ordinary salesman, to the sales force, and it just went downhill. When they put it back on to specialty sales again,
with engineers selling it, it's built right up again. And
so in some cases where there's a research and development
aspect to the sales, your technical talent is not being
wasted, it's really being used to show an intelligent engineering type what he has to do.

Comment: Sometimes the biggest problem is trying to educate
the marketing man, and usually the marketing man has other
things of a larger magnitude than the marketing staff is
concerned with like bringing in business in much greater
quantities. So the poor engineer really doesn't get the attention he deserves, and consequently he's forced to try
to sell it as an individual, and usually he does not succeed because he just doesn't have the attention of top
management.

John Blair: A great deal depends on whom you have to sell.
Certainly it would be a waste to try to put engineers on
the job of selling television sets. It's not a specialized
product. It's really one type of product that can serve a
very wide segment of the consumer population. And, indeed,
we have an established distribution channel for this: dis-

tributers, retailers, and so on. But in some of the other
areas where, for example, you are interfacing components
with computers, or where you're interfacing computers with
industrial process control, you have an entirely different
kind of buying population. By and large, the buying population in this segment is an engineer, or engineers, and
if you want to communicate with engineers, and if you put
a marketeer with just a superficial training on the job,
he is struck out even before he starts.

Wallace E. Vander Velde: I'd like to add to that. I see
the inside of a few large companies myself as a result of
consulting with them, and I see this happening all the
time with people I work with. They are usually doing somewhat innovative things and are doing their own selling. In
a large organization that has a well-established marketing
group, I think it's perfectly appropriate that the marketing group should coordinate these activities. If, for example, you have one program office going to a particular
customer for a $2 million program, you don't want that
same customer badgered by half a dozen other people who
are looking for $25,000 jobs. So the marketing groups serve
to coordinate the activities and in many cases to introduce the engineers to the right people. But there is no
doubt that the bulk of the actual selling ultimately has
to be done by the engineers involved.

John Blair: I'd like to just point out that engineers for
managers in this new technology area is another important

growth sector for employment. And in fact if you look at
even a relatively mature company as the Raytheon Company,
with which I am associated, and look at the top managerial
ranks, most everybody is an engineer. Our midmanagement in
marketing as well as in engineering and development, covering the whole spectrum, they all have engineering degrees.
So I'm sure this is going to be characteristic of the new
technology in industry that is just taking off the ground
and is developing. So there are more opportunities available than just R&D opportunities, and indeed what you
pointed out, that perhaps management training as part of
engineering training, is something that we might want to
look forward to is very valid.

Wallace E. Vander Velde: I'd like to ask a question of John
on that last point because we're interested in education.
Do you find that there is any particular management-oriented
discipline that is really of advantage to these people or
is it a matter of personal characteristics that go along
with general ability? In other words, what can we do in
education specifically to enhance this opportunity?

John Blair: I think that perhaps rather than to try to tie
it down to any specific discipline in the management sciences is not as important as trying to give the youngsters
who are growing up a feeling for what is involved in business and that feeling can be imparted through any number
of the management disciplines.

The panel then turned its attention to the problems arising from foreign competition.

Question: We've talked a lot about our engineering, but I gather there might be a tendency in the future to license foreign processes and foreign products. Does this take some special capability other than, say, language... I mean a special capability that we don't normally find in our engineers?

Wallace E. Vander Velde: We have had some experience in building foreign designs under license. It's been an unusual thing in our industry, but the Fokker F-27 has been built in some numbers in this country as a direct-licensed design. I don't think it takes anything special that our industry doesn't have. The aircraft industry has very good contact all over the world, primarily because of their marketing activities rather than because of their intent to buy something. Right now the Boeing Aircraft Company sells just about 40 percent of its product abroad. They know the world very well, so I think wherever there are opportunities to use foreign designs our companies are aware of it and will be able to do it without any difficulty.

Question: John Blair. Do you see possibilities of Americans exporting?

John Blair: It is a significant market right now, partic-

ularly in Europe. In many areas I'm quite familiar with
the significance of the export of integrated circuits to
Europe. This is an area where there's a need. They're
building computers and they're building instrumentation
in other forms of electronics. Their technology is not
developed to the level that ours is at this time in the
components area, and in fact the semiconductor industry
weathered the 1970 slump well because it was able to make
headway in Europe. Computers are being exported to Europe,
and some specialized tubes from the mature areas. Indeed,
as the European economy improves and gains momentum, at
least for the time being this is going to be a very lucra-
tive market for the electronics industry. The electronics
industry looks to Japan also as a market. For example, you
see all these very attractive Japanese mini-desk-calcula-
tors. The integrated circuits inside, at the present time,
are manufactured in the United States, shipped to Japan,
the computers are assembled, and they are reshipped to the
United States for sale. Just how long this is going on is
anybody's guess, but I can say that the Japanese as well
as the Europeans are building up very rapidly in these
high-technology areas.

Question: Could I ask you a question about exports. Could
you comment on why that is so effective and whether or not
you feel that that's a continuing thing. Is it a matter of
engineering, purely labor costs, or is it a little more
subtle?

John Blair: It started out to be purely as a matter of
labor cost, and I'm talking particularly about Japanese
imports, but this is no longer the case. The Japanese
electronics technology is highly developed in many areas,
and I don't foresee a very long period of time where they
will be relying on us very heavily still in the high-
technology aspects. Right now certainly the labor content
is less expensive in Japan, but we can hope for our sake
and the Japanese sake that primarily stimulated by their
advanced technology their standard of living is going to
rise as rapidly as their know-how in the high technology.
Perhaps when this happens they are not going to be quite
as labor competitive with us as they are at the present
time.

Comment: I think there was one startling statistic along
those lines that I read recently. If you compare the dollar of product produced per worker in the Toyota Automo-
tive plant to Detroit, the Japanese worker turns out about
twice the dollar value of product, which is probably due
more to their automation. Of course, he gets paid half as
much, too. What can we do about that?

Comment: From the consumer electronics aspect, the government situation in Japan is quite different from what it is
here in that they are strongly subsidizing export business
from Japan, in terms of lending the money at a very low
rate of interest, increasing the company's leverage, and
in performing effectively quality control and final inspec-

tion so that what does get out of the country as export
has been inspected approximately twice as hard than otherwise would be.

This is a situation that makes them, even if they were
paying the same dollar for their labor hour, have a substantial competitive advantage in the world market. Now,
I'm not proposing that we have to do the same thing here,
but it's a fact of life in competing with the Japanese.

Chapter 5

CAREER OPPORTUNITIES IN COMPUTERS
AND INFORMATION PROCESSING

*Employment opportunities in the new industries involved
in both computer hardware and software were discussed in
considerable detail. The general picture of the industries was presented by Mr. Robert W. Puffer, manager of
Peripherals Engineering of the Digital Equipment Corporation of Maynard, Massachusetts, and Mr. Arthur W. Heineck,
Jr., vice president of Inforex, Inc., of Burlington, Massachusetts.*

<u>Robert W. Puffer</u>: I would like to talk a little bit about
the computer industry and where I think it is going in the
next 3, 4, 5 years perhaps. Anything further than that
is pure speculation. In some respects, 12 months is pure
speculation. I think that I have an opportunity to be
what I should call cautiously optimistic. I am certainly
optimistic about the long term, and perhaps a little bit
more cautious about the short term. We have come on a
pretty fast ride during the last 10 years, as all of you
are well aware. I can toss out a few numbers that will
give you an idea of what has been going on in this business. First, I think it is appropriate to break the industry down into what I call general-purpose computers
that are, for lack of a better definition, whatever IBM
makes; minicomputers—it used to be under $100,000 but let
us say central processors that are $20,000 and under; and

then the peripheral equipment business which, although it
is dominated by the captive businesses of IBM and the major manufacturers, now has over 400 independent firms ac-
tively competing for pieces of the $4 billion in shipments
that were made last year.

 The general-purpose computer business witnessed about a
30 percent annual compound growth rate between 1965 and
1969. That is a pretty startling number when you understand that that 30 percent included a great many business
failures. It was a rather remarkable phenomenon. And it
was a purely American phenomenon. There was nothing
worldwide going on at all of that sort. In fact, the computer industry is still today pretty much of an American
business. This growth rate got us to shipments of domestic general-purpose machines of about $5 1/2 billion in
1969. For the first time last year the total numbers of
machines as measured by dollars actually decreased about
10 percent to about $5 billion. Now for an industry used
to growing 30 percent a year for 4 successive years to
go down 10 percent in a year is quite a remarkable turnaround. Obviously, a good deal of this was due to the
general downturn in the economy, and particularly hard
hit were those firms doing a predominance of their business with the aerospace industry. Some of the major firms
in this business which had done spectacularly well during
the 1960s actually operated at a loss last year. Another
factor last year was that the major manufacturers introduced their new generation of machines, the IBM 370 series
and so on. I do not imagine they intended it that way.

At the time they perhaps did not forecast economic conditions quite as accurately as they might have, but in any
case the introduction of a whole new series of equipment
obviously encourages customers to hold off for the better
thing tomorrow instead of buying today. On top of this,
the software end of the business has been lagging badly
behind the hardware end. There are many situations where,
although better and faster hardware is available, there
is not the software to make it work.

I think the next year is going to show an upturn, not a
remarkable one but at least a favorable one. A good number to shoot at is $5.2 billion worth of shipments domes-
tically, and then a resumed growth during 1972 and 1973,
getting to about $6 1/2 billion in 1973.

Within the general-purpose industry I see the small end
of the business, the $50,000 to maybe $200,000 end of the
business, being the strongest. The very large end, the
$1 1/2 million machines and up, will be quite strong for
the reason that there are some new machines being introduced which do not have any competiton right now. When
you start from zero, your percent increases can be very
large even if your total dollars are not.

There is a more level trend in the medium and large machine business, which is dominant historically, say the
$200,000 to $1,000,000 central processor price tag. There
is user migration to shared systems, to small systems, and
as the applications that are more and more appropriately
run on minicomputers get taken away from this segment of
the business we can expect it to level off.

Minicomputers are a little bit brighter story. The industry shipped about 10,000 units in 1970, and that works
out to an annualized growth rate for the past 5 years of
somewhere in the mid-30s percent. You can dig up all
sorts of forecasts that range anywhere from 20 percent
growth to 40 percent growth through 1975. Roughly, it is
a market of about $400 million right now, and by all mea-
sures the 1970 economic slowdown did not hurt the minicomputer market too much. The market did change appreciably
during the course of the year, it became ever more competitive, but it continued to grow. This is in no small
part because the minicomputer business has been historically less dependent on government sales than the larger
end of the business. Moreover, the general computing and
the education markets were up even though the laboratory
and industrial markets were down to some extent. And that,
plus an extremely favorable situation with foreign business, in Europe, Japan, Australia, let the minicomputer
business continue to grow.

The business is changing. Whereas computers at one time,
particularly small computers, were sold only to unsophisticated clientele, the broad base of the market is obviously with the great unwashed—businessman, store owner, and
so on. So minicomputers are getting themselves in more and
more everyday applications, and that is where the manufacturers are broadening their product lines in order to compete.

The peripheral business, which I talked about a little
bit earlier, is a real scramble right now. It has cer-

tainly been growing at fairly explosive rates although it
is hard to cite any specific percentage (maybe 40 percent
or 30 percent) just because so much of it is bundled in
with the dollars that everyone reports on a consolidated
basis. About 15 percent of the total dollars, which as I
said was about $4 billion last year, is being shipped by
independent people, and if you read the papers you find a
new company per day coming into this business and another
new company per day failing and going bankrupt.

The overall technology in the computer business is, I
think, pretty obvious to most of you. There is the
straightforward electronics technology that we share with
a good many other businesses today, the electronics of
semiconductors and electronics packaging. The increased
emphasis on peripherals of course is encouraging us to
make a lot more use of mechanical and electromechanical
design capabilities. And, as I said before, software,
which has been neglected during the past 3, 4, 5 years,
during the period of explosive hardware growth obviously
makes up a very important percentage of the total employment and the total number of dollars spent today. On top
of this, there are certain process technologies that are
associated with the captive businesses that each one of
the major companies runs: the people who make printed circuit boards, who stamp metal, who plate disc surfaces, and
string memories.

I find that there are relatively few opportunities in
this business for a true specialist. Now it is true that
every printed circuit board shop needs its chemist, but

that is one chemist for five or six or a hundred or a
thousand people working in some other area. In the engineering world we need logic designers and circuit designers, and certainly there are a good many programmers
around who are doing relatively specialized sorts of
things. But all of these people, if they are insensitive
to the competitive nature of the business, if they are
insensitive to the needs of the market, if they do not
understand what it means to make a profit, they are all
going to fail. So I look at this as an opportunity for
generalists, not an opportunity for specialists, people
who understand business, who understand competition, who
can perceive what a market wants because in this business
you are not measured by such abstractions as whether or
not you finished the design on time and it worked, you are
measured by whether or not anyone is going to buy it. It
is not quite like making toasters, but it is getting increasingly more that way.

  The sort of person I like to look for myself is someone
who is relatively young, and by that I mean 3 to 6, maybe
10 years out of school, someone who has a lot of business
horse sense, who understands why you should not have huge
inventories of stuff sitting around the cellar. Obviously
he has to have a pretty sound technical background and
some sort of record of accomplishment. But above all, he
has to be able to manage, and by that I mean he has to be
able to manage his own affairs and the affairs of his colleagues just as much as he may have to be able to manage
a project or a large group of people. All of those skills

that we tend to call management come into play today even
for the engineer doing what is relatively specialized design work. I think the persons least likely to succeed,
for my money, and I am speaking from a personal standpoint, are those people who have become highly specialized, the fellow who has been designing ablative coating
materials for an Apollo spacecraft for 10 years, someone
who is not used to being cost conscious, who is not used
to being cost measured by the real economic world that is
out there as opposed to a government contract, someone who
likes the comfort of a large organization with many services who is not used to doing things for himself and getting things done, somehow just figuring out how to do it
regardless of the fact that the personnel department is
no good and the accountants do not know what anything
costs, and on and on ad infinitum. Flexibility, I guess,
is a key word in what I am looking for.

   So, as I said, I think I am able to be cautiously optimistic. I think there are going to be a large number of
opportunities during the next few years in the industry.
The areas of the business that are growing most rapidly
right now are minicomputers and peripherals. And, as I
see it, the opportunities are for generalists with a great
deal of good horse sense on top of a reasonably good technical background.

Arthur W. Heineck, Jr.: The area of business that I should
like to speak about this afternoon is data entry and some
thing I call turn-key applications. Certainly data entry

is a neglected area of the computer world, one that is
getting much attention these days, though, and I think has
many opportunities for people in this room. Right today
there are some 500,000 to 700,000 key punch or verifiers
out in the field. These are the same pieces of equipment
that were used way back in the IBM 1400 days and the tab
days. More and more the managers of these pieces of equipment realize that they are not the world-beaters that they
used to be. There is a company called Mohawk Data Sciences
that really plowed up the ground there, and a lot of people are coming in behind them now and trying to benefit
from what they have done. Mohawk was the company that in
a sense freed people's minds from the concept of entering
data via keyboard and then punching a card.

If you look at a typical sequence of events that goes on
now, someone creates the information somewhere in the business and then somehow it manifests itself in the key-punch
room. One set of operators enters these data, another
set of operators, different girls, verifies the data, and
then all you have is a deck of cards. Even after verifi-
cation there are still many errors in those data because
the source material might have been bad, the verifier operator might have missed things, and so forth. So, first
they have to get the data onto tape in a separate operation. They take the cards into a tape room and then they
go card to tape. Now after the information is on tape,
they usually have what they call an edit run or reasonableness testing. The only purpose of that is to make
sure that all the data on the tape are basically correct

because if they are not correct when you send them to your
main processor, you know the one that costs $200 an hour,
the run is in trouble and the operators will have to get
that tape off and start all over again. So the whole concept in data entry is to get clean tapes made, clean in
the sense that the data are reasonable, the headings on
the tape are correct, the normal format that the normal
programs look for is correct. Keep in mind that there is
a series of steps here. The most damaging thing in this
series of steps is the person who really created the data
is nowhere in this process, and managers and computer operators and business people realize that, and they want to
get rid of key punchers, and it is going to evolve over
the next 10 years to 20 years. They are going to get to
the man who is creating the data, to the source, the man
who makes out the insurance policy, they want to get somehow to him because he knows what the correct data are.
They do not want to enter via one and verify it via another girl. They would just like him to enter the information
somehow, look at it and say, "Yes, this is correct," and
capture those data right at the source. The industry is
nowhere near that today, and there are fantastic opportunities to help industry get to that point.

What did Mohawk do? What Mohawk did, they said, "Well,
let's eliminate a couple of these steps here. What we can
do is instead of going from card to tape, we'll create a
tape right at the keyboard." A simple concept. Simple
concepts are things that make a lot of money. They just
saved that one step. One other thing that they did was

with the key punch operation. When the girl hits the skip
key or the dup key, it does that mechanically, it bump
bump bumps along. And all they did was to do that electronically. These are very simple things to do. What
they said was "by electronically skipping and duping, we
will save 10 percent of the key-punch time," and they did.
And if you think of 700,000 key punches in the country and
probably 1 million key-punch operators, you are saving
100,000 girls. You know, that is real money. A man can
see that. And they moved. Mohawk moved 25,000 of their
units out into the field on a simple concept like that.
Now, what happened with Mohawk is that at each station now
you are creating a tape, so you do not have a lot of cards,
you have a lot of tapes. If you have fifteen Mohawks in
your room, you get fifteen tapes at the end of each day.
So now they have to have a pooler, which is another piece
of equipment, some additional expense there.

   There is also a concept called batch balancing. Think
in terms of these supercomputers, think of what goes on in
the data entry area of the business. Somebody in one room
adds up all the data in one field on an adding machine and
he passes that sum along to the data entry room. After
these cards are all made, that same field is added up, and
if the sum on the adding machine tape agrees with the sum
that was created in the card to tape run then that batch
is in balance. Everybody breathes a sigh of relief, and
they send it on to the processing room. This whole area
is just in the horse-and-buggy days. It really is. So
the card to tape equipment did not solve that batch bal-

ancing problem. What they did is they put an adding machine on their card to tape unit. Really antiquated. So
some other people came along, and we are one of them, they
are many as you know. We have a key disc system. Many
people have a key disc system. What this is, it is a little processor, miniprocessor, and it controls up to eight
key stations, and it can do that simple thing called adding a field of numbers. So we check right then and there.
We do not have to go to a card-to-tape run; check right
then and there to see that this field is in balance with
the source. We still have not returned to the source yet,
by the way. And also we have eliminated several tape
drives, there is only one tape drive for eight girls, so
now you can do your pooling right in the system. And
there are many side effects. There are things like check
digits. You all have American Express cards with your
number, and there is a little check digit at the end there.
If a key-punch operator enters the number with the correct
check digit, the verifier operator does not have to recheck
that field. Just by definition, the check digit says it
is correct. People want to save verify key strokes and
they do. Again, these are all very, very simple concepts,
and the goal is to cut down on data entry time and verify
time and to get clean tapes to the big processor. The big
processor could be 100 miles away, it could be in the same
building.

Now more and more, people want to use the miniprocessor
that controls the data entry to do more of the reasonableness testing. They used to take the tape to a Mod-30, let

us say, or a DEC computer, do the reasonableness test
there and then go on to a Mod-65. Now they are doing it
all in one fell swoop right as the girl is entering it;
they are checking it right there for reasonableness. If
there is something wrong that she can correct, she corrects
it on the spot; she has not filed away the papers and
brought them back. So this is the way that the business
is evolving. Keep in mind that still they have not returned to the source yet. Some of the jobs they try to do
with careful hand printing, like perhaps 5 percent of the
jobs, and they run through on OCR equipment (Optical Char-
acter Recognition). This is very good. They are eliminating a pair of steps. Now for a while everyone thought
that OCR would eliminate all key punchers and verifiers,
but it did not quite do that. Of course, OCR lends itself
to only certain small segments of the work. But that is
a way now of minimizing some of these data entry costs.
Eventually as they get back to the source, what you want
to do is have very clever, single terminals or small clus-
ter terminals that can work economically over phone lines.
That is another problem. As managers get used to dealing
with telecommunications, they will get back to the source.
The reason they have not done as much today as they should
is that phone lines are so expensive. But they will move
back to the source. There will be much, much more done
in the way of phone line communications to get to the man
at the source.

  As you get to the source, you are not going to have a
main processor at that source. Here is a little remote

bank branch or branch of some kind of business. He does
not have a big processor there, and yet he has some of the
needs that go on where there is a big processor. He would
like to get some reports back. He would like to print out
checks locally rather than sending them out by mail because they take two or three extra days, so they want small
printers. Whole new pieces of equipment are necessary
here, low-cost modems, small printers, terminals with cathode-ray tubes on them, all because data entry is so antiquated today. There is a whole area here that has not really been tapped. And it is not a laser or cryogenic kind
of business, it is just a commonsense kind of thing. And
people are ready to move in this area. Just to run down
a list of companies that have started up here: Mohawk Data
Sciences inaugurated a key tape, and Sangamo entered the
key tape business, and Honeywell, and they all obtained
some part of that business; and IBM got excited and said
"What can we do to stop that trend?" and they came out
with a buffered key punch to eliminate the delay due to
mechanical skipping and duping, and you can backspace easily. If you make an error on the buffered key punch now
you do not have to feed that card through and duplicate
it up to the point of error. Some people tried key car-
tridges, it is not a key to magnetic tape, but it is a key
to a little tape, such as on your little recorders, but
now you need a special device to read that little cassette
into the main processor, and that extra step there is an-
noying and it does not seem to have gone over too well,
but maybe it will. Then there must be at least six OCR

companies: Recognition Equipment, Optical Scanning, and
Scan-Data. All these companies started because of opportunities in this data entry area. There are some small
printers coming on the market now. There must be at least
six or seven small printer companies on the market just
because of the need. This came on, I should say, in the
past 2 or 3 years. Then there is the key disc area that
we are in. There are ourselves, Logic, Honeywell is now
in this key disc area, Computer Machinery Corporation,
Systems Electronic Laboratory. The point that I am trying
to make is many, many businesses, whole companies are
springing up in this area. The opportunities are very
large and the technologies are not as dynamic as that,
not as drastic. It is just someone with common sense going out and filling these needs. That is why I should
like to say something about applications because the same
kind of thing is happening. Ross Perot's company does
nothing but supply turn-key operations. What he does is
he goes into a Blue Cross-Blue Shield operation where to
process one of their claims is a dollar. He comes in and
says to the manager, "I'll take over this whole operation—Michigan Blue Cross, California Blue Cross—and I'll
do it for 50 cents a claim. Guaranteed. And I'll sign
the contract today." And he has become a billionaire just
by doing that simple thing. That is incredible, isn't it?
And people are looking for that. People really do not
know how to do things economically. They are looking for
other people to come in and help them do those things economically.

Now some of the problems today are very simple ones.
Like the phone company. They get calls every day, you
know that very well, that say "I need some service." O.K.,
so they get that phone call. They try to enter it on
their file someplace, and they cannot get the man out
there soon enough. So maybe 6 or 7 hours later they get
another call from the same person, "I need service." Now
they have two requests in their file for service from the
same person, the same place, and somehow they have got to
connect them up. By the time they answer that one service
call, they have six requests in their file and it is causing them to go out of their mind. You cannot imagine how
a simple problem like that is going unattended. What people need is a way to enter information into a system rapidly, get it stored on a disc conveniently, and have it
shown back to the man or girl who needs it. It is a simple concept, and there are so many people with those needs.
When you go into a retail store you go up to the catalog
department and you would like to know when you are right
there if the item you are about to order is out. You do
not want to wait 3 weeks to find it is out and they did
not send it to you. If you knew it was out, you would go
somewhere else and get it. Retailers are going out of
their mind just trying to get that simple thing done.
That is interesting, isn't it? They would like to get
that done for $1000 a month. If someone here can do that
for them, you have got yourself a business. It is as simple as that.

People look for very, very clever and dynamic things,

and the business world is looking for simple solutions for very simple problems at a reasonable cost. And they are looking for turn-key applications. They do not want anyone to come in and say, "Here's a processor, use that processor and you can solve that problem." They do not want to hear that anymore; they want to hear, "Here's the solution *to your problem*. Here it is, it's a piece of software, it's a terminal. It's a whole system, $1000 a month. Do you want it?" They fall over backwards. They would give you an order for a thousand tomorrow.

There is a lot of opportunity in the sales area. In our own company, we are hiring salesmen now because our product is out there, it is reasonably established, and now you have to go into different towns. And the salesmen we hire are generally professional people. I think most of them are degree people. We have in our company fifteen or twenty engineers, and by the end of this year we shall probably be up to about sixty salesmen. This is an interesting area, sales. If you get with a company with the right product, a small company, it is a very challenging thing. You go out. You have to be able to meet the people. You have to know your product. You have to understand the people and see if somehow your product will be able to fit his need and, if not, then if there is a big enough market, take that need back to the company and say, "Here's a need. There's a hundred systems out there. A thousand systems." Sales opportunities are tremendous in this area. If you have not thought about sales, I encourage you to think about it, especially with young companies. Young companies in this area are looking for salesmen.

And the other opportunities, I should say they were modest in electronic engineering. You can do a great deal today with very few electronic engineers. Programming has more openings than electronic engineering. Mechanical engineering is not needed in large numbers. Again, with new companies there are opportunities in field engineering, making sure that equipment stays up and so forth.

But I should like you all to consider this area of data entry and turn-key applications. There are vast opportunities there that are still untapped.

The first part of the discussion was focused on the problems of the computer industry arising from the fact that it was a very new industry and had been growing very rapidly.

Question: To Mr. Puffer, with regard to your projections for the minicomputer field expansion at the rate of 30 percent. Is this on any rational basis or is this just an extension of the previous growth rate? Do you base this on any observable relationship, say between capital expenditures or projected capital expenditures, or do you have some other rational basis for predicting this resumption of a 30 percent growth rate?

Robert W. Puffer: I'm not an economist; I'm not sure what

rational base you're looking for. Let me say this. If
you look around, you discover a number of factors that obviously affect the industry's growth. The thing that you
cite is obviously one of them, the capital equipment policies that are going on today, government spending in various areas, but probably most important is just the plain
expansion of the bottom end of the market as cost keeps
coming down to make computers more and more economical in
more and more applications. That alone is certainly the
driving force in the minicomputer business and the expansion of it. Where I think the 30 percent comes from is in
looking over the studies that have been done in the past
3 to 6 months, I find the most sage observers of this
business coming up with ranges of numbers of from 20 to 40
percent and I'm saying, "Hey, I'm not any smarter than
they are, let's pick the middle ground."

Comment: There's some history that industries that have
overcapacity, while their volume production may increase
markedly, say 30 percent, the dollar value of this production levels off or even goes down.

Robert W. Puffer: I wouldn't want to argue that. In our
case we don't have overcapacity in general right now, and
I'm talking about the total dollars business as opposed
to units, which obviously are going to go up much faster
because progressively the cost is coming down by factors
of 2 every few years. I'm pretty optimistic. That's one
man's opinion on top of whatever literature I've been able

to survey. Just to see how far wrong forecasts can be in
this business, however, I happened to come across an article that was written no more than 18 months ago looking at
the memory field—this is a very comprehensive study—and
it projected that core memories would still be a fairly
major portion of the market today and through 1972, which
they are. It projected that thin films would be a relatively unimportant portion of the market, which they are.
It then went on to say semiconductor memories would be
terribly unimportant all the way out through 1972 and 1973
and, in fact, plated wire was the thing that was going to
sweep the industry by storm because prices would still be
in the 10 cents per bit area in 1972. Well, they're down
2 1/2 cents right now. And that was a study made only 18
months ago. So in an industry that's as volatile as this
and as subject to technological change, I think that your
guess is as good as Paul Samuelson's or any other distin-
guished person you'd like to cite. And I think we have a
good future and that if you look strictly at the market,
look at the applications, you can't help but be filled
with a little bit more optimism than you would like me to
believe you are filled with.

Comment: Then what you're saying is that you don't have
a rational basis for it. This is just optimism.

Robert W. Puffer: I'm just optimistic. I'm a "seat-of-
the pants" guy, and my rational basis is looking at all
the other people who are making projections and adding

them up and seeing if I believe them. I haven't done any
studies that indicate how many machine tools are going to
be bought in the next 3 months.

Comment: There's another aspect of the thing, too, that
you might relate it to, and that is the inflow of risk money into the field. Now there was a period when the inflow
of risk money due to stock flotations was very high. Practically anyone with an idea could get some money from Wall
Street. Now, this has been shut off for 6 months. It
looks to me as though it's going to be turned on again,
so your excess capacity is going to start increasing now,
again.

Robert W. Puffer: Oh, I believe a lot of people are going
to lose a lot of money, if that's what you're asking me.
Frankly, I don't share Arthur Heineck's pushing the sales
end of the business, and I think that must be because he's
a salesman. He did a damn good job of selling that idea.
I'm not as optimistic as that. I think for every company
that's a success there are going to be five that are failures in this business. And that probably goes for my end
of the business, too. But I think that overall, if you
look at the industry, and you have a reasonably good understanding of what the market is and what the applications for these machines are, including the ones that I've
talked about, we've got something that's going to grow
30 percent per year.

The discussion then turned to manpower desires of the industry in terms of the age and the educational attainments of applicants for jobs.

Comment: The older engineer who doesn't want to become a manager seems to be faced with a problem, and I wonder what the older engineer can learn and I wonder what industry managers are doing to change the way you look at it. Maybe one answer is the older engineer, to stay in his job, has to take a 30 percent cut in pay at some point in time, but has this so far created a question for you, and could you comment on it?

Robert W. Puffer: I'll take a shot at it. One of the things that I think is working against the older engineer—and I hate gross generalities that any specific case can prove wrong—is that they walk in and they have some credentials which relate to a series of different things that they've been doing which get more and more specialized and oftener than not tend to scare us away. Even with the older fellow who has been doing something we definitely understand, like designing digital logic or something like that, the trouble is that he comes in and strikes us as someone we just can't get as much out of, to put it in blunt terms, as someone who's 30 years old. This is a wild business, and the smaller the company, the wilder it gets. And the hours people work are crazy, and the sorts of thing that goes on are too. It's a very dynamic kind

of thing, and a person who comes in and projects even the
slightest amount of lethargy is just automatically failing
to communicate with the person who is potentially going to
hire him. If you look around my company, you'll find the
range of vice presidents is 36 to 43 years old. That's the
top management of the company. If you look around the
smaller companies, which have been successful for say 2,
3, or 4 years, those are all people in their late twenties
and early thirties. It really is a young man's business,
and I really don't have an answer as to what to do about
the fellow who comes in with what by all odds is good experience. How do we fit him in socially, if nothing else?

Question: Do you have a problem due to the pension policies
in the computer industries?

Arthur W. Heineck, Jr.: Let me make a comment on this.
I'd say it all comes out in dollars and cents, it's that
simple. We have programming to do in our system but it's
our assembler kind of a thing. We look for basically
young bright men or women who have recently come out of
school because all it takes to do the kind of programming
we have in mind is intelligence, just basic intelligence
and enthusiasm and the people coming out of school are low
cost. Now where there's a skill involved that we need
someone to work on, let's say a disc, and we don't have
that skill in-house, we go for someone in the industry
who's been working in the disc area 4, 5, 6 years, and
we're willing to pay for that *skill*.

Robert W. Puffer: Well, I tend to agree, except that I
don't like the person right out of school. I'd like to
have them fail somewhere else first. That sounds a little
bit snide perhaps, but one of the problems you run into is
the person right out of school doesn't have any way of
assessing the situation he happens to find himself in. In
the first job, he doesn't know whether he's working for a
great organization or a bad organization except by going
out and talking to somebody else. Everything is so sub-
jective that it's really tough for him to get a handle on
it. And there's a great tendency for people not to know
what they want and to be relatively insecure just because
of that. So the sort of person that I'd be most prone to
look at in a favorable light would be someone who'd been
out working for a couple of small companies perhaps. Maybe both of them had gone bankrupt. But the fact that they
had gone bankrupt and the fact that they weren't the
greatest place in the world to work had taught him something. By virtue of the fact that it was a small company,
he'd also, in the throes of some sort of financial problem
say, had to get close to a lot of problems. Maybe he
didn't get a paycheck on Thursday and he wanted to know
what the story was—that would have led him to go find out
something about the accounting department. Getting involved in those sorts of problems to me is a lot more valuable in the course of educating the young engineer who
knows how to design circuits than having him go to work in
a closet for a very large organization and find that he
never gets any exposure to the business problems that a

company has. This is really the question of how do you
train somebody to be a generally useful engineer with a
good understanding of the business. I'm a binary sort of
a guy who says either a guy's good enough to make a high
salary, say over $15,000 or $18,000 a year, or something
like that, or else he's bad enough so you don't pay him
over $10,000, and there's nothing ever in between. That's
a very simplistic way of looking at the world, but what
I'm really trying to say is that I don't mind paying someone if he has above-normal conceptual, or administrative,
or management, or engineering skills, and I don't really
have a place for anybody that doesn't have above-average
all of those things.

Sales is a little different in that most of the people
that our salesmen deal with are mature people. A lot of
them are vice presidents of companies, and we would hesi-
tate to send some wild-looking youngster out of school to
deal with those people. So in the sales area we do look
for more mature people, people who have been in business
awhile and particularly who have dealt with other people
and have some kind of a track record in some sales area.
So again, it depends on the situation and it depends on
the particular skill, the particular area you're talking
about.

Comment: I'd just like to make one comment along this line.
The firm I'm with has about twenty-five people. About a
couple of years ago, at one point there was an older gentleman working with us who was a programmer, and who was

quite a good programmer actually, but quite frankly, the place is very young, and the rest of us just about drove him crazy. We have a guy who works from midnight through eight in the morning, and other people coming in all the time and really, there is a kind of a communications problem just talking to his fellow workers of this social kind of thing. He really was a misfit, and he was very uncomfortable just being there. Particularly the other programmers, a pretty wild bunch. So I think that's not something to be underestimated. It really wasn't anything to do with his ability; he left by mutual agreement of all concerned. It was not anything to do with his technical competence but just the inability to communicate with those around him or to accept the idea of, well tonight he leaves at ten o'clock because something has to be done instead of the usual five-thirty without even thinking about it. It was more than he could cope with.

Another Comment: I have worked with both young groups and older ones in data systems operations, and while young groups are very exciting, there is a great deal of the hurry and flurry and long hours. Thank goodness they are young and have the energy to do it, they're ambitious. The older one is much more peaceful. In many ways he seems to get the job done a little more efficiently, with a little less fuss and muss, and at a much lower budget. It's well worth considering in my experience, in design engineering, and R&D, and pure research. There is a balance needed.

Question: I have a question about where the various companies like to pick up people, what academic level do you prefer to hire, or what breakdown you have on hiring?

Robert W. Puffer: Well, we're a relatively large company, and we have a corporate engineering area that has a large number of Ph.D.'s and masters in both engineering and the basic sciences. The manufacturing operations, however, have very few, if any. I only know of two Ph.D.'s in a manufacturing or product line marketing area, that is an area that's its own profit center. In our corporate engineering, I'd say a fourth of the professional staff have Ph.D.'s and another fourth are at the master's level, and the rest are bachelors. And I think it's a typical situation.

Arthur W. Heineck, Jr.: We have about 380 in our company, and I'd say—I know there are no doctors—we probably have about 6 masters, but we didn't hire them because they were masters, we hired them because of the skill they brought to the company. All of our salesmen are degree people. We have about 45 salesmen. Most of them are E.E.'s or some other engineering degree like that because we're in an area where we want to communicate. People have to know the product and know it very well. Actually in our engineering staff is probably where we have the fewest degree people.

Question: Do these people mean that they don't like

Ph.D.'s, or they don't like the salary they have to pay?
I wonder if you would clarify that point.

Arthur W. Heineck, Jr.: In our business there's no need
for a Ph.D. It's that simple. If the guy is a good guy
and he knows how to design a disc or a tape drive, if he
has no degree, it doesn't make any difference.

Question: You wouldn't care?

Arthur W. Heineck, Jr.: We wouldn't care. Right. If he
happened to have a Ph.D. and also could design a very good
disc drive, we'd take him. It's the skill that we look
for, the particular art or craft that the person brings
with him.

Chapter 6

CAREER OPPORTUNITIES IN THE MEDICAL FIELDS

The interest in possible employment of scientists and engineers in the health care fields was so great that two different workshops turned to discussing the opportunities in these areas. Two speakers focused attention on medical instrumentation. The first, Mr. Phillips R. Brooks, Jr., manager of Digital Instruments Research of the American Optical Corporation, and the second, Mr. Robert G. Foster, technical director of the Technical Products Group of the Corning Glass Works.

<u>Phillips R. Brooks, Jr.</u>: I have been asked to talk about career opportunities in health care; however, I will limit my remarks to the medical electronic equipment market. The entire health care system or health care industry is as big as the defense industry, taking into account all aspects, and I cannot undertake to discuss this whole area.

The medical electronic business has many opportunities for growth to many of the people here. The medical electronic market, according to one report by the U.S. Public Health Service was approximately $650 million in 1970. Most of that was for diagnostic equipment such as x-ray and nuclear medicine equipment. Therapeutic equipment took about $61 million, and this includes pacemakers, heart and lung machines, clinical laboratory instruments, and patient monitoring equipment. Electronic data processing is a large market in the health industry because hos-

pitals have found that they can use this type of technology from the business world; however, its use is limited
mostly to administration and research. A new field called
hospital information systems is an emerging market.

The medical electronic market is expected to double in
the next 5 or 6 years. New areas that are growing are for
multiphasic testing systems, miniaturized implantable electronic devices such as pacemakers and muscle stimulators
and pain suppressors, automated clinical laboratories, and
hospital information systems. Also, instrumentation will
be used in the area of preventive medicine where it is
generally agreed that, if large populations of healthy people could be screened to find and detect disease in its
early stages rather than waiting for the acutely ill to
enter the medical system, the cost of medical care could
be controlled.

The crisis in health care in this country is because
large segments of the population do not receive adequate
care. Furthermore, the costs have grown so high that most
people cannot afford to pay. Therefore, forces at the
government and popular level are working to change the
health industry, and this I believe will mean that more
medical electronic instrumentation will be required.

Some comments about the medical electronic equipment
market are in order. It is very fragmented, immature, and
no standards exist. Many very small companies specializ-
ing in many items have sprung up, and as a result it has
been called a cottage industry. The volume is not sufficient to take advantage of the manufacturing techniques

that have been developed in other industries. Also this
market fragmentation has been in part due to the history
of how medicine grew up in this country and how it has
been under control of the medical profession.

In the patient monitoring equipment business there are
over fifty companies competing for about $30 million worth
of business that may double in the next 5 years. Obviously, all fifty of these companies are not going to succeed.
At present three or four of these companies have about
half of the market and the other half is shared by the
remaining fifty.

One of the problems in this market is the excessive cost
of selling, marketing, and servicing. Scientific instruments can be purchased from companies like Hewlett-Packard
or Tektronix such as a low-cost oscilloscope for about
$500. This same oscilloscope with perhaps a meter added
to it sells for hospital monitoring applications for about
$1500. The quality and performance of this oscilloscope
may not be as good either. The reason for such a high
markup is because of the service that is behind a piece of
equipment for hospitals. This many people do not appreci-
ate. Hospital equipment is used in an environment by non-
technical people 24 hours a day, 7 days a week, and on
acutely ill patients where there is a high degree of ur-
gency and importance regarding its use. If an instrument
breaks down, it is expected that it will be fixed or re-
placed within the hour or a few hours at most. Therefore,
service organizations have to be organized, maintained,
and operated to satisfy this requirement. Most successful

manufacturers provide this service with their equipment.
Furthermore, since there are so many companies competing
for these dollars in patient monitoring, sales costs tend
to be excessive; however, there will be a shake-out in the
future of some of these marginal companies. This has already started because of the recession and other factors.

Any company however, large or small, has to be prepared
for the long haul to stay in the patient monitoring business profitably unless it has a very new innovative product. Of course, a profit must be made to stay in business,
but it may take several years before a product would become accepted by the medical profession, due to their con-
servatism regardless of how efficacious the product may be.

The role of the federal government in medical instrumentation is becoming larger. Already Medicare and Medi-
caid and other forms of governmental aid have had dramatic
effects on the day-to-day operation of hospitals, the population of the hospitals, their costs, and even physicians'
salaries. National health insurance, which is being talked
about today, will make it so that more people can enter
the health system. This will put even a greater strain
on the present facilities. Furthermore, legislation has
been introduced regarding specifications, performance,
safety standards, regulations of the industry, and this
will have an important effect on business.

A new kind of engineering profession is emerging in both
the hospital and the medical research laboratory, and it
is called the biomedical engineer, or medical engineer,
and it goes by other names. Some schools are even trying

biomedical engineering programs, but it is not clear yet
exactly what these people can do or how they fit into the
present system. Many of them are trained for research;
however, research funds are becoming scarce. Hospitals
are requiring more technological support than they have required in the past. As they use more equipment and the
systems become complicated, an in-house engineering department seems to be called for. Some large hospitals have
these today such as Massachusetts General Hospital. They
are manned by a cross section of engineers where flexibility is their claim—not narrow specialization. Usually it
is a common application of scientific principles, not high
technology, that is required in most hospital situations.

As the market grows, the number of manufacturers grows,
and they go in and out of this business; however, the net
number seems to be increasing. Many small companies with
new ideas try to enter, but they find the road tough because of the slowness of the acceptance of their products.

Testing and service organizations are growing, and this
is an area where entrepreneurs still have opportunities.
Since part of the game in the medical equipment is service,
it is usually the companies with good marketing and servicing capabilities that succeed. Innovation and low cost
are not as important as the total service one can provide
to a medical institution.

There is also a communication gap between the medical
profession and scientists and engineers, and it is a real
problem. However, it can be solved by using common sense
on both sides. I have found that the best way to overcome

it is to start with an attitude of flexibility, keep an
open mind, and try to understand how medicine is practiced,
what the problems are since most of them are not always
technical ones. There are many engineers today who have
been soured in medical engineering because they started
with an attitude that they had all the solutions because
of their training and background and just needed a chance
to apply these solutions to what looked like a simple
problem to them. Health care is primarily a service business, and the problems cover the whole gamut of human relations.

The medical instrumentation field is not a booming market, but certainly there is a continuity of demand. People are continually getting sick. Even though the recession has had its effect, the medical equipment market has
not been affected as severely as many of the other industries.

Many of the problems of the medical field such as coro-
nary heart disease, mental disease, and cancer are primarily medical and social where technology cannot help very
much. This is one of the real problems engineers have to
face. The state of the art of their technology has exceeded in some cases the state of the art of medicine;
however, if one keeps an open mind, is willing to work and
participate, he will find many opportunities.

Robert G. Foster: I should like to walk you through the
problems that we in Corning Glass have faced and what we
are doing about them, and I see that the same kind of

problems that I think you are feeling the symptoms of. I
will give you only one example of what we have done. We
have found that in our standard line we can grow only 5
percent a year. So how are we going to maintain this profit growth? We spend a great deal of money in trying to
identify those future things that are really going to grow,
and the areas that we have identified are in the services
type of field. There used to be a slogan at Corning—"If
it's made of glass, we're interested," and that slogan
changed to—"If there's glass in it, we're interested."
The slogan now is, "If there's money in it, we're interested." It is money that keeps you and me in jobs and
keeps us really challenged when we can see that we are
making a contribution and we are really bringing home something that is worthwhile. Now, the area we see ourselves
moving into is the health and biological materials field.
We have standing manpower requests for talents that have
strong technology and even smatterings of understanding of
physiology, blood chemistry, and related fields in health.
I am a mechanical engineer who went through M.I.T. some
years ago, and only in the past year have I tried to redirect my corporate and career objectives. I have elected
to go into the health areas. It is not too difficult,
and here is a budding industry that needs the kind of talents that we can bring to it if we just have a little bit
of understanding of how to talk to the receiver, who is
the doctor or the practitioner. We have been acquiring
corporations and companies that are in this field, and the
reason we are getting them is that the growth is so fan-

tastic that they run out of money. We are experienced in
running companies that have an exponential growth. But it
takes cash flow, and high finance, and a real source of
dollars to support that growth, and these companies just
cannot muster the resources they need. So in our case, we
are trying to put together for our technical people programs very much like what the United States government
does for the same area. Very specific core programs that
give you the meat of it. I am not interested in how we
name a chemical, I am interested in what happens when a
red blood cell breaks. But the instrumentation, the material, the logical approach to problem solving, we have,
and we propose to capitalize on it.

*Discussion was initiated by Mr. Charles M. Apt, a senior
staff member of Arthur D. Little, Inc., who acted as chairman of the workshop to which Mr. Foster addressed his remarks.*

Charles M. Apt: I was interested to hear about Corning's
concern with medical instrumentation and would like to
cite something that has got me a little bit puzzled about
that. Our health care group at Arthur D. Little asked me
to look into the question of what kind of medical instruments will be available that they might recommend to cli-
ents they are working for. Would I get some background
information on medical instrumentation for them? Well,
since they did not have any time for me to put in on this,
I decided that the easiest thing to do was to subscribe to

Medical Engineering News, which includes a big card with
each issue and it comes out every 2 months. So I circled
all the items that might be useful in medical instrumentation, and that was the sorriest day of my life. I have
now got to the point where I have three cabinets full of
catalogues that I have not even sorted out yet. I do not
know what I am doing for the medical instrumentation business, but the office supply business is doing very well.
Then the follow-up calls with the giveaways. I find that
the calls are: "We're not selling this instrument." "Why
did I write?" "What did I have in mind?" "Is there a
likelihood that I'll have some funds to be able to buy
this instrumentation?" Then we get into a little conversation; and the representative wants to know where will
the money come from to support the level of instrumentation that most people feel is needed in hospitals and clinics, not the teaching hospitals, they are probably saturated, but city hospitals, general hospitals, and
particularly for the doctor's office, let alone the commercial blood-analyzing laboratories and testing laboratories. At the moment my vision of it is, with all the
prefacing remarks about where I am getting it from, that
it is surprising to me that Corning should be interested
in getting into that field.

Robert G. Foster: Money. If you had to look back at what
put us in it, it was the specific glass technology that
enabled us to develop electrodes that would sense potas-
sium, sodium, chlorine, things like that, but that's a

very competitive field, and that was the opportunity to
expose us to the major kind of thing that is just about to
happen. We're just on the brink, I think of something major in this. I think I can summarize it by saying it's
going back to President Nixon's message—it is every citizen's right to be helped. That is far reaching, and when
you see the kind of technologies you see put into space,
put into medicine, and just have only a tiny insight into
it, it's just fantastic, and I can be as specific as you
all wish.

Charles M. Apt: No, I see your point now. There is going
to be one or another kind of health scheme; it's going to
be Kennedy's health scheme or the administration's, but
there is going to be one. In any case, what you're count-
ing on is that this will upgrade medical facilities, to
handle more people, which it probably will have to do as
Medicare had to make room for other people over sixty-five,
and that this will bring with it new and sophisticated
types of instrumentation to handle this broad population.
Can you project what the rate of growth is, I don't mean
in terms of absolute numbers—no one will do that—but is
it a 5-year, 10-year or 20-year thing? Is it something
like we met with in terms of even Medicare—the long-term
that was involved? Are we talking 20 years for this kind
of growth?

Robert G. Foster: Let me answer that by saying that we
have acquired three or four companies in this field—very

small—and they're in the $1-million type of business and
their growth has been, I would say, between the factor 5
and 10 per year. That's phenomenal.

When you want to do something, when you want to double
something, think how hard it is to do. Imagine the complexity of trying to go up an order of magnitude. These
are the numbers we are seeing, and it's not just in the
instrumentation, it's in the operating room, the handling
of the tools, the whole thing, diagnostic, therapeutic.

Question: I have a question along the lines of medical instrumentation. I was at a show at the Boston Auditorium
recently, and it seemed to me that I could already see
signs that the field is being invaded from overseas, particularly from Germany, France, and Japan. Would you care
to comment on this? They seem to be somewhat ahead of us
in styling design, sophistications, and backup software
for their medical instruments compared to our country.

Robert G. Foster: I think it is a very small fraction, the
impact. Yes, there are a number of them abroad. Those
abroad are being pretty much coupled to those in this
country. You are finding joint ventures—we have a number
with international firms—and I think the whole reason is
not for technology but to get into the markets, an opportunity to get in there where the problems are.

Question: Can you be a little more specific about what
kinds of skills would be required in this field? How they

relate to the products that you envision becoming volume
items?

Robert G. Foster: Yes. Let's talk about one or two specific examples that probably cut across the board in applications. The first one that we'll talk about is the field
of enzymology; in our own body system we probably have
about 50,000 enzymes that move about, that catalyze reactions that normally don't take place. They can catalyze
reactions millions and millions of times faster than a
reaction would normally take place. Urease is an enzyme
that converts the urea in your body to hydrogen and water,
to ammonia and water, and you can get it out. If someone
told you today, being an engineer, that I've found a cata-
lyst that catalyzes a reaction a billion times faster than
normal, your mind would go wild with the things you could
do with it. I guess the first enzyme was purified in 1936
or 1938, and right now they've identified and isolated and
purified maybe 200 or 300 of the 50,000. But let's give
you one example to what we are doing with those kinds of
enzymes and how this relates to that field.

In the health field, we have worked for the past 2 years
with the enzyme asparaginase, and it has turned out that
in leukemic cancer one of the things that has to be present in your body for that to propagate and grow is the
protein asparagine; without that it can't live. The particular variety that we are speaking of there is an enzyme
specific to asparagine—asparaginase, and the purpose of
that enzyme is to catalyze and break the asparagine apart

and do away with it. Our immediate reaction was, let's
take these people and give them an injection of asparaginase. But the body is too clever. It looks at that injection of asparaginase going in and says this is a for-
eigner to this body and the body system develops an
antibody that gets rid of asparaginase just as fast as you
put it in. That's the problem of artificial organ rejec-
tion and things like that. So, if you can take and couple
that asparaginase some way so that it cannot get attacked
by the body system, you can have some remarkable results,
and the results that we are seeing today on the lower mam-
mals that we have worked with is total remission—that is
a significant statement. We look forward greatly to the
chance to take the next step, but in this country it becomes very difficult, the Federal Drug Administration will
not allow that to happen.

Let me bring up one other point. You are talking to
medical people who have absolutely no technology at all.
You can be an absolute genius in there with those men,
and that's what they need, but you must be able to communicate with them, they say everything in Latin, and it
scares you to death. It was only the other day that I
found I had myocardium infarction—it meant that part of
my tissue has died because it has too much acid in it.
That meant a lot more to me than this fancy Latin word
that came out. We need to know enough so that we can communicate with them, and they can tell us their problems
and then we can come up with solutions.

Question: Mr. Brooks, in medical instrumentation what percentage of the medical instrumentation market is supported
by governmental grants?

Phillips R. Brooks, Jr.: I don't think that government
grants contribute directly to the medical instrumentation
market, at least in the hospitals that are buying patient
monitoring equipment for intensive care facilities. Surprisingly, hospitals are able to raise money from private
sources including private donors and foundations. If you
ever go into a hospital, you will see many plaques that
this room is given by so-and-so.

Question: This is for the real estate, but is it for the
equipment?

Phillips R. Brooks, Jr.: Yes. They also supply money to
buy equipment. I do not exactly know the breakdown as far
as government grants versus nongovernment support in hospitals. Many grants or government contracts are primarily
for research, and the large market today is for the clinical application of monitoring equipment. However, the
Defense Department through the Veteran's Administration
has a very large health system. This is a system that is
under their control, and they also have a strong influence
on the medical equipment by the standards and specifications they have set. Other hospitals are watching this
development and are following the practices of the VA.
The biomedical market is not an aerospace kind of market

in which you buy on a government basis. There is a lot of
federal money that helps keep the medical industry going
through NIH, through research grants for experimental use
as well as investigating health maintenance systems, but
it is not like the Defense Department. The percentage of
the total health care dollars that come from the federal
government I do not know, but there are economists who are
trying to break this down, including the government.

Question: How about the Veteran's Administration, do you
see any cutback in government funding in the medical electronic area that would make your cautiously optimistic
statement any more cautious or any less optimistic?

Phillips R. Brooks, Jr.: No. The Veteran's Administration
has let a large contract to several companies to design
and build a complete new hospital system using the latest
state-of-the-art technology. They are doing this because
they are finding their medical costs so high and they want
a new hospital system to help control the costs. They are
investing money in this, and will take several years before this hospital will be in operation. Also since the
number of veterans is increasing and because of the political clamor that the Vietnam veterans are not getting the
care that they deserve and need, I do not think the government will cut back but probably will increase expenditures.

Question: The question was raised this morning whether

high technology had any place in solving the social problems of today, the poverty problems, and maybe even health
care problems, education, and what have you. Do you subscribe to that? Do you feel that making things cheaper is
really the key, or do you see areas that haven't been explored yet in which various technologies can help?

Phillips R. Brooks, Jr.: There are many areas where technical knowledge can improve health care, but the cost effectiveness of this technology has to be closely looked at.
The political climate today is not so much to build computerized or high-technology medical systems but it is to
broaden the base of medical care and to extend it to more
people in such a way that they can afford it. This does
not lend itself to high technology, but there are many
small ways where technology can help.

Question: It seems to me that the medical industry in particular, in the first place, is ready for a lot of sales-
manship. From what I understand, the consumer for medical
technology is not prepared, as far as I can see it, to
accept some of the sophistication that technology is prepared to give him right now. So here is where salesman-
ship comes in. It seems to me that since in medical technology we are dealing with a customer who is totally
unsophisticated about what is available to him from a
technological point of view it might be more appropriate
to put that sophistication into the equipment and that
therefore in particular in this area it is necessary to

design equipment where the user doesn't have to put any
sophistication of his own in. I think the example was
pointed out where you can buy an oscilloscope from Hewlett-
Packard or Tektronix for $500, and if you sell it to the
hospital or to a physician you charge him $1500 because
of the service behind it. Well, if you take fifteen of
the thirty-five controls off the front panel so that the
user doesn't get confused by it, then maybe you will be
able to make it for $750, and you have to provide only
$250 worth of service instead of winding up with something
for $1500. It seems to me if you do that you might be
able to make some money. Could I get some comments on
that?

Phillips R. Brooks, Jr.: I think you have oversimplified
the problem somewhat. In order to sell an oscilloscope
to a hospital, it has to be made as simple as possible
with few knobs and controls regardless of the price. One
problem that increases the sales cost of hospital equipment is the fragmentation of the market. In some hospitals
the physician has control, in other places the nurses buy
equipment or the hospital administrator does. Sometimes
it is the hospital engineer or even worse a committee.
This is one of the problems in the medical industry.
There is no centralization or standardization. Each group
of physicians can consider itself an independent entity
that has its own preferences. To have a widely accepted
product, the lowest common denominator is used. The cost
is not always a critical factor. Of course, if you elim-

inate some of the controls and adjustments, you may have
fewer service calls, but if the knob is in the wrong position or if the nurse hasn't been trained how to use it,
this can result in false service calls because she did not
know how to operate it.

Hospitals are beginning to realize, however, that nurses
are poor users of technical equipment, and they are hiring
technicians or using some of the corpsmen from the service
or other paraprofessionals who enjoy this type of work and
leave the nurses to the tender, loving care, which they do
so well. This could help to standardize equipment and
cause fewer service calls.

Question: I got an inference in what you said that the
control of the hospital system may be shifting away from
the physicians. To whom?

Phillips R. Brooks, Jr.: I do not know, and I think many
physicians wish they knew, too, as well as everybody else.
This is a very interesting development. The hospital was
originally set up as a place for the doctor to practice
his business, and it was not a business in itself. Administrative people have looked at a hospital and concluded
that it is a very inefficient operation and the people who
run it do not know the first thing about running a business. They do not realize that a hospital is not a business, but a place for doctors to practice their business.
If you have been in a hospital, you will notice that each
doctor has his own preferences and practices and he can

have a lot of freedom as long as he stays within certain
broad constraints set by the medical profession. However,
because of the shortage of physicians and the demand for
more medical services and the high rising costs, there are
many political and popular factors that are trying to
change and improve this. Again I say get involved and try
to understand the field and take advantages of the opportunities that may be there as the system changes.

Question: Is it conceivable that it would go to a strong
administrative business manager concept and become sort of
a business in itself?

Phillips R. Brooks, Jr.: Yes. There are models and hospital setups operating in various ways to try to overcome
this problem. One is the Kaiser-Permente Medical Center
in California that some of you may be familiar with. It
is a closed system. To join the system you pay a premium
on a periodic basis, and in return the system takes care
of all of your health needs. The entry into the medical
system is not economic but is instead a health screening
system. They have set up a multiphasic testing center
that screens for abnormalities. This model has also been
set up in New York with the Health Insurance Plan. It is
being studied by both the government and the medical profession. Some physicians feel that this is a threat to
their patient-doctor relationship and are against it, but
I think some are taking a more flexible point of view.

*Firsthand experience with the health care delivery indus-
try was represented by Mr. Robert L. Biblo, executive director of the Harvard Community Health Plan.*

<u>Robert L. Biblo</u>: I am glad you pointed out that it is be-
ing referred to as an industry. It really is a nonsystem.
The Kaiser system is really an exception. The Harvard
Community Health Plan is an exception. One or two
thoughts, related to people who might be in this room,
might be of interest. This field is expanding as a result
of demand. There is a critical problem not only related
to the projected shortage of health care personnel but
also of distribution. Medical care is not available to
all people. Even middle-class people find problems getting
certain specialty care and then having to pay for it. And
for people in this room, the hue and cry raised about computerized medical records might be just that. It has not
proved to be an overwhelming success. Because health care
systems that are being developed and projected for the future on a much larger scale, like some form of a National
Health Care scheme, the technician who can come up with a
computerized medical record where the physician can get
back a clear printout with a turnaround time of less than
7 days to avoid having a patient revisit the physician and
not have the last encounter on the record in front of him,
could make a valuable contribution to the field.

    To go one step further, I think the multiphasic screen-
ing that is utilized in certain areas, that is the battery
of tests that a patient goes through, developed by a tech-

nician which can give the physician advance information
relative to the condition of the patient and supposedly
saves time and is more efficient and is medically valuable,
can do much if in fact it saves time for the physician
whose time is limited. This has not proved to be an overwhelming success. Health Improvement Plan in New York
City, which is a prepaid group practice program, is implementing the program and coming up with some very interesting information, one item of which is that the system needs
great development. If medical care is to be distributed
equitably, this could be a valuable tool. Anything else
that can relate to being an aid to the physician or can
help professionals who have to deliver care (and we do not
have enough of them) and anything that can help cut down
the time that he has to put into taking care of a patient,
without demeaning the patient, without having him feel
that he is becoming a robot, and without eliminating the
personal element, becomes extremely valuable. The nonsystem is going to have to become a system that is going
to have to be more equitably distributed. We do not have
the personnel necessary in the industry. The Harvard Community Health Plan is a good example. We can reach only
30,000 people right now, and we do not know what we will
do after we reach that number. For physicians, any valuable tools such as a workable computerized medical record,
a workable method of multiphasic screening, and those
which have not been projected become what the future and
near future will demand. This is a need that will have to
be filled in the medical care field.

Question: What kind of people are you looking for in the health industries?

Phillips R. Brooks, Jr.: Well I would say that we are not just looking for young people only. Our industry is growing in many directions and perhaps a little more stable than some others. We tend to look for people who have had some experience and who could immediately start contributing. The medical equipment market is very competitive, the cost is important but not a primary function. It is primarily selling a service, not a product, and this takes an experienced person. There is a great deal of personal relationship involved in selling to hospitals and physicians, and it takes a mature person to show that his company is reputable and can back up their service and overcome the communications problem that some laymen have.

Question: A question addressed to Mr. Foster. In your efforts to produce medical engineering devices, don't you run a very considerable risk of product liability suits, malpractice suits, and what do you do about them?

Robert G. Foster: That risk is there, and we have elected to go with it. That's a real concern. We built a significant staff in Washington, we have people in Federal Drug Administration, we do the very best, we can't protect the individual and yet still try to make advances, but we don't forget that for a second. That's a risk, and we just accept that and try to cover it.

Question: Well, is the profession of trying to work out
goals and a bill of risks a profession that an engineer
might be able to go into?

Robert G. Foster: Absolutely, a great deal of time is put
into that fail-safe device, just as how much redundancy
is in the Apollo craft.

Question: Perhaps, Mr. Foster could expand on the answer
to my earlier question in this way. In those areas that
you have gone into in this medical research field, are you
hiring and if you are hiring did you take engineering people?

Robert G. Foster: Yes, we're hiring. The types that we're
looking for fall into several categories. Specifically
bachelor's and master's types in electronics, electrical
engineering computer technology, physics, chemistry, and
chemical engineering, with understanding in the health-
related physiological fields, not necessarily degrees.
The chance of finding a man with working ability with the
hardware and the technical concepts and the degree also is
small, you just don't find those. We're after the inter-
preter, we're after the man who can translate technology
into a field.

Let me give you another example. If you ever go into a
hospital, see them count white blood cells; they take a
smear of blood on the slide, and they put it under a microscope and there are a number of people sitting at little

desks with their little counters, and they have eight little buttons and they look under the microscope and they
register the cells, and when that thing dings they've
counted a total of a hundred white blood cells. They look
and they have eight, so there is 8 percent of category one
leukocyte, which they recognize because it's got a long
tail on it. You can't imagine the facilities of a hospital that does that and the amount of time and the delay in
getting a report back. Let's suppose that instead of doing that, we take a tube and we scan it with a little tiny
smear of old blood under high magnification and we project
that onto the screen, and by looking at the different
white cells, and red cells—they have different densities—
and by working out some logarithms on optical density we
can automatically do the count. The medical man isn't
going to dream up that idea, and there's a fabulous opportunity right there in that one area that I've just suggested.

Chapter 7

CAREER OPPORTUNITIES IN OCEAN ENGINEERING
AND ELECTRIC POWER ENGINEERING

*Professor Alfred A. H. Keil, head of the Department of
Naval Architecture and Marine Engineering at M.I.T., discussed the broad aspects of his field as it related to
employment opportunities.*

Alfred A. H. Keil: I have a very difficult task to talk
about a field that is not really very well defined. As I
interpret ocean engineering, it means engineering for the
ocean environment—for the marine environment. Now, what
are the main uses of the marine environment? First, if
we look at in terms of economic importance, it is certainly ocean transportation. The country depends to an ever-
increasing extent on ocean transportation. Not necessarily on ships that are operated by U.S. owners but by ships
moving under foreign flags but which are in some ways
owned by the United States. If you look at the growing
rate of import of raw materials and the growing rate of
the import of fuels, you get two indications of the tremendous importance of this ocean transportation for the
national economy. In this whole area there have been
rather drastic changes in the last 10 years. I think one
of the best and most striking examples is the introduction
of the container ships which have revolutionized the shipment of processed goods across the oceans. And they did
that without any introduction of new technology. It was
a matter of using existing technologies but of putting

them together in a different fashion and looking at sea transportation not as moving something from pier to pier but looking at the total flow of cargo and trying to integrate it and use an integrated approach. So at the heart of this development was the gaining of the proper perspective and then having the courage to move. And it was done without government support.

The tanker development is a very similar one. It is strictly driven by the economics of transportation which favors larger tankers because the cost per ton to move cargo goes down the larger the ship is. Here I just want to mention the oil pollution problem. One way of fighting pollution is to prevent it from occurring. This could well be done on supertankers if there was a regulation that ship designers had to be forced to compartmentalize the ship to a much greater extent so that the loss of oil would be restricted to a small part of the ship. These kinds of rules do not exist. They would require international agreement, so you see, right away, in this whole field of engineering for the ocean environment, you get tangled up with international politics, with international agreements, and so on, and so on, and so on.

These industries are definitely growing, there is no question about it. If you look at the corresponding production in the United States, the shipbuilding industry, it is about a $1 million a year business including the repair business, on the commercial end. The present navy shipbuilding program is on the order of $3 million, and this over the next few years, and it will most certainly

grow. The trend, as I personally interpret it, is for the
Defense Department to put a major emphasis on the rebuilding of the navy because the navy at present suffers from
the fact that most of the ships are World War II ships and
something has to be done about it. This, naturally, has
a considerable impact on the industry, not only on the
shipbuilding industry but also on the related electronics
industry (the cost of the electronics aboard a ship is
probably 80 percent of the total acquisition cost).

In the area of navy application we see a rather substantial change, and I think this is clearly indicated by the
very recent statements of the Chief of Naval Operations.
A number of old ships have been laid up, in order to pre-
serve money to introduce new ships. What he is striving
for is introduction of new ship types by taking innovating
steps, breaking away from the slow evolutionary kind of
change which was the typical trend throughout the whole
development of the transportation industry and the navy.
So here is a chance that exists which should provide quite
a number of opportunities. However, at present there is
not much indication of the funding. I heard that recently
300 proposals for study came into the navy for innovative
approaches. There was a total of $40,000 available to
support the studies...$100 a study if everyone had been
accepted.

I have spoken about the transportation and ship industries. I should like to say a few words about another
facet of ocean engineering, and this is one that relates
to the ocean scientist—oceanography. I think it is im-

portant to realize that oceanography is undergoing a rather
drastic change. Oceanography used to be a basic science-
oriented effort, and it still is, but it is becoming more
and more sophisticated. Consider for instance satellite
oceanography and buoy systems. In addition we should see
a major funding in the area of applied oceanography that
is forecasting of weather, forecasting of hurricanes,
assessment of marine resources, and so on. And if you
think of oceanography in that term, you suddenly are in a
different ball park. You talk now for instance of making
synoptic measurements over a large portion of the ocean.
You talk about reliable data-gathering instruments that
have to last for a period of a year or two, not just last
for a few weeks, a period that is adequate if you are
taking measurements from a ship. You talk about integrated data processing, so you do not gather data just to
verify your theory but in order to make predictions, serve
as a predictive service. The weather prediction system
has been built along that basis. There is no operating
ocean prediction system except the one which the navy
slowly developed over the years and which is operating out
of Monterey, California, and which generated the weather
and wave prediction for the whole Pacific Ocean.

Now the major problem, as I see it, in all these developments in predictive oceanography for applications for
services to our society, is that it is going to be operated out of the National Oceanographic and Atmospheric
Agency, which was formed under the Commerce Department.

It suffers, at the moment, as I see it, from a lack of
direction.

It is quite apparent in my opinion that the large-scale
oceanography, which is a highly sophisticated oceanography,
is going to stay. The type of oceanography we used to
know, operating with ships and so on, is also going to
stay, but I do not think this part is going to grow. One
that is going to use buoys, satellites, and so on, that
is the part which I think will have the major growth during the next decade.

Now a few words about the pollution problem in the context of the ocean environment. What is needed is a rather
thorough understanding of some of the mixing processes of
the ocean, how whatever you put in the ocean is being distributed so that we know where to measure to make sure
that we learn what is really happening to the ocean environment. And this would require, again, this kind of
large-scale oceanography, which I described before.

There are a few sectors of "engineering in the ocean
environment" which have been growing rapidly and are still
growing, those especially related to the oil resources,
the offshore oil industry. I do not think I have to say
much about it because it is a quite well known subject.
It combines what I would call applied oceanography and
applied geology in the exploration process to determine
what resources are available and where they are, plus a
very thorough assessment of what these resources really
mean in terms of their practical usability. But a word of

caution here. We see many predictions on how many resources can be pulled out of the ocean, out of the ocean
bottom. It all sounds very good at first, especially if
you count the number of tons that are there, but then when
you look at the economics of the operation and what the
market is for the material and what the difficulties are
in processing, most of these pictures are suddenly not as
glamorous. I think the chemical industry certainly is
aware of it, and it is cautious. But many who want to
invest in such ocean industry could very well be misled
by some of these promises that are being made.

While the offshore oil industry is a healthy industry,
other industries are limping along, such as the fishing
industry. While the fishing industry on the West Coast
is doing well, the fishing industry on the East Coast is
not, because the federal government after World War II
supported the fisheries in Iceland, and the rebuilding of
Europe. How the East Coast fishing industry can be revi-
talized is a terribly difficult question because you talk
now suddenly about the interface between industry- and
government-supported public policy.

Other sectors of ocean engineering are related to military oceanography sponsored by the navy and the programs
of the U.S. Coast Guard, the U.S. Maritime Administration,
and the Environmental Protection Agency. At present it is
still more difficult to get into the contractual arrangements with the latter three than with the navy if you
have to make any for specific research or specific engineering developments. And it may take a few years before

those government agencies settle down to the point where
they can handle in an experienced way the interaction with
industry, the patent agreement, and so on, and so on. You
see now some of these negotiations going on. A typical
example is the national buoy study that was carried out
some 6 years ago and then slowly went through all the ap-
proval processes until the whole program was switched from
the U.S. Coast Guard to NOAA. Now they are beginning to
want to build the first prototype. One has to be aware
of these kinds of situations in dealing with some of the
agencies because you might well work on the wrong problem.

In general, I think the expenditures in respect to the
industry in toto with respect to ocean environment are
growing. How fast is a big question. Congress has made
many statements, the President has made many statements
about the maritime industry, the ocean industry. We have
not seen too much follow-through on these general promises,
but I am pretty sure that in a number of areas federal
investments have to be made and will be made because in
the end both Congress and the President must recognize
that we are a maritime-related nation.

Another perspective that I should mention is the interface between the separately growing ocean transportation
and the civil engineering aspects of port developments,
and the industrial developments that go with it. If you
look at countries that have to rebuild their industries,
you note that many locate their major industries and industrial complexes close to the shore: one example is the
Rotterdam Development. Rotterdam is not just a port, it

is a big industrial center at the same time. The Japanese
steel industry and the Japanese shipyards are big complexes
at the waterfront, eliminating as much as possible all the
land transportation problems in cargo.

*The audience had a number of questions about the financial
support for the professional engineer in oceanography.*

Question: I have heard it said that oceanography or ocean
science has been oversold in the last few years as a new
discipline, would you care to comment on that, Professor
Keil?

Alfred A. H. Keil: Well, at the heart of the matter is the
congressional decision, which was the Marine Resources and
Engineering Development Act, and I think this goes back
to 1966 or 1967. Prior to that time the largest part of
oceanographic support came from the navy. At the time the
navy funding began to drop and there had to be another
source for oceanographic research, and this, in essence,
has been switched to this national science contribution.
The navy still supports applied oceanographic research,
that means oceanographic research specifically applied
toward meeting its needs, like the prediction of sound
propagation, the prediction of surface waves, and so forth.
The basic oceanography now is with the National Science
Foundation. When the Marine Resources Act was passed, it
was directed at marine resources and engineering development, this is the actual title. It has often been quoted

as the Marine Science Act. A Marine Science Council was
formed, with its real title being the Marine Resources
and Engineering Development Council. The kind of oceanography that it supported out of these resources is the
application-oriented oceanography, oceanography oriented
at the utilization of the ocean and seeing what kind of
engineering developments it could initiate. This distinction between the two kinds of oceanography is often over-
looked. Oceanography for the sake of a basic understanding has to an extent been oversold. There has not been as
much support for it as was originally believed, and the
reason is that I think both the past and the present administration have tried to establish a balance between
more foundational science and specific applications-ori-
ented science in the oceans. If you look at the broad
spectrum, then it has not been oversold. If you are talking about basic oceanography, there was a hope that there
would be much more money here.

Question: Would Professor Keil please comment on what the
future is for the mineral extraction from the ocean other
than oil?

Alfred A. H. Keil: I briefly touched upon it, the fact is
that one finds certain mineral resources on the ocean bottom. Geological exploration is only an initial step toward determining whether this will really be an economically valuable resource. The manganese nodules are typical
examples: the original reaction was a most enthusiastic

one. A considerable drop of interest followed because
processing difficulties were anticipated. Now this interest is again rising substantially. We try to stress, in
our own education programs, that you have to look at finding the resources, assessing the resources, and the potential of economic development of the resources, and then
make the economic trade-offs.

Question: Is this also so in the context of marine agriculture?

Alfred A. H. Keil: Well, the only really active effort in
respect to aquaculture is in the areas of high-priced sea-
food. Oysters, it is really worthwhile doing; the Japanese invented the method (which is now spreading) of growing about one hundred times the amount of oysters per acre
than you do if you just let them grow on the bottom. The
potential for shrimp culture is definitely there; there
have been all kinds of research for the last 4 to 5 years,
and it is now coming to a head. You can now actually
raise shrimps from shrimp eggs. This is quite a difficult
process because shrimps in the natural environment switch
from living in the coastal estuaries and move out into the
ocean and come back, and you have to simulate that during
the artificial growth process. A lot of money could be
made if somebody could raise lobsters, although no one
has succeeded yet. Very little effort has been spent at
using the open ocean for ranching versus the raising of
fish in pools or restricted estuaries. The only broader

comments I heard on that line was to use the North Sea
systematically as a fish ranch by preparing certain micro-
organisms and growing them artificially and to put them
at the right spots when fish at a certain age of development would be there so that they have ample food: this
would be a natural enhancement.   It's like feeding cattle
on the ranch.   This was mentioned only as a potential, but
in order to be useful and applicable in the open ocean you
have to develop international agreements, and they are
awfully hard to get signed and even more difficult to
enforce.

*Attention was centered on the electric power industry with
a talk by Robert O. Bigelow, the assistant chief engineer
of the New England Electric System based in Westboro,
Massachusetts.*

Robert O. Bigelow: In essence, I am going to be talking
about the power industry, but specifically the electric
power industry, which, as I can characterize it, is fundamentally a production and service-minded industry as
against a sales and product-development type of industry.
I think in talking about it you have to say a little bit
about the industry before you can discuss its prospects
because it is unique in many ways from almost any other
type of industry.

In the first place, I should like to dispel the myth,
if I can, that has been around places like M.I.T. and
others for years that somehow back in 1903 Tom Edison

solved all the problems that there were, and the people
who flunked out of M.I.T. and went to the University of
Massachusetts and flunked out there went into the utility
industry and changed fuses and maybe set a pole occasionally because they were strong and good football players
and could dig. It is not true.

I want to pose a problem to those who are in a production type of industry as well as sales. Just suppose your
product required you to estimate precisely what your demand for that product would be, when your customer came to
you and said, "I would like a bucket of kilowatt hours,"
you could deliver it to him at 186,000 miles per second
from no inventory. You had to produce it instantly, and
if in any way you failed to meet his demand by 1 or 2
kilowatt hours, your system collapsed in a heap and you
made the headlines that said, "New York State and New
England have fallen flat on their tails." This is the
industry that allegedly has no challenge left, and I think
I can say that those of us who have been in it really do
not think this is true. It is also an industry that has,
I think, a tremendous satisfaction. I think that it is
absolutely vital to the economy. Where would the computer
business be if it did not have a reliable electric power
supply to run it?

This applies to almost every part of our economy, as
well as to our personal comfort and our present standard
of living. So you are dealing with something that has a
tremendous personal satisfaction and which has tremendous

challenges from both the technical and business point of
view.

Now I mentioned the subject of growth. We have been
growing in this industry here in New England at a pretty
steady 6 or 7 percent as far back as almost anybody can
remember. The growth has been accelerating, if anything,
in recent years, and we are now projecting at about 7 to
8 percent per year. In the last year alone just for construction of new production and distribution transmission
facilities some $700 million was spent just in New England
and something like $12 1/2 billion in the United States.
So it is a big industry that is doing a lot of work. It
is a very unique industry, as I have indicated, and one of
the things that makes it unique is that it has only one
product. If you are interested in product development,
we just have not got anything for you. We have only one
product, and it has been developed. It has a rather simple
figure of merit, and that is reliability. Either it is
there or it is not. And the only other thing you can measure reliability against is cost. How reliable is it, and
how much does it cost to make it more reliable? These are
the figures of merit that you are dealing with, and so you
develop quite a different psychology, if you will, in how
you run your business, how you select your people, and how
you operate. This is often quite misunderstood by people
dealing with the industry, and maybe I can help you a little bit, in talking about our prospects, to put it in this
context.

Because we have such an emphasis on reliability, because
we have a pretty steady growth, and because we have a single product, if you will, this has turned out to be an
extremely low turnover industry. It also has some unique
economics. Now while we have some very hard working sales
and promotion people, I think most of us on the engineering
side tend to forget what the sales group is promoting and
figure we are going to have the same amount of load growth
no matter what they do. As far as I can see, this has been
pretty much the case. We have a fairly fixed income, so
the only way we can make money is to keep our costs down.
On the other hand, we are in a very "political" industry.
The public expects absolute perfection of service. The
politicians do, and they exercise a lot of influence, so
that we have the same kind of pressures that a competitive
industry has but they are of a different nature. They do
affect how we develop and what our prospects are, however.

So it is an industry that has a lot of challenge and a
lot of satisfaction. But it is also an industry where,
to paraphrase the old cigarette ads on television about
Camel filters, "they're not for everybody." And I think
this applies here. I do not want to try to say, "Here's
an industry which everybody should try to get into" because it takes somebody who is satisfied with certain
types of accomplishments and can put up with certain types
of problems. It is a "black hat" industry. You wear a
"black hat" when you go to a cocktail party. You are a
polluter, or you are a guy who causes my lights to go out.
You have to be braced for these things. In our industry

cost is tremendously important, reliability is tremendously important. You are in a spot similar to a hockey ref-
eree—I have done a little bit of this and I know. When
I have done a good job and a game has gone well, I slink
off the ice and take off my striped shirt and nobody no-
tices me. But, if anybody says something to me I am in
trouble. They have noticed me. And this is the way it is
in our business. If you have made the papers, you are in
trouble. So you have got to be able to accept this kind
of a psychology, if you will, but you also get tremendous
satisfaction because you know you are doing a very important and very vital job. This is the framework; let us
turn a little bit now to what the industry needs.

The industry is predominantly technically oriented.
Most of the management as well as the professional people
have come in through the technical route; electrical engineers, mechanical engineers, civil engineers, people in
the operations research area, this kind of thing. All of
these people are being used by a large industry that has
a multitude of problems. In electrical engineering, for
example, there is a continual demand for power system engineering people, people with backgrounds who can deal
with the problems associated with building, developing,
and operating very large complex transmission and distribution networks. And the electromechanical problems that
go with them are very large. Electromechanical energy-con-
version devices, to use a term I think was invented here
at M.I.T., to convert fundamental chemical or other potential energy to an electrical form and get it to the cus-

tomer. The problems of doing this are varied, and there
is room for a whole variety of disciplines in these areas.
The same applies to civil engineering, structures, dams,
large buildings, power plants, and all the things that go
with them.

The whole field of computer applications is something
that the power industry really got into a little late, but
is undertaking tremendous development in. There are a lot
of opportunities in this whole field of applying computers
both to technical and to business problems.

The next question you may ask is, "Where do we get our
people?" And here is where we differ from many of the
other industries. We are not pushing people out the back
door while we are bringing them in the front door. Ours
is a very low turnover industry, as I indicated, and I
would say from my own experience that probably 50 percent
of the professional people that I have been associated
with are one-company people. They came out of school,
they went to work for one company, and they stayed with
it since they got out of school. I would not be surprised
if another 25 or 30 percent were maybe on their second
job since they got out of school. So it is a low-turnover
industry that tends to develop and promote from within.
This is not terribly encouraging as to openings in the industry for people in the age group in this seminar. As
was indicated, for the people coming out of school, there
is no problem. The industry is hiring as much as it ever
did, maybe more. It is replacing vacancies caused by re-
tirements and other attrition, and it is expanding mod-

estly. One industry's loss is another's gain, and with
the slowdown in the electronics industry, this would probably have been the ideal time for us to recruit or even
stockpile some of the top students whom we might not get
otherwise. Although the load is growing, inflationary
forces are pushing costs up, and the economic squeeze prevents the utilities from going all out in hiring available
people. As far as the young graduate is concerned, certainly the industry has as many openings as ever, actually
more, but not wildly more.

Well, then, what about the experienced people? Where
are the openings? There are openings, and there are areas
where the industry definitely needs help, where it can
utilize the talents, if you will, from other industries.
In saying this I should caution you, I think, that I am
not talking really large numbers, and I am not terribly
sure that I am talking either the kind of numbers that can
make any kind of a dent in the statistics. But there are
areas, and these are worth exploring.

The environment has become a big thing all of a sudden
in the utility industry. It was always with us, but all
of a sudden, we are overwhelmed with it. The politicians
have got hold of it, the public has got hold of it, and
it is a really serious problem. We are developing huge
amounts of energy-producing devices, which are obviously
not 100 percent efficient. There is a large amount of
waste energy and it creates problems. These problems need
to be studied, and answers need to be developed. We need
to know which ones are real and which ones are imaginary,

and what to do about the ones that are real and how to
convince people the imaginary ones are imaginary, if they
really are. There is a tremendous field in developing and
consulting services in this area. The utilities are trying
very hard to lick these problems. They do not really want
to wear a "black hat." They would like to take the "black
hat" off. They do not have large numbers of people with
expertise in many of these areas. And this is an area
that I think has a great many opportunities, some within
the utility industry, more in the consulting area.

The utility industry itself needs people who can help
pick the right consultant, can talk his language, can
understand the answers he comes back with. There is a
real need for people who can develop instrumentation in
these areas, who can collect data on the effects of low-
level things that happen in the environment as the result
of power plant operation and evaluate and interpret them.
These people must also be in a position to see the trade-
offs. What are we paying in the way of environmental
price to get this amount of energy? Is it too much to
pay? Is it reasonable? What are the alternatives? Are
they any better? Or are they worse? And beyond that
when you are through, you need answers that can be commu-
nicated to the public so they understand them, which is
one of the big problems. So here is an area where the
utility industry is finding itself in need of a great deal
of help, and where I think opportunities exist.

The nuclear field, there is no question but that we in
New England feel that nuclear production is the way we

ought to go for a large part of our future power generation.   In the Yankee Atomic Electric Company, formed 10 or
12 years ago from all the power companies in New England,
we now have probably the finest nuclear engineering team
in the country.   There is no question but what the two
Yankee plants operating here in New England now are the
two most successful plants in the country.   That is one
organization that was originally set up to build proto-
types and to get New England going; however all the utilities in New England are ultimately going to be developing
their own nuclear capability.   They are going to need help.
They are going to need people in these areas, but these
people are also going to have to learn the utility business and the many unique economic, psychological, and reliability factors that make the utility business go, that
make it unique.   The companies are going to tend to develop from within and bring in from the outside experts where
they need them to help develop these people and build
these additional teams.   One area in particular where the
nuclear industry and the nuclear power plant people are
particularly conscious of and are looking to outside industries for possible help is in reliability and quality
assurance.   The reliability techniques in the military,
for example, have made tremendous strides.   The nuclear
people, particularly, I think are reaching into this area
for help.

We heard quite a bit about the computer earlier as a
tool.   For example, in the development of large power systems and the analysis of how these systems are going to

operate, the digital computer today is our breadboard. We
cannot build large power systems in miniature and play
with them, putting a line here, taking it out, and trying
one there. It just does not work. So we simulate them
on the computer. The simulation of large power networks
and particularly their dynamic performance, as well as
their steady-state performance, and the economic and reliability analysis are all areas where we still have room
to borrow and develop expertise from other fields.

The computer as a control device: We have some very sophisticated control systems now in operation right here in
New England. We have what we call a dispatch computer
system consisting of a main computer-controlled center in
West Springfield and four other dispatch centers scattered
through New England. These currently are controlling and
operating the entire power production of the six-state
region. Furthermore, many of these individual plants, the
relatively new, large, steam-generating units, are also
using computers somewhat for control and a great deal for
monitoring, alarming, and allowing one or two operators to
operate a 650-megawatt unit, for example, where we used to
have eight or ten operators operating a 100-megawatt unit.
This is the kind of thing that is developing and where
there is still room to borrow from the experienced people
in other fields to help out.

Maybe the area with the most potential is that of business application, information systems, operations research.
This is an area where the utilities have lots of room to
learn and where there is reason to think there might be

openings. Operations research has not really "arrived" in
the utilities industry. Only lip service has been paid to
it. Many companies have an operations research officer or
an operations research man of some sort off in a corner by
himself, but he has not really made the big splash yet
that he is going to.

These are the areas where we will look for help, but
through all of this I think I should emphasize that for
the most part the utilities are going to develop their
people from within. They are going to bring in some outside people to help them where they need special expertise.
But they will be individually specialized in most cases
and not sought for in terms of large numbers of experienced people.

I think that in the consulting engineering field and the
manufacturing areas associated with the industry this is
less so, but it varies. It is still somewhat the nature
of the industry.

To summarize then, the point that I want to get over is
that the electric power industry is a challenging and re-
warding industry. It has tremendous importance to the
public, tremendous technical challenge, and there is no
question but what it has relative economic security compared to many other technological industries. It has the
disadvantage that it is difficult to break into. You have
to have something to sell because fundamentally there is
not much turnover, the development is from within, and to
break in you have to offer something that they need. It
is an industry where you are not always the most popular

person around. You have to learn to live with it. It is
an industry where if you do not like big companies you may
miss the opportunity to deal with the most challenging
problems because many of the big challenges we have are
the result of bigness. Much of the really innovative work,
if that is the word I am looking for, is done by the large
company; the relatively smaller ones, which might be a lot
more fun to work with, tend to be followers rather than
leaders.

*A lively discussion ensued, with the audience seeking more
information not only on technical details but particularly
on the characteristics that the power industry was looking
for in its job applicants.*

Question: For Mr. Bigelow. As to the need for peaking
units, gas turbines, and possibly M.H.D. (magnetohydro-
dynamics) in the system, I believe Boston is going to ex-
periment with it.

Robert O. Bigelow: I don't think peaking units as such but
the whole area of developing new means of converting non-
electric energy to electrical energy is an area that
clearly needs research, particularly with the emphasis on
the environment. I think it does open up areas. M.H.D.
is one example where you bypass the turbine and produce
electricity directly from heat through the flow of an
ionized gas. Gas turbines have come in just recently as
a source of peaking power and have undoubtedly created

some openings, particularly for experienced people from
the aircraft industry. But in general, the mechanical engineering and operating departments of these companies
have one expert around to lead them into special features
of these particular problems. Mind you now, I'm talking
something like a gas turbine, which isn't very new or un-
conventional. Bring in some M.H.D. and get a working system operating, then I think you'll definitely create some
jobs within the utility companies with somebody that's got
familiarity in that area, but right now this is strictly
in the research stage and hasn't really arrived with the
utility yet as a workable entity. The present operating
and engineering people seem to be able to handle gas turbines with maybe an occasional expert to come in and clue
them in on the intricacies of these particular devices.

Question: To your knowledge, has anyone actually tried to
apply something like M.H.D. to a power plant realistically?

Robert O. Bigelow: There is a research project now going
on at Avco, sponsored by the New England Utilities and
Edison Electric Institute, particularly Boston Edison,
and I know they have been working on the possible application of a 60-megawatt system. It's in that order of magnitude. Up until now I think the biggest one they could
produce was a 20-megawatt unit, and that was experimental
and could operate only for seconds or minutes, not contin-
uously. But there is a research project that is in the
looking-for-funding stage where the preliminary specifica-

tions for development of this thing have been worked up,
and Avco would like to see the industries support them in
developing this thing and they believe they can develop a
practical unit. These are not government contracts.
These have been primarily supported by the Edison Electric
Institute, which is the electric utility trade organization. The government may also be in on it. I'm not sure
of the details of the funding, but my understanding is
that the major part of the money has been from EEI.

Comment: Mr. Bigelow specifically mentioned that the older
engineer who doesn't want to become a manager seems to be
faced with a problem, and I wonder if you would care to
comment from the point of view of your industry.

Robert O. Bigelow: I think we're in better shape in our
area, for the older engineer in the power industry. In
the first place, there is much less tendency to lay him
off, so there are very few of them wandering around looking. The consulting engineering firms have often been
quite happy to pick up people who've retired in the 65 to
70 age bracket and put them to work for another 5 or 10
years in consulting work, particularly the engineer who
has experience with developing projects, substations, power plants, transmission lines, and has worked with construction projects. It is a type of job that takes a certain type of personality, a fellow who maybe isn't terribly
strong on the mathematics, but is long on the practical
end of the problem. He's had a great deal of experience

dealing with construction and design people. Many of
these people are the type who may go as far as being a
project leader in a power project but not go much further,
who have a lot of technical background and a lot of experience, and these kinds of people I think are being taken
care of. The problem we do have though is the fellow who
comes to us from another industry and who's an older engineer. And this sort of person we really have a problem
with because it's an industry that's built itself around
a low turnover. We tend to promote from within. You
bring in a senior man, you're bringing him over men who
feel they've been earning their way up in an industry
where they're sometimes accused of not having rapid enough
development. You bring someone in above them, and they're
pretty unhappy about it, especially if this person is not
experienced in the area, doesn't have something to bring,
we're not in a position to retrain him. So we can help
some but not all.

Question: Are you in a position to use him as a consultant,
an individual consultant?

Robert O. Bigelow: In special cases, yes. When I say consultants, I'm thinking of the architect-engineering firms,
the Stone & Websters, the Chas. T. Mains, they tend to
pick up these people, quite often, especially if they've
got experience with the utilities which are their customer
type of firm.

Question: Is this low turnover due to your pension policies?

Robert O. Bigelow: Oh, I think there's definitely a tendency for people to lock themselves in. There's no question but what, whether it's intentional or unintentional, it works that way, and I'm not privy to the councils of how these things are developed, but there's no question but that if you've been with an outfit 25 or 30 years, you're locked in. It costs you so damn much money to move no matter what conditions you're in.

Question: But you're often locked out too, aren't you?

Robert O. Bigelow: Not to my knowledge. I've never been told that I can't hire a guy I want because he doesn't fit into the pension policy.

Question: Mr. Bigelow, I had the impression that as a result of your personnel policies, it has produced the effect that the utilities are extremely resistive to innovation of all kinds. Now you mentioned bringing in outside consultants for this purpose, but recalling that you described how large the public utilities are throughout the United States, I should think that it is large enough so that these outside consultants were in fact part of the industry as a whole, that they didn't have to consult in any other line. Isn't that either true or should be true?

Don't you have enough business to keep a lot of consultants busy all the time?

Robert O. Bigelow: The answer to your question is yes, and
at the moment there's a shortage of them. What I was trying to say is that here's an area where there is opportunity. I think there are firms developing in this area
because the need is growing faster than there are people
who are qualified.

*Professor Gerald L. Wilson, the director of the Electric
Power Systems Engineering Laboratory at M.I.T., had a more
optimistic view of career opportunities in the electric
power industry.*

Gerald L. Wilson: I'm on the faculty here and I've been
involved with a group at M.I.T. that started about 5 years
ago called the Electric Power Systems Engineering Laboratory and I'd like to describe my view of the situation,
which is somewhat different from Mr. Bigelow's. We've
been doing research at M.I.T. on a level that's probably
considered by most of you as very small; on a level of
about $145,000 to $150,000 a year. This work has been
supported by General Electric, Westinghouse, American
Electric Power, Edison Electric Institute, and so on.
From our own point of view, the opportunities and technological growth in the utility industry are going to get
great very fast, for if they don't get great very fast the

utilities are going to lose out to the government and government control. There are pollution problems of great
variety and even more so there are technological problems.
I think the future is going to be both with corporations
like Westinghouse and General Electric and with the utilities. What's happened in the last 10 or 15 years is that
where Westinghouse and General Electric used to provide
analytical services and research kinds of services, the
utilities now find that they have to provide them themselves. A company like American Electric Power has a
large and expanding research budget. Consolidated Edison
is going in for a 1 percent rate increase right now which
is all going to go for research. The ERC Council is
talking about spending $300 million a year in research,
and they're beginning to try to organize the utilities together. There's a lot of question about the politics involved in how this is going to be done. There are problems in developing sources of energy with higher
efficiencies involving design work on all kinds of new
units. There's great possibility for using binary systems,
to build bottoming cycles to reduce the waste heat.
There's a great need for people in gas physics, plasmas,
breakdown, and electrohydrodynamics. There are problems
involved in system modeling and using the computer because
the computer is not quite big enough to handle all the
digital problems.

  So we find that our group has grown from something like
two faculty and two students to four faculty and thirty-
five students. We send out about four or five students a

year. They have on the average about three or four offers.
The biggest problem for the older engineer, and there's
no way around it, is to spend some time to retrain, to
retool, and learn about the power industry. In the last
15 years, especially at M.I.T., it's been completely ignored—both M.I.T.'s fault and the industry's fault. We
had many engineers who left here who had no appreciation
for the utility business. And although there are plenty
in the electronics business, for example, looking at digital computer applications to the power industry, very few
people realize the reliability aspect. If one little con-
troller in a power plant unnecessarily trips a 650-million
watt unit that's making $9000 an hour, it's not going to
be looked on very happily. There is a strong need for reliable and unique control devices. I think if one looks
at the power industry and looks at what is happening there,
he will begin to understand that there is a great need for
people.

Robert O. Bigelow: Jerry Wilson is one of the finest salesmen we've got, and I highly endorse everything he says.
My feeling, and maybe I was trying to be conservative in
my approach here, was not to offer vast amounts of encouragement to the experienced people. I think there is a
tremendous opportunity for the youngsters coming out of
school, and this is where the heavy hiring is being done.
All of these outfits that can take an experienced man and
use his talents will most certainly do so. And there are
tremendous areas where work needs to be done. But whether

we like it or not, and whether it's right or wrong (I'm
not trying to sell this as a policy), the general practice
within the industry is to start with younger people and
develop them within the industry. This work has got to be
done, but I think it's going to be done, for the most
part, by people who are developed within the industry and
are recruited in their fairly formative years rather than
with the older people. This may not be good news, from
this point of view, but I think it's a fact of life.

Gerald L. Wilson: I guess where the difference is maybe
my optimism or maybe my lack of experience, I'm not sure
which, that I feel that it's going to change, and change
fast. There's talk, for example, of ten regional research
areas where utilities will be plowing in $200 to $300 million a year. And if they don't, I'm afraid we're all head-
ing for trouble. And if they do, I think there'll be
plenty of jobs for qualified people.

Robert O. Bigelow: I think this goes back to a speech made
by Mr. Nassikas, the chairman of the Federal Power Commission, where he urged that "utilities put 1 percent of
their gross revenue into research." Several utilities
have grabbed at this and are now appearing before the Federal Power Commission in rate cases requesting allowance
of an additional 1 percent for this research. You may
laugh, but this is the key to it. If the government, or
the various powers that be, really want research, they've
got to be prepared to have it show up somewhere in the

rates because there's only one source of income, and that's
the customer. If you can't build it into the rate structure, it will never get done. It's just politics, pure
and simple. And if that 1 percent is accepted as government policy, everything he says is absolutely right.

Question: I have a question about where the various people
like to pick up people, what academic level do you prefer
to hire, or what breakdown you have on hiring?

Robert O. Bigelow: I think as far as we're concerned, it
is the master's degree man predominantly we're looking at
out of today's engineering education. We hire a great
many fellows with bachelor's degrees, but we find that at
the master's level the electrical engineer, particularly,
gets away from the general electrical science, if you will,
into his specific engineering discipline. Here is where
we get them with at least a grounding in the problems that
deal with the power industry. Doctorates are very few and
far between, at least in the utility area. You see a few
in the consulting and manufacturing companies, and the
research, but they're a very small number out of the total.
We have a significant number of nondegree engineers who,
for my money, in some cases are putting out well beyond
their colleagues with degrees. When someone comes in to
talk to me about a job, unless he's right out of school
and I don't have anything else to work from, I tend to
weigh the academic end of his qualifications down on the
list, maybe 25 percent or so. I'd really rather talk to

him and see what he's done rather than what school he went
to if he's been out of school for more than 3 years, say.
I recently had a young fellow ask me this question. He's
a fellow who just got his master's degree: Should he go on
for a doctorate? And the answer that I gave him was that
as far as I could see if he wanted to push his career,
this was a career in the power industry, the time that he
would spend getting that doctorate would be relatively un-
productive relative to the type of experience he would get
in industry. At the end of whatever number of years it
took him to get that doctorate, if he really wanted to
come into the power industry, he would be behind the man
who had spent the time learning something about the business rather than continuing in the academic field. Now,
when he comes to be hired, he expects to be paid at a level where it gets to be an economic problem. The fact that
he's spent all this time makes him dissatisfied because
after all this work it hasn't moved him ahead that much.
I've got nothing against his having a doctorate, but my
feeling is that he probably will be unhappy with me because he'll find that he's behind people his own age who
have developed experience plus the fact that he wants more
money than he's worth to us at this point. In another
case, the Ph.D. comes in and says, "Look, I'll take anything. I'll take your lowest salary." Then a year later
things turn around. You spend a year training him in your
business, but he just can't wait to get away from you.
He's just marking time with you. You've got to be convinced that he really wants to get into this industry, be-

cause we're an organization that is developing people for
the long pull.

Question: I'd like to have the last comment expanded upon
a little bit. This is a problem that a lot of people are
having. The prospective employers are giving us this argument of overqualification, that there's no question but
that you would work out on the short range, but as soon as
things turn around you're not going to stay with us, and
that I think is a big reason why a lot of you are having
trouble getting jobs, especially people who have Ph.D.'s
or people who have been in high-technology areas and are
now trying to get into low- or middle-technology areas and
are willing to do this, and I think many of them indeed
would be happy doing this. It's not that they're married
to high technology. It's just that that's where they were
needed in the past 5 or 10 years and they're no longer
needed in this area, and now they have to cope with this
barrier that the employer apparently puts up to them saying
that they feel that they're not going to be able to hold
on to this person when things turn around. My question
is, I guess, do you really have any hard evidence, or is
this just a feeling? Are there real hard examples one way
or the other?

Robert O. Bigelow: Absolutely not. I can honestly say
from my own experience, that it's purely a gut feeling.
The problem is that right now we're in a position where
fellows right out of school, or a year out of school,

really bright young fellows, are coming along who want to
come to work at reasonable starting salaries. A man who
has got a Ph.D. in solid state physics comes to a power
company, and my instinct is that fundamentally he's going
to be unhappy with us. We're not a research and development oriented outfit. We're not developing a product.
We're dealing with applications work. This man's got to
go out and work in a power plant with construction people,
learn how things are put together and how they're built,
you've got to deal with union problems, you've got to deal
with all kinds of engineering problems that go with design
and construction as well as with the system problems of
building a model on the computer and developing the differential equations for solving change and stability problems.
It's an entirely different type of business. I'm not des-
perate for people now. I've got more people applying than
I can take, so my instinct is to put my money where I think
my best bet is. It's as simple as that. It's not a conscious desire to exclude anybody, but it's that kind of a
market and the tendency is to take the man you think you've
got the best long-range prospects with. Now, there are
always going to be exceptions. A fellow comes along who
maybe has some experience in this area, or you need somebody who can do a certain thing and he is it, or maybe you
know him personally. There are many ways that the barrier
is broken, but if you're sitting there playing the odds
that's what you've got to do.

Chapter 8

CAREER OPPORTUNITIES IN FINANCE, CONSUMER GOODS,
AND HOUSING

*The availability of employment of engineers in the fields
of finance, the consumer goods industry, and the housing
industry was discussed by Glenn P. Strehle, vice president
of the Colonial Management Associates, Inc.; Ward J. Haas,
vice president of Warner-Lambert, Inc.; and Antony Herrey,
director of the Institute Real Estate Office.*

Glenn P. Strehle: It is my pleasure to talk about the financial industries this morning. I have defined in Table 8.1
the seven major subcategories of the financial industry. In
preparing my talk, I tried to define the reason why I went
into the investment business 9 years ago. During those 9
years I have given a number of M.I.T. people and other
technically oriented people advice on whether they should
go in the investment business, and which firms or specific
areas were of most appeal. Looking back over those 9 years,
I have had a perfect record—nobody ever took my advice.
Maybe you have had the same experience when people have
asked you about career opportunities.

Many of you may consider the financial industries unlikely
areas for M.I.T. people to go into today. I think these industries offer as good an opportunity as in the past. If
you know the various categories of the financial industry,
you will find M.I.T. people at the top of many of the companies in these industries. For example, one of the largest

Table 8.1. The Seven Major Categories of the Financial Industry

Profession	Marketing	Financial Analysis	Administration	Legal
Commercial Banking	+		+	
Finance Companies		+	+	
Insurance	+	+	+	+
Investment Advisory	+	+		
Investment Banking	+			+
Stock Brokerage	+		+	
Trust Department		+	+	+

+ Areas of primary activity

finance companies and one of the largest investment advisory firms name M.I.T. graduates at the top. For several years, the largest brokerage firm in the country had an M.I.T. graduate as president. One of the largest banks in the country is run by an M.I.T. graduate.

I think that in looking at these fields there are some things that M.I.T. people have brought to them in the past and will bring to them in the future that provide better than the usual opportunities for success. I think the scientific approach to problem solving has been needed in these industries in the past and is going to be needed to

even a greater extent in the future. An improvement in the
quantitative approach to problem solving has been particularly needed in the investment fields as well as the banking fields. Certainly the problems of the stock brokerage
firms in the last few years has illustrated the need and
the demand for people with scientific training. People
with backgrounds in accounting and computers have long
been sought to take a subordinate role in those firms, but
in the future I think we are going to see an increasing
number of people with this kind of background taking positions of leadership with these firms. A background in
operations or financial analysis may replace marketing as
the experience requirement for top management. I have divided the financial field into seven industries: commercial banking; finance companies, which is a catchall for
the specialized lenders such as finance companies, savings
and loans, mutual savings banks, venture capital, and so
on; the third category is insurance, both fire and casualty
and life insurance; the fourth is investment advisory, that
would include mutual funds, independent investment advisory
firms, managing college endowments, pension funds, and so
on; the next one is investment banking that involves the
underwriting of new issues; stock brokerage, Merrill Lynch,
Bache & Co., and so forth; and the last one is trust departments, bank trust departments are a very large business. In looking at those seven categories, I have left
out accounting, which many M.I.T. graduates have entered.
I am not as familiar with accounting as the other industries mentioned, and in addition, accounting would probably

need a little more specialized background. Any one of these
industries mentioned earlier could probably be entered by
anyone in this room today, and they would find a useful job
with whatever their background happened to be.

Looking at those seven industries again, commercial banking has revenues over $10 billion, with the total revenues
of finance companies, savings and loan, and so forth, about
the same size, and the industry is also quite large. The
stock brokerage business is smaller, but still a multibil-
lion business. These industries employ the great majority
of the people in the seven financial fields. The fourth
one, investment advisory, has estimated gross revenues of
between $1/4 billion and $1/2 billion a year. It is much
smaller than the banking, finance, or insurance. Investment banking would be about the same category of size and
is usually part of a stock brokerage firm. Bank trust departments have annual revenues of about $1/2 billion a year.
My personal experience for the past 9 years has been in the
investment advisory field, but as a security analyst I have
followed most of the other industries. In the case of the
stock brokerage industry, which has only recently been pub-
licly owned, I have had close associations with many of the
people in brokerage firms.

Now I know there are many people who work in the financial
areas who would not want to generalize about those seven industry categories, as I have done in Table 8.1. They would
describe the differences in these companies which, I ac-
knowledge, are substantial. When you take a look at all the
companies in American industry, however, the financial com-

panies have similarities that are different from most other
industry categories. First of all, they are functionally
divided into four general categories: marketing; financial
analysis; administration, which is a catchall for controllership, computer operations and accounting, and the legal
activities, which also covers the regulatory and statutory
reporting functions. Each one of these seven industries
has substantial activities in all four of those areas. In
my own company we are divided into those four areas: marketing, financial analysis, which is labeled "investments,"
administration, and legal.

Let us look at each one of these areas and see what they
cover. These companies are primarily marketing-oriented
companies. That is true of even those such as the finance
companies and the trust departments, which I have not put
a plus sign on as being predominantly marketing oriented.

The marketing I would divide into two categories, the
retail-oriented marketing—this is the sale of insurance
to individuals, the operation of a bank's branch operation,
the sale of mutual funds to the public by investment advisory firms, and trust departments dealing with personal
trusts. You could take each one of the companies in these
industries, and you would find within it a department which
you could label retail sales. In the case of the life insurance industry, it would be called the ordinary life department. Then you would find a second category, which I
would call institutional sales, wholesale sales, or industrial sales. In the case of a life insurance company,
that would be the group life operation, and in the case of

an investment advisory it would be the institutional sales
activity to pension or endowment funds. In the case of a
bank, it would be their national banking operation, in
which their bank officers travel around the country visit-
ing with large corporations.

   In the area of financial analysis, I would subdivide that
into investment research, which is the analysis of market-
able securities such as stocks or bonds. Investment research should eventually lead into what we might call investment management. In commercial banking you do not have
either investment research or investment management, for
these are in the bank's trust department, but you do have
credit analysis. Under the finance companies I have put a
plus sign under financial analysis, and what I am talking
about is credit analysis. In the insurance industry, they
have large investment departments, but the marketing and
administrative functions of the insurance industry are more
important particularly as they might relate to a possible
entry into the industry by M.I.T. graduates. I could go
down each of the seven categories, and you would find substantially investment activities or credit analysis activities in all seven industries.

   The third category is administration. This has been the
fastest growing area in the financial industry during the
past few years. Part of this growth has been caused in the
stock brokerage business by the business failures they have
had in the last several years, and I would trace those
failures in part to the domination by marketing people and
investment banking people who were not professional managers.

That is an oversimplification, but when you see what they
are doing today in the brokerage business, you find that
most of the growth and most of the pay increases are taking
place in what I would call administration. You might call
it bookkeeping, controllership, or accounting, but they
are all doing the same kind of thing; processing the tremendous volume of paperwork that takes place in all seven
industries. Let me just give you one example: In the finance company industry there is a subcategory you might
call factoring, and a factor is a lender who takes all the
risk for accounts receivable that he finances. Because of
this risk, the factor will duplicate and follow every single
account receivable on which he has assumed risk. This is a
very substantial bookkeeping operation. You can find a large
bookkeeping activity going on in my own industry, investment
advisory, where the mutual funds generate a tremendous
amount of paperwork. I categorized this under the trust department area rather than investment advisory area because
so much of it takes place in commercial bank trust departments rather than in the investment advisory firms themselves.

And finally, the fourth category is legal. Some of you
may be surprised that this is included since I am talking
to an M.I.T. group. I think it is important to realize that
all seven of these industries are highly regulated. The
commercial banks, obviously are very highly regulated. The
finance companies are regulated more by the states, and the
savings and loans are regulated by both the states and the
federal government. As you break down each category in those

seven industries, you will find very substantial regulation. Insurance companies, for those of you who may be interested in looking into that field, are regulated far
more by the states than they are by the federal government. And, in fact, the insurance industry is largely regulated by the insurance commissioner of the state of New
York.

Now, let us look at some of the other characteristics of
the companies in the financial industry. Most of these companies are what I would describe as small or smaller companies. There are only a few you could even call medium-size
companies. Very few companies in these seven categories,
for example, have over 10,000 employees. There are in this
country almost 2000 life insurance companies, and there
are well over 10,000 banks. Part of the reason for this
large number of companies in this industry relates to the
regulation that I described under legal. For various reasons banks cannot branch either outside their own state or
in some cases outside their own county. If you are planning
to work in this industry, I suspect the chances are pretty
good that you are going to work for a smaller company, and
it will have the characteristics of a smaller company. One
of these characteristics is the nature of control exercised
by the operating management. Many of the companies in these
industries are controlled by a single person, often the
founder, or they are controlled by a single family, or they
are controlled by one single person or a relatively small
number of persons who either took over the company or developed in it over a number of years. I realize this is true

of some big companies, but I suggest you find out who runs
any company you visit in the financial industry. Quite often, you will find out it is someone who founded the company whether it is a bank, an insurance company, investment banking, or stock brokerage.

I think most of the companies you look at will be managed
by marketing people or marketing-oriented people. Sales are
what makes most of these companies go. They are small companies. Many of them, as was certainly illustrated in the
stock brokerage business in 1969 and 1970, depend on continued high volume of sales, and they cannot afford to have
a slow-up in sales for any length of time.

Almost every one of these companies has this characteristic, a very large number of clerical people and a small
number of professional people divided among the various
specialties. In a typical investment advisory firm, you
will find one or two lawyers, and you will find from ten to
one hundred people in the investment department. You will
find perhaps half that number in the marketing department.
I am talking about the professional people. In addition,
you may have from 100 to 1000 clerks, depending upon the
amount of work you are doing yourself or the amount that
you farmed out to banks, computer service companies, and so
forth. On the professional level these companies traditionally have had low pay except for the marketing people and
top management. Furthermore, they have traditionally had
low starting pay. I would say that in most of these industries you will find much better starting pay situations
than you did 10 years ago, but still somewhat below the

starting pay in the technological industries. The exceptions, not in starting pay but in eventual pay, is that
the marketing people in most of these industries tend to
get a disproportionately large amount of the income. In
an insurance company, you will find a few salesmen, operating as independent agents, earning more than the president of the company. In the stock brokerage business, you
will find the partner who runs a branch office or even the
whole company earning less money than his top half-dozen
stock producers. I think this characteristic is one that
is important for you to look at when you decide you are
not going to go into marketing with these companies.

Another characteristic that is unique of almost every
one of them is their balance sheet. They are highly leveraged from a financial standpoint. Commercial banks have
about $10 to $15 in deposits for $1 of stockholder's net
worth. In the investment banking and stock brokerage areas, you will find very substantial financial leverage. Insurance companies do not borrow money, but they have insurance reserves that they hold for policyholders; and
again, these are many times the stockholder's net worth.
Most of this leverage is appropriate, but I think it is
important to realize what the financial leverage is and
to look at it if you are going to work for a company in
this industry because you want to be able to weigh the
potential risk or failure. Certainly anybody who went into
the stock brokerage business a few years ago would have
been able to spot some of the difficult problems and avoid
the companies with those problems if he had looked at the

balance sheets and checked with the people in the industry
to see who were having problems.

What are the growth expectations for the financial industry? Well, my own feeling is that during the next few
years the growth expectations of these seven industries
are substantially better than the overall economy. Because
there are so many smaller companies in this industry, it
is not difficult to identify a company, oftentimes a large,
well-managed company, with a traditional growth rate of 10
or 15 percent a year or more and with a noncyclical growth
rate and a steady expansion in the number of employees.
What kind of companies would you find? Well, for example,
commercial banking: in many areas of the country you will
find commercial banks that are growing at 10 to 15 percent
a year. In insurance, you can identify quite a few insurance companies with that growth rate. In the investment
advisory field my own firm would expect to grow at about
the rate that I described over the next 5 years. Investment banking and stock brokerage are quite cyclical. Looking at trust departments, you will find a growth rate of
10 to 15 percent a year in most of the large bank trust
departments. As a result, I think that the growth rate we
are going to see in the next few years in these industries
is better than for the overall economy. What about beyond
the next few years, and again, let's go back to that legal
column, and the substantial regulation. Regulation can
change this industry. Just let me give you one example.
The fire and casualty industry had regulation affecting it
because of the continued rise in auto premiums. This regu-

lation is known as "no fault" auto insurance. The fire and
casualty insurance industry, with a better than a 10 percent growth rate in premiums, is obviously attractive until you look at the very substantial losses of the industry and the governmental concern about it.

What about the job environment? I think it is an advantage for anybody going into these industries to have an
M.B.A. or a Sloan-type master's degree. On the other hand,
we are hiring people who have had substantial experience
in industry. We are interested in people with a number of
years of industrial experience, hopefully together with
some financial experience. If this kind of individual is
willing to work hard, and he is reasonably bright, we are
very anxious to talk to him or to her.

That brings me finally to what is the job situation right
now, and let us go down each one of the categories. I have
talked to people over the past week, so I think I have a
reasonable feeling for the job situation with New York and
Boston firms.

Commercial banking job opportunities are fewer now than
they have been for as long as anybody could remember. The
reason is that many banks have expanded their personnel
about 10 percent a year for several years, and their total
labor costs, because of wage increases, have been rising
at 15 or 20 percent a year. Many of the commercial banks
are cutting back; although, as far as I know, all of them
are still talking to job prospects. There are two categories
in commercial banking you might be interested in. First is
the loan officer, the fellow who makes the bank's loans.

And obviously anybody who has some industrial experience
in an area where bank loans are made, which includes virtually all industries, might look into that field.

Second would be the computer operations, which we have
titled under administration. Banks have very substantial
computer operations, and anyone with a background in computers could find any of the large banks willing to talk
to him.

The next category includes the finance companies and
savings and loans. There is not too much activity in this
area, and the starting pay scales are fairly low, but I
think in those categories you could find a few job opportunities.

Insurance industries are hiring on a selective basis.
I talked to the largest insurance company in Boston yesterday, and they told me, I think the way they described
it was, that their personnel needs are better met this
year than they ever had been in the past. I said, "That
means you're not hiring." Well, they allowed they might
hire one or two people this year. I do know of a life insurance company that had openings for about twenty professional people that are in the Boston area.

Next is the investment advisory area. There are at least
fifteen investment advisory firms in Boston, and Boston
probably has more investment advisory firms and more jobs
than any place else in the country, except New York. I
would estimate that there are about twenty-five investment advisory jobs available in Boston investment firms
primarily for people to be security analysts, eventually

working up to being portfolio managers. If they do a good
job, I suppose, they can become president of the firm. One
of the reasons there are jobs available is that last summer some of the firms, fortunately not mine, decided to
clean house for various reasons. You probably know the
stock market was not too good then.

The investment banking field has some openings, primarily
New York. There are very few investment banking jobs in
Boston.

Last are the stock brokerage firms; most of them are
hiring stock brokers. They are hiring in the financial
analysis field in a limited way, and the qualification, as
I mentioned earlier, is a business education, but you could
substitute some financial experience with your own company.
The stock brokerage firms I know are also offering very
good starting salaries in computer operations. This varies
from firm to firm, but there are jobs available. Bank trust
departments are hiring to a limited extent in investments
and of course again in the computer operations.

I hope you will consider the opportunities in the financial fields if you are planning a job change.

Question: We heard yesterday morning that it hurts to have
a doctor's degree. I was wondering whether any of the people on this panel now have any definite feelings on the
subject?

Glenn P. Strehle: Well, I know in the financial field it's
not a detriment. I can think of one of the large invest-

ment advisory firms that recently hired two Ph.D.'s in non-
financial fields to do investment research for them.

Ward J. Haas: I had a hopeful feeling I could come up and
say, "Consumer goods is this, fellows; it's recession-
proof. It never grows up like this, but it doesn't fall
off like that. It's a nice steady line." I was sure that
there were a few blips because when the textile people
guess wrong on that skirt length, they are really dead,
but if you stay out of that kind of end of things, you are
all right. It is not quite so. The figures indicate in the
past couple of years, that the dollar volumes pretty well
stayed up. Things stayed pretty even. On the nondurable
business the sales went up about $1 million on a $30 million from 1968 to 1969 to 1970 but there has been a 6 percent inflation factor, or more. So what you are talking
about is an actual complete evenness or dropoff on unit
volume. And then of course it varies widely from field to
field. So the consumer goods outfits are hiring now, they
are not hurting like the aerospace people. They are not
even hurting like the brokerage operations, but they are
hurting, and the net result is the damnedest body-count
business you ever saw. We have a morning report situation.
And the line manager who wants to go in and add a body has
a real fight on his hands. So it is not all that rosy even
in the places that are doing the best. But there is something in this recession-proof story. It is not in the nondurable area a cyclical industry. Durable consumer goods
I am sure I do not have to tell you anything about. They

fluctuate about as wildly as anything does—automobiles
being the biggest single factor.

So with that kind of an economic background, and I find
nobody keeps any figures on the different types of industries' employment statistics by type of people, professionals versus nonprofessionals, and so on, that are really meaningful. They come out of the Labor Department, but
it has a big long lag in it and has all the uncertainties
of unemployment statistics themselves, and I do not think
it is any help. So what really might be helpful is talk
about what it is like.

I am a prisoner in the Listerine Fortune Cookie Factory.
I am inside, looking out. What does it look like? What
sort of thing is it? You do not know what it is like until
you have been there 3 years and there is absolutely no way
to scenario this until you get a real feeling for it. And
you cannot do it completely rationally. It is something
you have to do yourself, but it has got to be done with a
very high quotient of ESP and clairvoyance because there
is no rational way to do it.

Anyhow, Warner-Lambert is a consumer goods operation. It
is a big one. It is a $1.3 billion company cut into $1/4
billion chunks. I had better tell you I am a technical guy
gone sour. I have a technical background, and I play the
management game in a qualitative sense. The operations research people drive me up a wall because they are always
coming in with a lot of extra details. So this is a very
personal viewpoint of what a broad-scale consumer goods
outfit looks like. It has a dazzling multiplicity of dif-

ferent products. A consumer goods operation may have a
single product like Mr. Bigelow's electrical business.
Coca-Cola people sell Coca-Cola. It is an extremely complex business, but it has one product in it. It cannot be
like Warner-Lambert. I have never counted our product
line, but it is something more than 1000 single items.
There is a dazzling range of distribution and sales methods—the way the goods, which are not necessarily always
a tangible, are delivered to the ultimate consumer.

It ranges from the kind of business you have in text-
books and educational aids of various kinds and ethical
drugs, which if you remember are the two places where the
consumer has no choice in what he buys. When you are a
student you take the text that the teacher says you should
pick up at the Coop, and if you are sick and you go to the
doctor and you buy the drug at the drugstore that he tells
you to buy and you do not have any say in what product you
are actually getting. It ranges from that all the way over
to a point of sale at a checkout counter in a supermarket
on an impulse buy where you have not even heard it advertised but it looks pretty. And a dazzling chain of difference in the amount of fluctuation that goes on with the
product line, from high fashion goods to the skirt business or cosmetics, something that has not really changed
basically from the consumer benefit in more than fifty
years, like chewing gum. We make Chiclets. There is a very
broad range in the amount of R&D resources on the sales
dollar or any other way you want to measure them. Even in
our own company we have divisions or operations where the

percent of sales going into what you and I would call R&D
is less that 1 percent to one or two operations in the
pharmaceutical end where it runs to 13 to 15 percent of
sales.

There is an equally broad range on the innovation of
product cycle. You can change a television advertisement
and it will have a dramatic effect on your business in
about 90 days. If you come up with the right one, for example, the Volkswagen campaign or the Avis campaign, or
the latest one we had was that "Dentyne gives you the
freshest breath in town," and it has just enough erotic
undertone that sales on the West Coast went right through
the roof when they tried it. It is an extremely important
innovation, but it takes only 90 days to bring off from
the start where the man at the copy desk or the brand
manager or what-have-you had this stroke of genius to
where the dollars are rolling in. In the ethical drug business, from the time when somebody comes up with a new compound that looks interesting it may be 10 to 15 years before it is actually going out into medicine somewhere and
being paid for and money coming back into the firm and
hopefully helping people in the process.

There's a tremendous range in public attitude toward
the consumer goods. Generally speaking, consumer goods
people wear gray hats. In fact, at this present time I
think that this is part of that *mal du siècle* that Secor
Browne was talking about because I do not know anybody in
the industry who is wearing a white hat anymore. But it
fluctuates, it is dramatically different, but generally it

is a gray hat. And it is very hard to take. It does affect your attitude. You are a gray-hatted guy and you worry about it.

Now what is the main conclusion out of this? I think it boils down to this kind of difference in sort of a quantitative type of frame of reference for you. The consumer goods industry is different from the aerospace kind of business, the systems-oriented industry, basically in the respect that in general the consumer goods industry makes relatively simple products. They have certainly on the average less than 1000 components. That does not mean that American Optical Corporation is not making a research microscope that is as complicated as anything you ever saw, but in general they have less than 10,000 components. And they sell these simple goods to considerably more than 1 million customers, whereas in the aerospace industry you are making very complicated products. They generally run to more than 1 million components, but your customers run below 100 and in some cases below 10.

That overall phenomenon covering this broad diversity of things I am talking about has an inevitable, immediate, and most important consequence: this business is dominated by sales. Sales is the line operation. It is the decision-making operation. It is the thing that counts. The sales activity in a consumer goods activity, and I do not care whether it is automobiles or chewing gum, is in the same situation that the political process is on the aerospace kind of industries. Jerome Wiesner talked about the inside

story a little on the space race, and if you remember what
he said was that President Kennedy said, "I'm not even sure
that this is good for society. There may be a helluva lot
of better things to do so you geniuses in the back room,
now come up with something that will carry the same political clout and get me more Brownie points with the electorate and make me a hero as the space race and I'll do that
instead for you because I'm a public spirited citizen, I'm
President, I want to do great things for society." And the
geniuses failed him. They did not come up with anything
that had the same political clout.

Now in the consumer goods industry, in our company and
myriads of companies like it, the thing that counts, the
measure of effectiveness is, are you going to make a sale?
Sales dominates. This has a very definite attitudinal effect on the operation and the kinds of things that go on
and where technical people in particular fit in, or if they
have technical backgrounds where do they go and what happens?

The industry has a number of characteristics in operations that come out of the fact that if you do not make
the sale, you are dead. There is not cost plus. There is
no way to go back and do it over. There are no overruns.
Nobody ever heard of this. The name of the game in staying
alive in this business is to meet a real need. Now the
needs may be a very definite and tangible one or it may be
a triviality from the viewpoint of people who have a liberal standard or who worry a little bit about what we ought
to be doing. To meet this need is to get there and be not

necessarily first but mostest. There is a military analog,
"to penetrate, capture, and hold" what, for want of a better term, is a market franchise Warner-Lambert was the
first to break into the feminine hygiene area as a felt
consumer need with the changing times and the new sexual
freedom and all that. Some of you probably read in *Time*
magazine about two years ago the first ad advertising the
innovation that talked about that unmentionable area that
only the French have handled so well in the past, with
apologies to any ladies in the audience. We were first.
We were out there. We had the product. We had the advertising program. We now have something like 10 percent of
the market because we did not have any flankers. We had an
innovation. In this case, not a laboratory innovation but
a sales innovation, a marketing innovation, if you will.
It was good, but we were not there with the follow-through,
and that's the kind of problem that makes heads roll in our
industry. That is the equivalent of the cost overrun, but
nobody comes around and bails out the line manager.

There is another consequence. Our industry is patent oriented, monopoly oriented. If we cannot see a way to go and
hold it, we should not go. One of the biggest weaknesses I
have seen in our R&D shop is that those men do not think
patents. Our Patent Department thinks how can we get patents
from the Patent Office. They are all patent lawyers working
for the Patent Office in our concern. I am exaggerating a
little. But the idea that the patent is something that en-
ables you to hold territory until you can fill in with an
adequate marketing campaign and flanking innovations and

really get a major marketing franchise that nobody can wipe
you off the map with is very foreign to patent people. They
just do not think this way. They do not think of patents as
offensive marketing tools, and yet that is the name of the
game in the consumer goods industry. I am not talking about
antitrust, collaboration, automobile starter nonsense, I am
talking about a good offensive patent that slows your com-
petitor down. And you may lose the patent. It may not hold
together if he ever takes you to court, but it gives you a
breather. It gives you time to get there. And it is something that has to be ingrained in the attitude of success
in the consumer goods industry.

There is something else that happens that is a little
hard to think about because I think on the aerospace side
of things it goes on but it goes on very slowly. Mr. Secor
Browne talked about an example of it in the public transportation business last year, what has happened to the
DC-3? And what happened to the 707's when they brought the
747's out, and what is going to happen when the supersonics
hit? And the name of this in our business and the consumer
goods business is called marginal effect. The chewing gum
people sell a brand some of you may chew, the one I just
talked about with a nice advertising claim, Dentyne. The
claim on this was, you know, it is good for your teeth. We
changed this to saying it has got the freshest breath in
town, and the sales went way up because that man who came
up with the halitotis slogan in the 1920s was a consumer
marketing genius, and we still all worry about what nobody
will tell us. At the same time they have come into this

market with something called "Cert," which you see on the
candy counter. It is a Lifesaver with an extra benefit, it
makes your breath stay fresher longer than just a plain
sugar mint does. And it has done very well. Now we have
that franchise in the market so the competition, and I
think this is good thinking, say, "Let's see if we can't
extend that further—this military flanking operation. We
are going to occupy more territory. We're going to fan out
from where we are." And they develop a stick gum with the
same breath-freshening stuff kind of things in it, and they
introduced this thing. And it caught, because as the Cert
gum stick sales go up, the Dentyne sales go down. And you
say to your people, "What's the matter with you. It was
obvious. There's only so many dirty breaths out there. And
you're dropping shrapnel bombs on your own troops, and you
should have seen this and brought it in on the projected
profit and loss." Well, they did not. I am sorry it is
so much easier to talk about the things that go wrong when
you are trying to dramatize, but I am trying to emphasize
the importance that whether you are in the lab or you are
out in the sales field, you have to think about what the
effect is going to be in this sort of military analogy on
that market target, and marginal effects are extremely important.

Now what do you try to do when you work in this business
to encompass these things, to become comfortable with them,
to do something that will make it work? Of course, you are
dealing with people always. It is a very people kind of
thing no matter how much technology gets into it. And there

is no real way to conceptualize an abstract but I think
there are probably two areas that worry the management,
and if you are going to get ahead in our game you have got
to think in management terms. One of them is that you make
a real attempt to come up with what marketing ought to be.
And if you are a member of our industry, marketing is the
putting together of production and sales so the production
people make what the sales people can sell. They do not
tell the sales people, "Look, you guys ought to sell it
because we make it." And at the same time the sales force
is not arguing with the production people and saying, "Why
the hell don't you make what we can sell?" Both of these
groups find out on what the need is and work together.

Well, that is what it is like inside. Whether you are
working away as a junior chemist trying to come up with a
somewhat more stable antacid so that it can stay on the
shelf longer or working over in Chicle labs and you are
worrying about the fact that the gum gets stale when your
competition at Wrigley's picks it up every week at the
checkout counter and your line management does not want
to throw that extra resource into picking up gum so they
tell you, "Make it last longer." There are the factors
that are at play. What does it mean about people outside
the industry? Do you want to play this game? There is a
certain amount of fun in it. Well, there is certainly no
question that we have a requirement in the consumer goods
kind of business, whether it is health goods, pharmaceuti-
cals, biomedical things, or what have you, for a wide diversity of every kind of skill you can think of. There is

no way to select the consumer goods skill. We use everything a little bit. The thing that will not happen is you
will not find a consumer goods company that says, "We're
going in to just area X and we're going to stick there
forever on a technical base. You'll be in area X. We're
very big in the mouthwash business because we have a market
franchise." Our president comes from a food company, and
his philosophy, and I think it is a very straightforward
one, is, "When I was working for the food company and anything threatened Jello, we clobbered them." And that is the
way you play the game.

   There is no difficulty in consumer goods in coming in at
the bottom. Breaking in the middle is tough. It can be
done. You have to earn your passage. And you earn it the
way the industry plays the game. It is the old private en-
terprise way. You earn it by doing something that is meaningful in sales. And I would say there are probably two
ways you can go. You can start your own business. Some of
you fellows have heard on the radio, I think it's called
Pearl Drops toothpaste. A little business with soft polymer
granules in it, and you brush your teeth with it. Somebody
had this idea. Makes a little in the back room, and he
starts working the local area. It is a plow. And this is
going on all the time. People are going into the consumer
business, and they are ending up as millionaires just as
your friend who started in the twenties with the investment banking business. I do not know what the failure rate
is, but it is something like 999 out of 1000. But there is
enough of it that people are making it this way. And then

we buy them. They do not have to stay there the rest of their life, we buy them. We take the business partially grown. When I say we, I do not mean just Warner-Lambert. There are a dozen, two dozen, three dozen firms that do this. We buy them for the product. Or if they have a patent position and it looks like its something that could go, we will buy them on a royalty basis, or what-have-you.

The other way you can do it is go into the sales end and sell. Move the goods. The men who come up, who have broken in, are the fellows who make the sale. Your management people, the people who have real careers in the consumer goods industry generally are people who were good detail men and, no matter what happened in their business, they knew their customer better than the competition, and they had better sales figures.

So those are the two ways at midcareer. And they are both tough. And they have a high failure rate. I do not know of any other way. Either you have the basic low technology that you own in some way and show that it will sell, or you just come in and go selling.

Now I thought I might end up broadening my horizons a bit. What the consumer goods orientation says to you, if you look at how this works, is that it has a tremendous advantage from the viewpoint of overall society. It has a very close-in, immediate feedback, figure of merit, measure of effectiveness, criterion, or whatever you like, sales in dollars, profits. Very quick. If you are out of whack, you know it. There is no bailing out. No subsidy. Some other plant, some other social organism grows instead. This is a

very effective way of keeping the thing going in the direction that the criteria indicate. And I think what I would
say, from my experience now in the consumer goods field for
a few years, is that what we really need to do to avoid
the kind of crisis we are in at this point is not start a
lot of subsidies, centrally managed programs, the Russian
kind of analogous system. The state plan sort of business,
as far as I know, always leads to major dislocations. What
we need to do is find a way, a mechanism, or a series of
mechanisms, to get market forces—the same kind of thing
that operates in the consumer goods industry to express
social costs. That is maybe the job for the next generation because nobody knows how to do it. If we can get
market forces to express social costs, then we are going
to be able to trim ship and sail. Anything else is bound,
sooner or later, to end up with an even more major disloca-
tion than we are going through now.

Antony Herrey: I do not think I qualify as an expert on
the Housing Industry generally. It is a very difficult industry to be an expert on because it is so broad, and my
vantage point comes from the real estate development field.
I have been in that as an entrepreneur myself and 5 years
ago came to M.I.T. to help the Institute initiate nonprofit
real estate development in the city of Cambridge. Right now
we are developing about 1000 dwelling units off the campus
in Cambridge for a total cost of about $35 million. And I
have had an interesting personal look at our topic today
because of the difficulty of finding capable people to as-

sist us in this development effort. The housing industry
is a huge industry. It is regarded by many as the biggest
industry in the country. And housing is a very large portion of it. Last year there were approximately 1.6 million
dwelling units built, not including mobile homes. Depending on the kind of figures you want to use, that is a $20
to $30 billion industry alone. And that does not include
associated fields such as dormitory housing, hotels and
motels, vacation homes, and various other types or special
sectors of the general housing industry, which are quite
similar in many respects. It is a highly fragmented industry. There are many operators who build only a few houses
a year. There are many brokers and insurance agents and
many other types of professional and related services that
are one-man operations with a strong local flavor. At the
same time giant corporations such as ITT Levitt, Boise
Cascade, and Alcoa have entered the industry. More and more
these days we find many of the *Fortune* 500 firms staking
out a position in the housing field because of what they
recognize as a tremendous national demand.

I would like to talk a little bit about the demand because if any of you are seriously considering changing
careers you ought to be doing a fairly dispassionate, ob-
jective analysis of what field you are going to enter. You
obviously want to get into a field that is on the verge of
tremendous expansion rather than one that is level or even
on a downward trend. The most well known recent estimate
that has been made of housing needs was by the so-called
Kaiser Committee. Some experts question the bases and as-

sumptions underlying the Kaiser Committee's statistics, but
it is the best-known and one of the best-researched contemporary estimates of the housing needs in the United
States. They estimated that about 26.7 million units were
needed in the decade starting in 1969. Contrast that with
the production in the previous decade of a little bit over
14 million, not a slack decade in terms of housing production. So from 1959 to 1969 a little over 14 million, from
1969 to 1979, something like 26.7 million, a figure close
to doubling that production. And, again, that does not include vacation houses, hotels, dormitories, nursing homes,
convalescent centers, and the like. Professor Dietz told
me recently that the state of New York needs 6 million
square feet of dormitory space in the next 5 years, just
for the state of New York university system. There is no
question that the demand is enormous; other experts, who
may vary from the 26.7 million estimate, do not vary sig-
nificantly.

The real question is how this demand will give rise to
actual production because, unfortunately, the housing industry is perhaps unique—I think Mr. Strehle would con-
firm that—in its sensitive dependence on the availability
of capital and the cost of borrowing such capital. A small
change in interest rates or in the liquidity of lending institutions has a dramatic immediate impact on the housing
field. That is probably due in the first instance to the
high leverage typical for the housing industry. Most of
the capital used to produce housing is borrowed, causing
the debt service cost to account for a large part of the

total cost of housing. Due to the Vietnam War and the fiscal
manipulations (if I may use that term) of the Johnson administration, there was a sharp drop in construction in
1966, owing to the credit restrictions placed on the economy and the monetary efforts to control inflation. The
impact was felt so severely in the housing industry that
production plummeted that year and has risen only very
gently since (until this year).

I personally believe that the pressure in the country,
particularly in the urban centers, for housing is so great
that from the political standpoint alone, without examining
all the esoteric fiscal and economic problems involved, any
national administration is going to have to undertake far
more substantial efforts to release the funds needed by the
housing industry. The obvious real demand must for political
reasons be turned into effective demand. If I were looking
into a change in career to enter the housing industry, I
would be confident that housing production in this country
will approach the levels called for by the Kaiser Committee
within 2 to 3 years. If you forget about the United States,
you can look at worldwide needs. Almost any part of the
world today is suffering housing shortages to an alarming
degree. More and more we find multinational companies that
are interested in producing housing not only in this country
but abroad. ITT Levitt is perhaps one of the best-known
American companies building abroad. Thus, even if the United
States began to meet its demand, there will continue to be
enormous demand in other parts of the world.

Let us examine for a moment the kind of skills needed in

the housing field, assuming that there is this enormous
pent-up demand, because if you find that your skills are
not transferable it will not help you much even if production does increase with attendant needs for more personnel.

A wide variety of fields are pertinent in one sense or
another to housing. It is not an easily structured or
easily described industry. I have amused myself from time
to time in drawing charts to try to transmit to others a
little bit more effectively than is usually the case the
many fields and professional services that relate to housing. At the center of these charts is the owner or devel-
oper of real estate, and around the center there is a need
for some twenty to thirty boxes representing various industries. I will review these briefly to give you an idea
of the variety. Construction is only one area, but I will
begin with that.

The construction field today is, as everyone has heard,
inefficient and not at the professional level often found
in the fields that probably most of you come from. The
construction industry operates in many cases without truly
professional personnel. To a large degree the people in it
are strong in experience, perhaps, but not in professional
skills. And I am not talking here about Turner Construction Company or Fuller Construction Company, but rather
about the average construction companies that actually
produce most of the housing in the country. The large firms
account for a very small percentage of the housing produced.
Once you get past the major contractors you find a low
level of skill and professional expertise. Most contrac-

tors are poor in scheduling. They are poor in management
information systems. They are poor in organizational techniques. I presume many of you have considerably more sophistication in these areas. As the construction industry
is becoming more aware of the need for higher skills and
sophistication in these areas, I foresee a relatively easy
transfer for the possessors of skills in these specialties
to the construction industry.

There is the whole area of finance, which is absolutely
critical to the production of housing. There are many "institutions" in the financial area which are indispensable
to the housing industry. There are the lending institutions,
both for construction loans and permanent loans. There are
tens of thousands of institutions across the country cater-
ing to the demand for capital in the housing industry:
mortgage banking firms, commercial banks, real estate investments funds of different descriptions, pension funds;
I cannot go into all the details that are actually closer
to what Mr. Strehle talked about, but the different types
of organization for financing housing comprise a tremendous
variety of financial institutions. It should be possible to
find attractive opportunities in some of those firms for
people determined to enter the housing field in the financial area.

Innovation is needed in the financing of housing. Congressional committees are studying and debating important
new approaches to financing. The experts in the field are
constantly studying this problem because of the rigid and

inflexible current techniques of financing housing. New
ideas will have eager listeners.

Many opportunities exist in the legal and in the organizational field. Many problems must be solved in the areas
of land conveyance, in making the ownership of housing
available to lower-income people. We have recently seen
the embarrassment of the Romney administration by its program to give home ownership to low-income groups and at-
tacks in Congress on some of the scandals that undoubtedly
did occur in this field. Romney has evidently decided that
"Section 235" (the program in question) will have to come
to an end. In spite of the failure of that particular program, home ownership will have to be made available to low-
income families for several reasons. To accomplish this,
extensive innovation in the legal and organizational areas
will be necessary, and you do not have to be a lawyer to
be effective in this field. This leads right to the opportunities in government at various levels such as the
U.S. Department of Housing and Urban Development or a
state agency such as the New York State Urban Development
Corporation. The most recent production target of the latter agency was about 43,000 dwelling units throughout the
state of New York. This is a new organization. Other states
are planning to adopt similar agencies. Governor Sargent
has proposed an agency of this kind in Massachusetts. Such
organizations will have to staff up with new people capable of implementing the complex giant programs that are
being demanded.

There are many needs at the local level in the different

government agencies. Besides the old, established agencies
in the cities, there is the Model Cities Program—though
its future may be doubtful—and new types of agencies are
necessary on the local level. The established agencies such
as the housing authorities and the planning boards are
badly in need of better ideas, more efficient methods, more
imagination, and greater ability to get things done in city
after city. The need for capable people at all levels and
in many specialties among these different tired agencies
is enormous. This may not be the kind of job opportunity
that you were seeking, but I think that as time goes on we
are going to find more attractive possibilities among these
types of agency. Otherwise they just will not attract the
people they need.

There are many technical positions in the engineering-
architectural-planning areas essential to housing. We have
seen the tremendous growth in the mobile home industry,
which was based on the trailer housing of earlier years.
The mobile home industry has become a significant factor
in housing nationally, producing close to 1/2 million units
a year. Mobile homes, as well as sectional and modular
housing, are being produced under factory conditions.
There is a need now for people who are strong in production and industrial engineering as opposed to conventional
site-oriented construction. Operation of factories utiliz-
ing assembly-line techniques requires the kind of expertise
found in the manufacturing industry regardless of product,
but there is a severe shortage of such people familiar with
housing. If you look through the newspaper want ads, you

will find interesting evidence. In *The Wall Street Journal*
of last Friday there is a large ad by Kaufman and Broad,
one of the larger national producers, desperately seeking
"qualified candidates for sales, purchasing, manufacturing,
and general management because we have just completed the
first phase, increasing from two to seven manufacturing
facilities of a planned expansion program." I noticed in
the same paper by coincidence that in the dividend news
Kaufman and Broad is planning a three-for-two or two-for-
one stock split because of their tremendous growth and increasing earnings. This is an example of a company that is
extremely successful. The company is about only 10 years
old, and month after month, they are seeking qualified
people. Read the list of fields again: candidates for sales,
purchasing, manufacturing, and general management. I can
imagine that people with good qualifications in another
field, with an effective presentation to Kaufman and Broad,
can be persuasive in this situation where they desperately
need people.

Public relations is another large new field. In housing,
especially in urban areas, with the relentless pressure
from citizen groups for more participation in the decisions as to where housing goes, what it will be like, who
will live in it, and so forth, it is becoming clear that
the traditional developers and contractors are not equipped
to deal with these groups. They find it necessary to hire
people skilled in public relations, who are able to go out
and work with citizen groups and to take the flak, to negotiate with them, and persuade them to accept what is be-

ing proposed. Too many projects after years of planning
have finally had to be dropped because of popular opposition. We at M.I.T. have just emerged successfully from a
major effort of this kind in Cambridge, where M.I.T. faced
citizen opposition in some cases. We have worked extremely
hard for 3 years to win the confidence of citizen groups.
We have been very successful, but if we had not spent 3
years and thousands of man-hours in very carefully preparing the ground we would never have achieved acceptance
by citizen groups of our "Housing Program in Cambridge,"
a program that is actually in their interest. The major
corporations are also realizing the need for this kind of
skill, so even if you do not have a technical background
but have experience or flair for public relations, for
negotiating with ordinary citizen groups, for putting your
best foot forward, for understanding the project requirements and being able to translate them into readily understandable terms, this may be an area that could become a
satisfying career for you.

Let me talk briefly about the means of entry into this
industry. Compared to other fields, the housing industry
can be entered easily. It is not as difficult as the more
rigorous, more formally prepared fields of engineering and
science.

The real estate brokerage business is easy to enter in
most states, including those states that have license requirements. These are quite trivial for anyone with a college education. If you are really seriously interested in
entering the field, it is quite possible to become a broker

in your spare time. You can work on weekends, in the eve-
nings, and you can earn some income for a period of time
while you prepare the way for a full-time occupation as a
broker.

If you have an entrepreneurial bent, you can try the investment side of real estate. It is possible to make small
investments; $10,000 can go quite a long way in local in-
vestment in real estate. It is the best way to become familiar with the mode of operations, with how things are
done, with the kinds of risks and activities that are necessary. You have probably all seen for years the best sel-
ler, *How I Made a Million Dollars in Real Estate in My
Spare Time*. Well, this is not a unique story. Maybe there
are not many who have made a million dollars, but they have
made enough so they could leave their jobs and devote all
their time to their real estate investments. This can be
done without a dramatic switch and prematurely giving up
a prior career by waiting until your investments have developed to the point where you can leave your present means
of support and live off the investments. You can do this
with partners or groups where all participants pool their
capital in order to acquire larger and better properties.
Furthermore, $1 million invested in good real estate might
make it possible for you to live from the income on that
investment. Now $1 million does not require necessarily a
large investment of your own. Some people have invested
$1 million without putting in a single dollar of their own.
There are highly leveraged positions possible. It may be
possible with $50,000 to develop or acquire a $1 million

property, and the income from that might be enough to give
up a previous position.

There are, of course, many, many engineering and archi-
tectural firms working in the housing field. Those of you
with technical skills may be able to transfer from one engineering field to another, although there is a longer
learning process and the difficulty of meeting the requirements for specific credentials in a field such as struc-
tural or mechanical engineering. It is also a field in
which layoffs can occur almost as easily as in the aerospace industry. But nevertheless there are large numbers
of engineers working in the general field of housing, construction, and planning.

In the financial institutions there are many other possibilities in such areas as accounting, actuarial studies,
fiscal analysis. There are some new types of financial institutions that have developed in recent years in an effort to provide more capital for the housing industry.
There are the mortgage funds, the real estate investment
trusts, and other funds interested especially in real estate, which have had to staff up rapidly in order to provide the kinds of services they offer the public. These
are possible openings for people who have a background in
finance, accounting, and similar fields.

Government agencies should be relatively easy to enter
because of the continuous need for qualified personnel.
There is a severe shortage of capable people in the governments of the large and medium-sized cities. In New York
City, for example, Mayor Lindsay has dramatized the tre-

mendous need, and as a result many professional people from
very different backgrounds have joined his administration.
The need is at least as great in many other cities.

As I have mentioned, many major corporations have recently entered the field and are looking for personnel to staff
their new activities. Some of them are simply aiming to
have a foot in the door in case the industry "takes off."
Many of them recognize that it might not "take off," in
which case they will just drop the new operation. Others
are going into it more seriously, so if you are familiar
with the large corporate environment, it may be possible
for you to move into a corporation that has recently entered
the housing field in your own specialty that is not necessarily specifically related to housing such as personnel,
finance, administration, or organization. At least you can
then be on the periphery of housing as it begins in some
corporation. Recently I talked to one of the men in Alcoa.
Alcoa started in the housing field originally in order to
market more aluminum in construction. Then they found it
was such a good investment that they began to invest in it
simply to apply some of their earnings. Now real estate is
a part of the company's normal operations with about $1/2
billion invested. It is part of their profit-making activities, and the emphasis on selling aluminum has simply
stopped.

Nonprofit institutions offer other possibilities. Foundations, church groups, labor unions, and other nonprofit institutions are entering the housing field for programmatic
reasons or because of outside pressures. These institutions

do not have personnel experienced or familiar with housing,
and once again it is relatively easy for someone without
the full professional background to enter here. It is quite
possible that a university or foundation or similar organization may be interested in finding a capable management
person to assist it in the kinds of programs it is anxious
to enter. The funding for such activities is sometimes in-
adequate or unreliable, but there are possibilities in this
area.

If you have a law degree or an M.B.A., you are obviously
much better off even if you do not have experience in the
housing or construction field. One of the Project Managers
in my office is now going to law school at night and will
get his degree in 4 years. Then he can add to his credentials a law degree, which can be very important in the
housing industry. Another member of my office is going to
night school to get an M.B.A. It may be possible for you
to pursue such a course of study at one of your local universities. Even if you cannot present a résumé with deep
experience in housing or construction or real estate, you
could then at least present legal or business administration training. Because of the dearth of people with this
kind of qualification in the field, you would often enjoy
an advantage over someone who may have practical experience
but may not have legal or business training. I can tell you
from my own personal experience in hiring that it does make
a difference if someone has a business or legal education
even at the expense of specific experience in the housing
or construction field.

I would say again, in closing, that the best thing you
can do is to make a dispassionate analysis of the field
and of your own abilities to provide some necessary skill
or expertise. I would look at the high growth areas, such
as California, Florida, Colorado, Arizona, and then I would
look at the most rapidly growing fields in those areas
(those may be industrialized housing, modular housing, or
sectional housing), and then I would look at the most
highly demanded skill, the one that is hardest to find in
those areas (such as the ad I described here by Kaufman
and Broad), and then I would make a very intensive effort
to sell my skills to one of the companies involved in that
kind of activity in that part of the country. The rate of
growth in those regions and in those specific fields is
explosive. These companies need people desperately and
will be more inclined to gamble with a professional lacking
the necessary experience.

   If these opportunities appear attractive to you, I urge
you to try. You live only once. Good luck!

The discussion period ranged from questions for clarification to the value of advanced degrees in the finance and consumer goods industries.

Question: You mentioned Kaufman and Broad. Who are some of
the other larger companies in preconstructed housing, and
do you see their growth perhaps thwarted by union opposition and traditions in the construction industry?

Antony Herrey: This is certainly a controversial subject
right now. However, there are many firms, perhaps a hundred, producing mobile homes around the country in a factory environment with assembly lines, relatively highly
mechanized and automated compared to on-site construction.
These are located mostly in areas where union controls are
weak, that is, in the rural and suburban areas and rarely
in the middle of the large cities where the unions are
powerful. Many of these companies are in the Midwest, the
South, and Southwest. Some major corporations like Boise
Cascade and ITT Levitt and Alcoa are either already
in manufactured housing or planning to be. I don't think
it's going to be possible to withstand the trend in that
direction, and the more responsible union leadership understands this. How big a field it will become is not possible to tell at this time. I wonder if Professor Dietz
would like to say something about this.

*Professor Albert G. H. Dietz is professor of Building En-
gineering in the Department of Architecture at M.I.T.*

Albert G. H. Dietz: I think what Tony Herrey has said is
certainly true, and as matters stand the problem of organized labor in these factories is not particularly important because, as you say, most of them are nonunion.
There is a trend in that direction, however, and some of
the larger operators in this field, those who are going
into Operation Breakthrough, are already negotiating with

the unions to organize the shops but not along the traditional union craft lines. You may have several crafts involved, but some one of those crafts will take the job of
organizing the shop and running the shop as a whole, and
you won't have to negotiate with five or six different
unions within the same shop. That seems to be the trend
right now. The unions involved will still be the craft
unions. The industrial people, of course, would like very
much to get in there, and if the craft unions don't find
some way of making the craft unions set up work along the
lines we're talking about here the industrial people will
try to take over. The Teamsters already are pushing hard
to take over this kind of industry because they are trans-
porting the units. Having control over the shipment of the
units, they'd like to take over the shops too.

Question: What threats do you see in local regulation, local building codes, local wiring codes, and other restrictions for modular housing? I understand that the codes have
been somewhat of a brake on modular housing development.

Antony Herrey: Certain states, such as California, have
passed statewide codes applicable to manufactured housing
specifically; these codes apply to any community in the
state and supersede all local building codes. This means
that the manufacturer needs only to meet the requirements
of the single code, no matter what community is involved.
These codes are so new that it is difficult to tell what
the effect will be, but I think something like fourteen

states have either passed or are very close to passing such
a statewide code just for industrialized housing. At the
same time a long-term effort is under way to pass statewide codes that, while they don't apply specifically to
industrialized housing, create one code that applies to
every municipality throughout the state. This makes it
much easier for the manufacturer of housing at least to
meet the requirements of every community in a given state
with one standard set of plans and specifications. It's
still a very complex problem, and it will take years to
standardize all the different code requirements from one
community to another. The federal government is beginning
to use its influence in this area. In spite of the difficulties, many businesses are already producing manufactured
units, especially outside the urban centers.

Question: What's the nature of the financing structure on
industrialized housing? Is it primarily financed through
manufacturers or their financing agency or is it mostly
through local banks?

Antony Herrey: There's a big difference between mobile
homes and the financing techniques used for them and what
you might call "conventional" housing even when constructed
in a factory. The factory-built units, such as modular
units, are eventually attached to the ground in a permanent
fashion; thus, they can be financed just like any other
housing. Mobile homes, where the units can be easily moved
from one site to another, are still treated as personal

property, such as trailers or autos, where the terms of
financing are more onerous—shorter amortization terms,
much higher interest rates, larger down payments. The dividing line is drawn on the basis of how mobile the unit
is; the more mobile it is, the poorer the financing.

Question: Mr. Herrey, you spoke of the possibility of going into the real estate business, investing in a situation of very high leverage. Could you enlarge on that. Just
how do you get into such a spot, say with $50,000, to swing
$1 million?

Antony Herrey: In last Friday's *The Wall Street Journal* I
put red rings around the want ads that relate to this whole
field. One of the most frequent types of ads you'll find
in here, for example, reads "F.H.A. Subsidized Housing
Projects Wanted. We are willing to purchase outright or
enter into a joint venture or partnership if you have an
F.H.A. project with feasibility or commitment letter. We
will supply capital and our development expertise to the
project." The ad is large, in bold type. Now these are
probably syndicators in New York City, consisting of wealthy
investors who need a depreciation shelter, who are search-
ing for people all around the country who have an F.H.A.
project ready to build but who don't have the capital or
the expertise to get it done though they have been able
to "seed" it. There is a strong demand for these situations. With your local knowledge of your community and with
your local contacts, you may be able to find the land that

is necessary, make sure that it's zoned properly and has
the local approvals, and can get an F.H.A. (Federal Housing
Administration) commitment. If you can accomplish this,
then your situation will be attractive to the people who
placed this ad. A profit-oriented project requires offi-
cially only a 10 percent equity investment; with a little
skill and some luck you might reduce that 10 percent down
to a smaller percentage. If the owner of the land, for example, is willing to contribute the land without payment
in return for an equity interest, you can form a partnership and get it to the point where a well-capitalized entity could be interested in financing it and taking it
over. We can't turn this into a real estate investment
seminar, but there are many opportunities of that kind.
They can be risky, which is the disadvantage, of course.
You have to recognize that when you enter this field you've
got to be able to lose the money that you're going to invest.

Question: Mr. Haas mentioned a statement that I didn't understand but it interested me. Something about market forces
to express social costs. Can you give me a quick, simple
answer to what you mean by that?

Ward J. Haas: No, but I'll try to make it clear. It's just
very difficult to see how you do it. We've just had a tremendous 20-year boom. Everybody has been making more and
more everything until some of the younger generation feel
that they're getting sick to their stomach with this stuff—

more and more, chewing gum, automobiles. Somebody last
night said, "Do you necessarily have to go faster?" We've
had what the economists would call a very definite economic
growth rate of about 3 or 4 percent a year or something of
the sort in real terms of more wealth, goods, and services
produced. This has been done with a number of social factors not paid for. We've run them down in the bank, essentially the pollution and ecology problem. We haven't met
the social cost of the highways. It's the game that I guess
our friends the economists and city planners and so on all
play. The only trouble is that if it's wrong, like the
Vietnam War, it's so badly wrong that everything goes down
at once and the thing collapses. In the consumer goods
business, you don't go as badly wrong for as long. I use a
trivial example of the skirt business. If the maxi skirt
doesn't sell, the garment manufacturers are broke in a
year and then you make shorter skirts again. If we could
get the social cost of the highway, of the automobile, or
of whatever major changes are going express in dollar terms
where market choice could be made by the consumer more
readily, we would be able to keep going forward toward
society's objectives in a much cleaner fashion, with less
play between the gears.

Possibly, the example that would help is to talk about
the university. Universities now get their funding from
Uncle Sam, in large amounts. There's all kinds of federal
grants, Uncle Sam gathers money in out of the income tax
and pumps it back in. The suggestion was made years and
years ago that we do away with federal grants to education

at universities completely and that instead we change the
tax structure so that anybody can give money to any university he wishes or any college, or any educational venture, and when he does he gets the same benefit on his income tax that a man in the 90 percent bracket does. You
remove the mechanism from central planning to free play of
market. And all the schools then go out with big development drives, and those that want to feature football teams
in order to get money, feature football teams, and others
feature other things, and you get back to a pluralistic
market meeting the full social costs of education. That's
probably as clean-cut an example as you can think of. If
there was some way you could rig the social costs into
transportation, into health care, so that you had free
market forces playing, you would get much better response
times and you would probably then waste less effort.

Question: We heard yesterday morning, that it hurts to have
a doctor's degree. I was wondering whether any of the people
on the panel now have any definite feelings on the subject?

Glenn P. Strehle: Well, I know in the financial field it's
not a detriment. I can think of one of the large investment advisory firms that recently hired two Ph.D.'s in non-
financial fields to do investment research for them.

Ward J. Haas: In our kind of business, the consumer business, it depends where. It would be relatively difficult to
grow adequately in the ethical drug discovery and develop-

ment operation without being thoroughly grounded in one of
the necessary disciplines. This would imply the doctorate,
but generally across all of the situation I don't think we
would look at whether a man had the Ph.D. or not. We'd try
to look at what he could bring. I'm talking now of the
technical shop. I have a personal feeling that you don't
go and get a doctorate because you think you're going to
earn it back. You get a doctorate because you're interested in the subject, you want to know something about it,
you're getting a breadth of education. So, if you're interested in the subject matter, and you want to know something about it, and you get a kick out of doing that, fine.
But, don't get a Ph.D. because you'll earn more money than
the man who didn't get the doctorate. That is a red herring.

Chapter 9

CHANGING CAREERS

*Robert K. Weatherall, the assistant dean of the Graduate
School and director of Placement at M.I.T., introduced a
panel discussion by explaining its purpose.*

Robert K. Weatherall: This session gives us all a chance
to look at some of the personal considerations that apply
as people look at their careers in midstream, as they look
at possible career changes they might wish to make, and
the personal side of a developing career and changes in
career pattern. We've put together here somewhat intuitively a panel to lead off the discussion. First of all the
panelists are three of your number, Willard J. Basner,
Class of '69, Bradford Bates, Class of '59, and Brian
O'Brien, Jr., Class of '49. There's a symmetry there,
which I will tell you was purely coincidental. With them
is Professor Edgar H. Schein of the Sloan School, whose
field is organizational psychology and management. He's a
very appropriate person to have joined with us in our
scholarly way and pull our thoughts together.

Edgar H. Schein: Since this was an intuitively put together
panel, we thought we ought to do a little bit of intuitive
planning. We decided that what we really wanted to accomplish here is not to see this so much as an exchange of
facts as a kind of a joint inquiry into what some of the
issues are, particularly the personal issues of career

switching at different stages of the career. We would like
to make this like a group interview where you may join in
as a member of the group as the spirit moves you. We would
encourage you to ask questions, to relate your own experiences, to give examples where a panelist may have brought
something to your mind that you feel could be shared, with
the goal that we go away from here with a somewhat better
understanding of some of the personal issues that are involved in career switching. We decided the best way into
this is to have each panelist tell us just a little bit
about his own career and the kind of issues he sees in
thinking about it.

Brian O'Brien, Jr.: My background has been relatively broad,
although until relatively recently my switching has been
more one of environment than of career. I did my undergraduate work at the University of Rochester, starting out
in chemistry for one year and then switching to optics,
combining that with the chemistry later on. I then came to
M.I.T. for physics, and got immediately out of any of those
and into graphics arts research with the American Newspaper
Publishers Association in photoengraving research, printing
processes, and this sort of thing.

  After that I was with American Optical in the motion picture field. They were venturing into the Todd-AO motion
picture program—again, development of hardware in picture
production equipment and this sort of thing, gradually trying to broaden there into the transition development type
of area of getting products from research into useful prod-

ucts. From there I went to Itek Corporation, when Itek was
only less than a year old and had big ideas in the information handling, specifically the graphic information handling, area. At Itek, again the environment changed numerous times, in fact I went through I think it was fifteen
or sixteen bosses. They were not very durable. I was there
for 12 years, and starting initially for the first 5 in the
graphic information handling field, and they gave that up
to bid in the reprography area, and then in their main
field, reconnaissance photography, and relatively pure
work in photographic image analysis, image evaluation.
Well this went on for 12 years, as I say, which is a long
time to be in any company these days, and the aerospace
crunch hit Itek, and me, and all of a sudden for the first
time in my career I was looking for a job.

    I was in the very fortunate position of not being forced
to jump. We do not have any children, so that we were not
in an extremely tight economic bind, and so I was in the
fortunate position of being able to sit back and relax for
the first time in quite a while and look around. In fact,
my wife sometimes made comments about how she was getting
sick and tired of supporting me by teaching. Actually, I
was looking from February of last year until May. I had
always been interested, even when I went to Itek, in a
product type of commercial business, and Itek, it turned
out, was not the place for that. I was looking for use of
engineering in the management side because, regardless of
what any company's stated philosophy is of how they bring
their technical people and their management types together,

there is still only one president of a corporation. So this
was my aim, and I was very fortunate in finding actually
through a friend of mine, another former Iteker, a relatively small, and completely commercial corporation, the
Kaylard-Victor Corporation, they're in the audiovisual
equipment field, and this is about as much of a wrench and
switch from Itek as you could imagine. This is the area of
the 11-cent transistor, and if you pay more than 6 cents
for a diode, you're in trouble. We use where we can Japanese
components, although the Japanese are having problems with
Japanese labor costing too much, and they're getting their
work done in Korea and Hong Kong.

   I think I'm somewhat atypical as far as the psychological,
the emotional portion of this because, as I say, at that
point in my career, I rather enjoyed the chance to sit back,
take account of stock, relax, and look carefully toward the
future. It also got me shaken out of my lethargy that had
been building up, and interested me more in self-broadening.
It suddenly dawned on me that this sort of thing is extremely useful. Even if you're in a broad industry such as
Itek with a wide variety of things, your perspective gets
often very much narrowed. And so to me it was, I think, a
very fortunate thing personally that this happened. Many
of my friends unfortunately are not in as good shape.

Question: Did you consider, or would you consider a year
back at M.I.T., let's say, to help you to switch?

Brian O'Brien, Jr.: I have considered this sort of thing, be

it here or elsewhere. It would not be in my case an aiming
at technical updating, but broadening, for example, in
financial matters. I would be very interested in going into
general management, marketing techniques, market details,
this sort of thing. If I considered further formal education, I think it would be probably in these lines rather
than now back at M.I.T. Of course, Sloan School didn't exist when I was here. This might well be an area that I
could find very useful. Right at the moment I'm in a very
good spot. I'm getting very good experience in a completely
different area than past experience and it's well worth
sticking with.

Comment: I'd like to address a question to Mr. O'Brien.
Apparently, you've had several jobs so you're not in the
same situation that I am in. I've been with the same company for 26 years and I'm a little hung up on the fact that
I have 4 weeks' vacation and a lot of retirement credit and
yet I'm in this seesaw position. I don't know whether I'm
going to be allowed to stay or not, and I'm at the point
where I think I ought to move out because, if I don't go
under with this wave of unemployment, a few years from now
I may go under, and I'll be that much worse off. Have you
had any problems in that area? I certainly did. This was
some of that lethargy. My good wife had been saying for
quite a while, "Why don't you get to heck out." I'd come
home griping about this, griping about that, but it was
4 weeks' vacation in my case that held me. There was enough
variety in the job, technically it was very interesting

and challenging, so it was much easier to stay until I finally got booted.

Question: If there was an educational system that provided
you with an opportunity a couple weeks or a month after
you were terminated such as the Sloan School on a monthly
starting date, would you have gone for something like that?

Brian O'Brien, Jr.: Yes, I think I would. In fact, I'm sure
I would. In fact, I did something a little bit different.
A very good friend of mine has his own proprietary personnel testing program, and he kindly offered one of his ses-
sions on that, again, for broadening. Yes, I definitely
would have considered this if it had been something I had
known about.

Question: But faced with the probability that you could only
engage in an activity like this, say, starting in September
with a February termination would you then consider it seriously?

Brian O'Brien, Jr.: I'd certainly consider it. Again, depending on the timing, I think it would probably be foolish
to quit looking in the meantime. I'd like to keep the op-
tions open, and again depending on one's immediate economic
situation, but a concentrated broadening formal training
type of thing could be extremely valuable. I wouldn't have
gone into this at Itek. If this had come up while I was

comfortably in a niche there, I might very well not have.
Just plain laziness.

Edgar H. Schein: I might make a couple of comments on this.
I hear two different functions being talked about that are
worth identifying. One would be the kind of training program that would help people shake out of their lethargy,
so to speak. And I do know from having run lots of these
groups that that is one of things that does happen in sensitivity training. When people go to a training group of
this sort that's often one of the major outputs. They discover by talking to other people who are in other companies
and other situations that they had lost perspective on
themselves and where they are trying to get to, and they
come out of the group with a much better sense of "who am
I and where am I trying to go." The other function that
you identify, though, which is an intriguing one to think
about, is a kind of picking up of the pieces, helping
people readjust, helping people deal with the shock, which
is quite a different thing. That would have to be available
after a person has been terminated and would have to be
available on a regular basis since the termination process
has no clear-cut time dimension to it. And each of those
is an interesting thing to bear in mind. I know the former
exists, one can go to programs where one can take stock of
oneself; the latter, I'm not aware that it exists anywhere.

Comment: I think we are pointing now to what I see as the

lesson of these discussions, that the employment picture
is moving away from the employment of the extreme specialist and moving more and more now toward employing the man
who can see himself as someone with a foot in one of several camps, with more than two feet, perhaps. I think that
was emphasized by Mr. Foster from Corning, who spoke about
their need for people with training in technology who could
talk to physicians and understand what the physicians
needed. And I think that Mr. O'Brien's statement now is
the same kind of thing. He was successful because he was
able to see himself as having skills interfacing with several areas. And I think that the lesson from these meetings
is that we should look very carefully at ourselves, not as
specialists, but to try to see if we have skills that can
be carried in to other areas.

Bradford Bates: I have changed jobs several times in my
career, although not recently, and I thought I'd try to
draw attention to something rather different. Any of you
people who have had training in business management at all
have most likely been introduced to a problem that is always around in industry and has some very classic examples.
Industry often has a hard time deciding what business they
are in. Two classic examples that are always brought out
in management training have to do with the railroads and
movies. The railroads thought they were in the railroad
business. The truckers came along and the truckers knew
that they were in the transportation business. Now had the
railroads not finally figured out what business they were

in, they probably would be out of business. Twentieth Century Fox and Metro-Goldwyn-Mayer all thought they were in the movie business. Along comes TV and they're in trouble. They came probably closer to going out of business than the railroads did. When someone finally figured out that they really weren't in the movie business, and now things are better than they ever were in the old movie companies days.

Now, there's an interesting hint of a problem on the horizon right now, I think in that the network TV people are getting threatened by cable TV, and we may see another problem and another reanalysis of what business any of these people are particularly in. I think the point that I want to generate here is that my personal feeling is that many, many engineers don't know what kind of work they're in. They don't understand what they do, or what their real contribution is. Certainly somebody in a very specialized field may be able to put his finger on it very carefully, but in general I suspect that most engineers don't understand just exactly what their contribution is, and what talents they have that they're bringing to bear in doing their own job. I think if people could identify what talents they really are bringing to bear on the work that they do and what aspects of the job that they're doing or that they think they would like to do really brings them the greatest satisfaction, they would be much better off. There is very likely some industry somewhere that would dearly love to have these people with these talents and goals, and they just can't get together. This matching, of course, is always the big problem. If you could properly identify the various aspects of talents or goals and get them on the appropriate scales and forms, then I guess the actual matching would be a trivial process. Computers do that day in and day out. Finding out what things are worth matching is a problem that at least I haven't seen a great deal of information on. Indeed the process that I, personally, am trying to go through right now, just to identify what things we ought to use as a match basis seems unknown. Then, after we can establish that, we'll go hunt around to see what people would like to match up on the other end of the stick.

That's the basis of what I'd like to bring to you. I could go through in a little more detail what my career has been if anyone is interested. I'm right on the norm in that I've been out of school about 12 years and I've had four jobs. And as we heard yesterday, every 3 years is the norm. So, I'm Mr. Average that way. And I'm not sure it would be very interesting. I did switch in and out of commercial and aerospace and things of this sort in a very careful set of steps to broaden my background. So now I'm at the point where I think I've done all the background broadening that I need to do and I've got all the horsepower behind me, and now I really want to find a place to apply it very carefully.

Question: What kinds of steps have helped you to sort out who you really are occupationally? How have you gone about this?

Bradford Bates: I didn't mean to imply that I've done this
yet. I think that the kinds of steps that have got me thinking along this direction at least have to do with comments
by other people. Some people that I have worked with or for
have identified qualities in my work that are a little unusual in terms of looking in the newspaper and trying to
find a job. Many people have commented that they think
I'm very resourceful, very inventive; things like this are
things that you don't find in the newspaper. You can't go
into the newspaper and find an ad that says, "Hey, we're
looking for a resourceful guy." So here are talents that
have been identified by other people, and as I explore myself carefully I think I agree with them. Yes, indeed,
that's the talent I can really bring to bear in the world.
Now that doesn't have to be in electrical engineering. That
happens to be where I graduated. I've never designed an
electrical circuit in my life. I left M.I.T. and went directly into computer logic design, which is allied with
electrical things but has really nothing to do with elec-
trons running around. So I'm not an electrical engineer,
and I don't have much to offer as an electrical engineer
to the world. But I have a great deal to offer to the world
with respect to a breadth of knowledge, having been in
aerospace, and consumer products, right on down to being
inventive, being resourceful, being known for being able
to get a job done. It's surprising how few people in industry can get a job done. We have several people, and they
work forever but they just don't get the job done.

Edgar H. Schein: You know your comments trigger an immediate reaction in me of how our concept of writing a résumé
probably biases this process because the résumé is often
constructed in terms of a stereotype of yourself. It's very
hard to dig out these unique characteristics when people
look at the degree and what you graduated in, and right
away they know all about you because they know what electrical engineers are like, and then you have to overcome
that stereotype if you're lucky enough to get interviewed,
and it raises a question of whether we could also invent
a clearer a better way of presenting ourselves through our
résumé that would give a potential employer a picture of
where we're really at.

Antony Herrey: I think that the point that this gentleman
has made is proof along the lines of what Professor Schein
was just saying when it comes to persuading someone or
some organization that you are the person that it should
employ. Too often the candidate just lists these items that
we're talking about without any real analysis of what the
employer is looking for. In fact, the employer, if he's
any good at all, has got his eye very specifically on his
needs and how Mr. X sitting there can fulfill those needs
most effectively, so that the point of view of the prospective employer is how can this gentleman do for me what I
need. Well, it's very difficult for the candidate to tell
Mr. Employer how he can fulfill the needs of that employer
unless he is absolutely clear about his own strengths and
weaknesses because there can't be a match unless he is. It

seems to me that looking down the road to when you're actually facing Mr. Employer to persuade him that you are
the man he needs, you've got to have analyzed from the beginning what you're saying so that you can then make very
clear to the employer that you are providing exactly what
he needs. I've talked to too many people, whether it's a
secretarial candidate or a project manager candidate, who
tell me a long line of things that are perhaps interesting
but which have no application to what I'm looking for when
I'm trying to find someone to fill a spot. And I think it's
very difficult to get the dispassionate analysis that you're
talking about, yet it is crucial.

Edgar H. Schein: But you're also saying something else—
that it is more important to be truthful than to do a good
sales job because if you sell yourself on an erroneous
basis either because you're kidding yourself or because
you're a good huckster, 6 months later the thing will all
come crashing down. You're better getting turned down initially on the basis of who you really are than to be hired
for what you are not.

Comment: I'd like to comment on this question of specialization versus diversity. I was recently interviewed for one
of the most reputable research organizations in the country,
I won't mention its name, it's not M.I.T., and the people
were out for a specialist in a specific field, but they
wanted a young graduate who had just done his Ph.D. in that
field. Well, I'm not a young graduate who had just done my

Ph.D. in that area, but I had done three years' work in
that specific thing. Well, that was good. But then the
interviewer said, "But you can do this and that besides,"
and when I said "No," he said, "that's very bad."

Edgar H. Schein: Well, I think what you're saying is important, that while it may be on the average true that companies are looking for breadth, it is certainly not true
for all companies. There are clearly in this exploding
technology a lot of companies who are in a very special
business and probably have very special needs, and obviously you came up against an employer who had very special
needs. It seems to me that both points of view are correct,
and in a way they're tied together by breadth. At least
you've got to know where you're at and hope that the company knows where it's at so that kind of a good match can
be made.

Comment: I think this discussion suggests that we should
throw out any résumés that could be classified as résumés
because most of the résumés develop a serial-type identifi-
cation that is superfluous and actually prevents you from
getting your message across that you can solve the type of
problems that the employer wants solved. So what I suggest
is that we start a movement that eliminates the stereotype
résumés and provides a problem-oriented presentation of
what you can do for them, of course, based on your previous analysis of what the employer wants.

Comment: I think before you write the résumé you ought to
think about what it is that you as an engineer do, and in
thinking about that for myself I think I'm identified as
having ability to think and solve problems, and I happen
to have a particular bag of tricks that I got at M.I.T. in
a particular kind of problem that I work on. But if I want
to change fields or go into something that's not exactly
what I've been doing, I think the main thing that we as
engineers have to offer is the ability to solve problems,
come up with a solution, and do something about it. I have
in my own résumé written that down before I've written
down anything else that I do, all the B.A. degrees that I
have, or the experience that I have, so that the people
who are evaluating me know that what I like to do, and
what I do do. I think that that's what people are really
looking for even though they haven't identified it themselves. They want people who can think.

Comment: As a reader of résumés on occasion, this is a good
idea except that it doesn't tell me a great deal because
usually, in my case as a director of engineering, I am
looking for some specific talents. For example, we were
looking at one point for a fellow to work specifically on
design of 16mm motion picture mechanisms. What I do when
I see the résumé, if I see any motion picture or similar
types of things, I underline that, and if there are several
underlines in that one, it's worth considering, and if
there aren't, forget it. I look at that, I look at salary,

age, then education, but I tend to look at the stereotype
things but in these particular cases, the specific engineering contributory talent that I happen to need at the
moment. All engineers think they're creative and can solve
problems, and so on. Some can, and some can't, but they're
all going to say they can. It's a balance, I agree, but
you've got to have specifics, too.

Question: On the sensitivity group, what sort of facilities
are available for doing this, for getting involved in this,
the Sloan School, or something like this? What's available?

Edgar H. Schein: There are some sensitivity training groups
that are given by universities. The only one I'm aware of
in this neck of the woods that does it is B.U. The Sloan
School or M.I.T. does not actually offer that kind of program on any kind of public or alumni basis. But in addition to university-based programs, there are usually programs run around the country by the N.T.L. Institute of
Applied Behavioral Science, you can send for brochures.
This N.T.L. is the organization that kind of invented and
is the oldest purveyor of these. It stands for the National
Training Labs, and they usually have programs all around
the country that individuals can sign up for. Then in the
West there are comparable kinds or organizations that do
that on the West Coast and in the Mountain regions. Any of
you who are interested, the best thing would be simply to
write for general information to the university closest to
you to see if they offer it. If not, get some advice as to

who in that region runs a reputable organization that does
offer it. There is a problem of an awful lot of fly-by-
nighters who simply advertise encounter groups, but you
have no way of knowing whether it's a quality operation or
not. The best thing to do is to write your local university's psychology department and get them to give you the
names of organizations in your region that give reputable
sensitivity training groups.

Question: Do you have anything to say about the professional
commercial groups of this nature that advertise in newspapers and are generally, from what I understand, fairly
expensive deals? A couple of hundred to a thousand dollars.

Edgar H. Schein: I'm not aware of any that are that expensive. It's hard, unfortunately, to generalize about a
category like commercial groups. N.T.L. is in a sense a
commercial group. It tries to sustain itself by the fees
it charges, though it's basically nonprofit. But among
these advertised groups there will be maybe two or three
that are perfectly reputable consulting firms that are providing this kind of service, but there may be three or four
others that are not. So that's why you're kind of stuck with
having to get someone else's advice before you plunk your
money down and go. And certainly don't go to anything that
offers a 1-day or 1-evening kind of encounter group. I
think 3 to 5 days is the absolute minimum for these programs, so anything that offers to give you this kind of experience in less time is probably doing it without responsibility.

Question: What type of person would profit from going to these organizations?

Edgar H. Schein: A person who wants to have an opportunity to spend some time thinking and talking about himself. The time to go to a sensitivity training group is when you're motivated to do so. It's not a good place for people to be sent, but if you know you're at a point in your career where you want to have an opportunity to share your thoughts with others and you want to get a little more self-insight and you feel the need of some sounding boards and some feedback from others, that's the time to think about going.

Question: I'd like to ask you a very standard question that I have found to be almost impossible to answer on my own, but it seems that you might have it better analyzed in view of the moves that you make. To what extent would you define an ultimate long-term goal that might give you the framework for making the decisions as to what move you're going to make? Can you define to a prospective employer your goal in life projectionally?

Bradford Bates: It's a good question. And it is certainly a question that every employer will ask you, even the people that you're employed with now. I would guess that having changed jobs three times and applied for four, the goals are probably changed a little bit each time. When you first get out of school you just want to get charging

and tear up the world, be the president of the company,
and so forth. And I know in my own case the goals have
shifted somewhat just as perhaps as are some of the goals
of this era as opposed to when I was in college. Just being president of a company and making a million dollars
doesn't appeal to me quite so much now as it did when I
first got out of college. Getting my kids grown up and off
on a useful productive life, things of this sort start to
take on a little bit more interest. I lived about half my
life in New England and half on the West Coast, I moved
back and forth two or three times, and there was a period
in my life when I thought that anybody who didn't live in
southern California was nuts. As I got a little older, all
of a sudden I began to realize that perhaps life wasn't
all sunshine and flowers and there was perhaps more to it
than just being warm and having roses around your house,
and maybe New England wasn't so bad after all. So, I'm
back again. Now who knows what will happen 10 years from
now. I may get tired of shoveling snow 10 years from now
and decide that maybe Southern California is the place.

I think these goals shift constantly, and presumably,
for some people the goals keep getting higher, and maybe
for some people they keep dropping some. I have some
people who work for me who are technicians going to night
school trying to get their degrees, and I'm sure that their
goals tend to be increasing as they find they really can
accomplish more. I never had any trouble accomplishing
anything I wanted to do, so that in some sense I guess
some of my goals are tending to drop back as I get a little

more pleasure out of spending a little more time with my
kids, helping them to understand some of the basics in life,
at least some of my values of what's good and bad, and the
goal of being a president doesn't interest me. I don't
want to be the president at all.

Willard J. Basner, Jr.: I'd like to give you a brief idea
of my own personal experiences. I think in comparison to
those of my colleagues here on the panel, mine could be
described as a sort of résumé at this point. I finished
4 years of study here in aerospace, and I worked for Avco
during the summer, and at that time I decided I would like
to go to grad school for a while. So I went out to Michigan
and attended Horace Rackham and finished up my M.S. Then
I came back with high hopes. Well, about a hundred letters
and résumés and three hundred telephone calls later I decided that a change was in order and started beating the
streets. First I tried to get a job as a technician to give
me a little experience, and I couldn't even do that because
they told me I was overqualified. I tried to impress them
with the fact that maybe I could handle the job of three
of their technicians, but it didn't seem to sell. And then
because I've always been afflicted with angling fever, I
tried to get a job as manager of a sporting goods department in a local retail store. That didn't work out too well
either. In short, I didn't have a lot to offer except a
couple of degrees, and then a neighbor came up to me with
a terrific promise of a fine job. He took me out to the
Tewksbury, Mass., and asked me if I'd like to work in their

cow barn. Well, I wasn't quite ready for that. As a last
resort I went down to Boston to the Division of Employment
Security, and the lady down there spoke to me for a while
and she asked me if I had a huge interest in math, and I
said I did. So she suggested that I look into teaching.
This sparked an interest, so I decided to. I went to several schools but was told it was no go without a teaching
certificate. I decided I had to be a little more aggres-
sive. A comely secretary at the front desk told me to go
away. I indicated I wanted to see the man in charge, and
at that time a superintendent of the school happened to be
in the hallway and he was talking to some various people.
I guess they were looking for jobs, too. So I walked right
up to him and tapped him on the shoulder and told him I
wanted an interview. I went in and spoke to him for a while,
and I was fortunate to land a job. They had a meeting of
the school committee that night, and I decided to give it
a go. I must say that I've been a little bit happier than
I would have been in an unemployed state since then. At
this stage I'm not sure whether I want to stay in teaching,
at least now I have a little bit of security. Of course,
I'm trying to decide what I'd like to do eventually.

Question: You're in a high school teaching job?

Willard J. Basner, Jr.: Yes. It's a vocational-technical
high school.

Question: Are you certified?

Willard J. Basner, Jr.: No, I'm not. If I retain this present job, I'll be taking courses this summer toward that
end.

Comment: It's a tragic and horrible waste that someone with
your talents and education wasn't able to find a job in
your field, and I think it's a crying shame that nobody
was there to tell you not to go into aerospace 4 years ago
when you signed up for it.

On a personal basis, it's very tragic, and I think there
is some moral responsibility at M.I.T. to tell people they
are in the wrong field because if they can project and see
what's happening 2 years ahead they ought to speak up and
say something because with a man's career and life ahead
of him, I think that somehow, somewhere, something is miss-
ing, and I wish I could put my finger on it.

Robert K. Weatherall: I'd like to say in regard to that
that we are working now at trying to predict for the M.I.T.
community, the students here, better than they have had in
the past, what the future has in store. Dean Sanborn C.
Brown here and I and Professor Paul W. MacAvoy from the
Sloan School of Management and Paul Penfield have been
getting together to try and work out ways of mapping the
future. I ought to also say how difficult it is, but we're
certainly looking, but at the Placement Office, which I
run, we're trying to offer seminars and meetings where
students can talk and explore more the future. I should
also say that students seem quite responsive to the chang-

ing situation, and I think the registration of students in
the sophomore year and the junior year for aerospace at
M.I.T. for example, has fallen off.

Comment: I'd like to support you in one sense, I was in
Toronto last Friday and picked up the morning paper there
and read about a Canadian survey that was done, I guess
with government funds, of the employment of chemists, and
the figures there were that of the Class of '70 something
like 20 percent had jobs and 80 percent were still looking.
Really frightening figures, considering the fact that many
of these were masters and Ph.D.'s and they were having as
much or more difficulty finding jobs as the bachelor chemists. Now, the thing that struck me about this was that
the Canadian government had put a good deal of money into
getting this kind of information fast so that a feedback
loop could be built that would be useful. I think the resources of the university are not such that we would probably be able to do the kind of large-scale surveying that
would really be necessary to develop this information in
time to make it useful. I think some way would have to be
found to finance the kind of data gathering that would be
necessary really to get an idea of how typical some particular experience is, what the percentages are, where in
the country the jobs are if there is indeed a shortage, all
of which is a very difficult data-gathering operation, and
certainly an expensive one.

Comment: I don't see how anyone or anything, even something

as great as M.I.T., could possibly predict that things
would happen in the way that they did, so I'd rather talk
about what we can do about the situation now that we're
in. There are groups in this area, for example there's a
group in Sudbury, of unemployed engineers who have found
themselves having been in one company or one industry for
20 years or so out of a job—and it's a frightening pros-
pect, and it is tragic, and I think it's important to be
able to talk about tragicness and cry on somebody else's
shoulder a little bit. But you can only do this for a little
while, and then it's awfully, awfully important that you
forget about the tragedy and get on with life. I'm a salesman and I know that no one likes a salesman who comes in
griping about the weather. Optimism and enthusiasm are the
key words. And I think it's important for us either to do
it or try to do it. Maybe you can help us figure out some
ways to build up the enthusiasm and the optimism that we
need to get back into industry again if we're out of it,
or even if we're in an industry that's become obsolete. We
still have the job, but it is still just as shocking to
know that you aren't going to have it a year from now.

Edgar H. Schein: Maybe the answer is neither pessimism nor
optimism but realism. A lot of what I've heard here suggests that if we're going to get any kind of real bead on
ourselves as to who we are and what our talents are and
where we want to be and where our careers are going to be,
optimism can be just as much of a problem as pessimism.
And the trick, I guess, is to get over the shock and to be

able, with the help of others, or with the help of your
family, or by yourselves, if your bent is that way, to
take a look at where you are and where you're going and
what kind of a situation you're in and do it in a way that
Brad Bates was somewhat pointing out—to look for what
your unique talents are rather than your average talents,
and see what kind of thoughts that leads to in terms of a
career.

Comment: In line with the previous comment, I think the
point is very well put, that we should pay a little more
attention to where the problems are and to see to what extent we can utilize the abilities we have acquired even
though they may not be directly in line with the problems
at the present time, than to worry about the problems that
we could have solved that are no longer problems of great
interest. I think that there is nothing wrong with a career
in teaching if that's what you like to do. I don't know if
Mr. Basner likes to teach, but if you like to teach I certainly think that my kids are entitled to the best education that they could possibly get and if he likes to teach,
I think that an M.I.T. education is a fine way to get a
teacher.

Willard J. Basner, Jr.: Well, let me respond to that. I do
enjoy teaching very much. It's an immense amount of personal satisfaction. However, I still think I may be a little
too young and impetuous to direct my entire career in this
particular area at this stage, so right now I'm trying to

look at other alternatives or the possibility of getting
back into engineering.

Question: Could I ask a question in this particular case
because I think it's interesting in general. What motivated
you originally to go into aeronautics as a sophomore
wherever you were? What inputs came to you at that time
to decide for you into that area?

Willard J. Basner, Jr.: Well, it was sort of a lifelong
interest. Back in grammar school my vanity aroused the
idea of wanting to be the first man to set foot on the
moon about the time of Sputnik I. And then there was the
cry for more scientists and engineers, so it looked like
a wide-open field for me at the time and I just developed
a real interest in it.

Comment: So it wasn't a coincidence. It was a long interest.

Willard J. Basner, Jr.: Yes. There was a lot of planning
behind it, really. In fact, I was in R.O.T.C. for a while,
and I thought I'd be in the Air Force, then they eliminated
me from the program on medical reasons.

Comment: On the subject of self-evaluation, in 1957 wanting
some help in self-evaluation and in an industry situation
that was still reasonably healthy I came to M.I.T. and asked
for some guidance in where I could get such guidance. I

think it was Mrs. Yates who sent me across the river to a strange little outfit on Beacon Street that spent several days and charged me some little money and gave me very little help. And that was about all anybody could advise me to do at that time. Do you have any other advice now?

Robert K. Weatherall: Oh, by the way, Mrs. Yates, who is in charge of our alumni placement, didn't necessarily say that this was a wonder outfit. It was just about the only one she knew about.

Edgar H. Schein: I think that that situation I suspect has changed now. There are lots of places.

Robert K. Weatherall: Evelyn Yates is here, as a matter of fact. She always tells me that we should be questioning the value of these outfits that people ask about. There are many alumni who come in and say, "Is there any testing outfit here in Boston that will tell me everything I need to know about myself?" I don't think there is, but there are places who attempt it. I think Evelyn might want to say something.

Evelyn Yates: I really don't know very much about these places that test. I know they're very successful in pin-pointing career—they may or may not be the right ones—for very young people when their families take their high school children in—shall they be dentists or chemists—and I know there are a lot of very reputable companies that

will give you long tests, but around Boston we've not had
much experience.

Edgar H. Schein: Let me ask this group. How many of you
here, could I have a show of hands, have ever been exposed
to one of these outfits? Could we just see. (A few)
    How many of you feel it was helpful?—Very few.

Comment: I may have been lucky, but 7 years ago Haldane Associates helped me to get a job and did it well. They have
a program to write the story of your life, what did you enjoy most, and then get it organized and build a résumé
around what you like to do most. They're pretty good at
coaching you on the politics and the personalities of in-
terviewers, for instance. They're a hand-holding outfit.
They won't line up interviews for you. They hand out advice on the politics of getting along on your new job.
They'll coach you for 6 months into your new job. For me,
it worked.

Comment: I was one of the fellows who put his hand up and
then put it down for those two questions. And yet, I wish
that there were a situation that I could get into that I
could put my hand up and leave it up. But I do feel that
there probably isn't one, looking for the golden goose sort
of a thing. You encouraged me to feel that way when you,
the "expert" on the panel in this area, asked Brad if he
had found any techniques that would help him to analyze himself. Am I right in assuming that there are no academic

approaches in this area as apparently there are in such as
sensitivity training? I guess maybe you told us that sensitivity training was a possible way of knowing oneself or
trying to evaluate oneself.

Edgar H. Schein: I guess I would say that I gave the nod
to sensitivity training because I've seen that to be very
helpful, and I would say that the same is true for a lot
of these psychological services because I've heard many
people say that they were helped very much. However, what
has come out of this discussion, which I think needs to be
very strongly underlined, is that the way in which any one
person in this room can be helped is not necessarily the
same as for any other person. So even the kind of help you
need requires initially a bit of self-study and self-insight before you go out and pay somebody good money, because the odds are that various peoples' needs for help in
this room are different. If you're with a reputable group,
they will vary the kind of help that they will give, they
won't run you through a standard testing mill, they will
counsel those people who need to be counseled and they will
test those who need to be tested, and they'll do what seems
to them to be the most helpful. And I know that such organizations exist, ones that will try to sense what your
needs are and then try to respond to those needs rather than
simply grinding you through some kind of a program. But
whether for any given individual there is that golden goose
is, of course, impossible to answer because it's not clear
what your particular needs are.